WINGS OF GOLD

The Story of the First Women Naval Aviators

BEVERLY WEINTRAUB

LYONS
PRESS

Guilford, Connecticut

An imprint of Globe Pequot, the trade division of The Rowman & Littlefield Publishing Group, Inc.
4501 Forbes Blvd., Ste. 200
Lanham, MD 20706
www.rowman.com

Distributed by NATIONAL BOOK NETWORK

British Library Cataloguing in Publication Information available

Library of Congress Cataloging-in-Publication Data available

Names: Weintraub, Beverly, 1961- author.
Title: Wings of gold : the story of the first women naval aviators /
   Beverly Weintraub.
Other titles: Story of the first women naval aviators
Description: Guilford, Connecticut : Lyons Press, [2021] | Includes
   bibliographical references and index. |
Identifiers: LCCN 2021034044 (print) | LCCN 2021034045 (ebook) | ISBN
   9781493055111 (hardcover) | ISBN 9781493055128 (epub)
Subjects: LCSH: United States. Navy—Aviation. | Women air pilots—United
   States—History. | Women in aeronautics—United States—History. |
   United States. Navy—Officer. | Air pilots, Military—United States. |
   Aeronautics, Military—United States. | United States. Navy—Biography.
Classification: LCC VG93 .W45 2021 (print) | LCC VG93 (ebook) | DDC
   359.9/40820973—dc23
LC record available at https://lccn.loc.gov/2021034044
LC ebook record available at https://lccn.loc.gov/202103404

∞™ The paper used in this publication meets the minimum requirements of American National Standard for Information Sciences—Permanence of Paper for Printed Library Materials, ANSI/NISO Z39.48-1992.

Contents

ACKNOWLEDGMENTS

WHEN I'D TELL PEOPLE I WAS WRITING A BOOK ABOUT AN EXPERIMENtal program that brought women into US military flight training in the 1970s, I'd get about three sentences in before they'd stop me: "You mean World War II, right?"

The 1,074 members of WASP—the Women Airforce Service Pilots, who flew for the US Army between 1942 and 1944—have, at long last, gotten the recognition they so deserve. But the first six pioneering female naval aviators, who were subjects of tremendous publicity at the start of their careers and paved the way for thousands of women military pilots who followed, have largely vanished from the history they both bore witness to and made.

I am honored that they're letting me tell their stories.

First and foremost, my gratitude to an extraordinary group of women, who, with their families, graciously allowed me into their lives (and, in several cases, their homes) to share their personal tales of tenacity and triumph: Judith Neuffer Bruner (Captain, US Navy/Reserve, Retired), Jane Skiles O'Dea (Captain, US Navy, Retired), Joellen Drag Oslund (Captain, US Navy/Reserve, Retired), former lieutenant Ana Maria Scott (US Navy), John C. Rainey (Captain, US Navy/Reserve, Retired), Tommy Mariner (Commander, US Navy, Retired), former petty officer second class Tom O'Dea (US Navy), and Dwayne Oslund (Captain, US Navy, Retired).

My heartfelt thanks to Mary Louise Jorgensen Griffin (Captain, US Navy, Retired), an indefatigable font of knowledge, insight, and information, and a nexus of the female naval aviator community, for welcoming me in;

to former lieutenant commander and Southwest Airlines captain Tammie Jo Shults (US Navy/Reserve), Patricia Welling Leugers (Commander, US Navy, Retired), Jerry Leugers (Lieutenant Commander, US Navy, Retired), and Wendi Carpenter (Rear Admiral, US Navy, Retired), for their invaluable recollections, perspective, and context;

to Melissa Washington of the Women Veterans Alliance and Linda Maloney of Women Veteran Speakers, for helping to connect me to this most impressive community;

to Marc Levitt (National Naval Aviation Museum), Shelia Bickle (Texas Woman's University), Erin Sidwell and Gary Johnson (Library of Congress), Madeleine Stix (CNN), Penny White (University of Virginia library system), and Mort Greenberg (*Navy Times*), for unearthing long-forgotten archival material at a time when a global pandemic had shuttered archives and made travel ill-advised;

to Linda Balink-White (Captain, US Navy, Retired), Paulette French, and the late Senator John Warner, for their quick responses to queries seeking decades-old information;

to Christine Negroni; Carl Malamud; Janis D. Jorgensen (Commander, US Naval Reserve, Retired) of the US Naval Institute; Petty Officer 3rd Class Randy L. Adams II, Laura A. Waayers, Senior Chief Petty Officer Timothy L. Francis, and Jonathan M. Roscoe of the Naval History and Heritage Command; Kelly Murphy and Nancy Bink of Women in Aviation International; and my former *New York Daily News* colleague Corky Siemaszko and Elizabeth Chuck of NBC News, for pointing me in the right direction;

to ex-*News*ers Linda Hervieux and Monique El-Faizy, Howard Yoon, Robert Kern, Gary Ireland, George Robinson, Margalit Fox, Deborah Hofmann Asimov, Susan Raihofer, and Christina Wilsdon, for their sage advice to a novice book author dipping her toe in the water. Also, to Chris for the logo;

to Mary Jo Murphy, whose invitation to write for the *Washington Post* introduced me to the late captain Rosemary Mariner, and to Stephanie Scott, who saw book potential in this inspiring story;

to Beth Hawkins, a brilliant feature writer making her first acquaintance with naval aviation, for her excellent feedback from a civilian point of view;

to my offspring, Abigail Leib and Josh Leib, for their technical assistance, grammatical guidance, and patient indulgence during this yearlong endeavor;

to the New York / Rome / London Zoom crew—Annamaria, Annie, Charmaine, David, Debbie, Linda, Liz, Susan, and Virginia;

to my sister Ninety-Nines. Blue skies!

And, finally, to Rick Rinehart, Kristen Mellitt, and Melissa Hayes of Lyons Press, for seeing the project through.

PROLOGUE: THE FLYOVER

ON FEBRUARY 2, 2019, THE SKIES OVER MAYNARDVILLE, TENNESSEE, filled with the roar of four F/A-18F Super Hornets streaking overhead in close formation. In each aircraft were two young female fliers, executing the first all-woman missing man formation flyover in navy history. As the four jet strike fighters reached New Loyston Cemetery from the northeast, the second pilot from the right pulled up, climbing toward the heavens in an aerial salute to a fallen comrade. The other three flew on, the gap in the formation symbolizing the emptiness of a wingman lost.

The singular honor that winter day was a fitting memorial for Captain Rosemary Mariner—a groundbreaking navy jet pilot; an inspiring military commander; a "badass pilot," as one friend described her (though she likely would have bristled at the phrase); and a determined and dedicated leader—whose drive to ensure that the US military had its choice of the best America had to offer, both men and women, broke down barriers and opened doors for female aviators wanting to serve their country.

In her twenty-four-year military career, begun as one of just eight women chosen for flight training as an experiment in 1972, Mariner racked up an impressive roster of achievements, and firsts. She was the first woman to fly a tactical jet aircraft, in 1974; the first woman to command an aviation squadron, in 1990; one of the first women to serve aboard a navy warship, the World War II–era aircraft carrier USS *Lexington*, and to qualify as a surface warfare officer. She logged more than 3,500 flight hours in fifteen types of military aircraft, from the A-4C Skyhawk and QF-86 Sabre to the S-2 Tracker and A-7E Corsair II. She made seventeen aircraft carrier landings, known as traps. She held a master's degree in national security strategy from the National War

College; was a staff member for the Joint Chiefs of Staff; and chairman of the Joint Chiefs' Chair in Military Strategy at the National War College. Leading by example, and by confrontation when necessary, Rosemary Mariner blazed a trail for women toward the highest levels of command, taking on deep skepticism within the fleet and empowering the men and women in her squadron to be their best. Step by step, she worked to broaden the opportunities available to navy women—to fly increasingly sophisticated aircraft, land on an aircraft carrier, serve at sea, become test pilots and astronauts—to equal those that were open to navy men. And she and her fellow female naval aviators, as they were sometimes designated, challenged and eventually helped win the repeal of rules excluding women from combat, a career-limiting restriction that, given the technology and logistics of modern-day aerial warfare, had no practical meaning but reinforced institutional prejudice within the military.

Her guiding principle was simple: Aircraft don't know the gender of the pilot doing the flying, only the aeronautical skill.

The trajectory of Mariner's life seems to have followed a course perfectly suited to someone of her aptitude and talents. But that path was by no means clear at the beginning; not for Mariner—born Rosemary Ann Bryant—or for the other five graduates in that inaugural group of female pilot trainees: Barbara Ann Allen Rainey, Judith Ann Neuffer Bruner, Jane Skiles O'Dea, Joellen Drag Oslund, and Ana Maria Scott.

Some came from military families, but not all. Some already held rank in the navy, but others, like Rosemary, were civilians with no particular inclination toward military life before signing up. Some already possessed pilot certificates; some had never been pilot in command of an aircraft of any kind.

Barbara Allen, the first female naval aviator, was already a commissioned officer when she earned her Wings of Gold in February 1974. The daughter of a naval commander, Barb was the first navy woman to qualify as a military pilot. She was killed in 1982 while giving flight instruction to a young ensign at Middleton Field in Alabama.

Judy Neuffer, too, was a naval officer when she was accepted for flight training, the first of the group to sign on. Her father, who flew combat in the US Army Air Corps during World War II, taught her to fly a

Piper Cub when she was sixteen. She became the first female Hurricane Hunter, and was the first woman to fly into the eye of a hurricane. After ten years of active duty, Judy joined the US Naval Reserve and then fulfilled a childhood dream when she began working at NASA, ultimately becoming a senior manager at NASA's Goddard Space Flight Center. Judy, who had once said she would like to be considered for astronaut duty "if the opportunity came along," retired from the Reserve as a captain in 1998.

Jane Skiles was a civilian, a graduate of Iowa State University with a degree in political science. Her parents had both served in World War II, her father as a naval aviator and her mother as a supply corps officer in the Reserve. The first woman to train in and fly C-130s, Jane was outspoken about the limitations placed on women wanting to serve. "It's very discouraging to know the best you can play on is the junior varsity team no matter how good you are," she said in a 1984 interview. The nation's first pregnant military pilot, Jane retired in 1997 with the rank of captain.

Joellen Drag was also a civilian with a political science degree, hers from California State University, when she heard the navy was seeking women to fly, "and it looked better than a legislative internship at Sacramento." After being sworn in by her father, a retired navy commander, she became the military's first female helicopter pilot.

But she wasn't permitted to hover over a ship, let alone land on one—not even to deliver mail. In 1977 Joellen joined a class-action suit challenging duty restrictions imposed on female service members under federal law, on the grounds that she was evaluated on the same basis as her male counterparts but not permitted to perform the same duties or gain the same experience. The limitations, she argued, deprived her of flying time—and robbed the navy of a qualified pilot. Judge John Sirica, of Watergate fame, ruled in her favor in 1978. Joellen retired from the US Naval Reserve as a captain in 1998.

Ana Maria Scott, another civilian, was a private pilot and a political science graduate of University of California at Santa Barbara. She was considering applying for the diplomatic corps when her father saw a newspaper story about the new program for female pilots. Intrigued, she jumped at the chance, found a navy recruiter, and signed on. Ana Maria became the navy's second female helicopter pilot—secretly landing on a ship while restrictions on female aviators were still in place—and left the service in 1980 to pursue a flying career.

Rosemary Merims—she was using her stepfather's name at the time—was the last of the six to earn her wings, but she would come to occupy perhaps the most prominent place in the public eye. She wrote op-eds, gave speeches, appeared on TV news shows, and was the subject of newspaper profiles. She was named one of Ten Outstanding Working Women of 1982 in *Glamour* magazine, and appeared on *What's My Line?*, a TV game show in which celebrity panelists tried to guess the guest's profession (in Rosemary's case, they did).

For Rosemary, the seeds had been planted early. She was the daughter of an air force captain—a World War II US Army Air Forces veteran who died in a crash when she was three—and a World War II US Navy nurse who supported her daughter's fascination with aviation. One of Rosemary's greatest joys growing up in San Diego was watching the airplanes take off and land at Naval Air Station Miramar.

Rosemary earned her private pilot certificate at seventeen, cleaning houses and washing planes to pay for lessons, and was the first woman to graduate from the professional pilot program in Purdue University's aviation technology department. At nineteen, she received her bachelor's degree, hurrying through a four-year course of study in two and a half years when the navy announced it was opening the door—just a crack—for women fliers.

But from the start, Rosemary's dreams of piloting jets like those from her childhood near Miramar were not consistent with the navy's plans for its inaugural group of flygirls. That 1973 program was devised by a maverick chief of naval operations, Admiral Elmo Zumwalt Jr., against the backdrop of the women's liberation movement and a looming personnel shortage caused by the upcoming end of the military draft and the winding down of the Vietnam War, which had made navy service a much more palatable alternative to the army. Zumwalt, an outspoken supporter of greater opportunity for female enlistees and officers, saw an untapped resource and viewed his experiment as a first step toward fundamentally changing the role of women in the navy. Others in the chain of command expected the endeavor would be short-lived.

The six who made it through earned their commissions in Women's Officer School, where they were taught that it "was undignified for female officers to sit atop barstools," among other lessons. They earned their Wings of Gold—the official winged-anchor insignia denoting a naval aviator—in the same training program as male pilots. But they were not allowed aircraft carrier qualification, a defining achievement for navy fliers and a prerequisite for command. And though they were fully qualified to fly, they were not permitted to exercise those skills where their country might need them most: in combat.

The public response to installing women in navy cockpits was, in general, surprised condescension. Newspaper coverage of the time invariably mentioned the new pilots' physical traits—"blue-eyed," "petite," "blonde," "brunette," with "fetching bangs." Also, marital status. As noted by the *New York Times* in January 1973, "There will be no prohibition against their carrying feminine gear such as makeup in the capacious pockets of their flight suits, should they desire." The writer added helpfully that "a man pilot is allowed to carry personal objects" as well.

How they pushed back against ingrained resistance to the idea that women could do "men's" jobs as ably as males, how they faced down men waiting for them to fail, and how they used the chain of command to challenge artificial limits that impeded their advancement is an amazing story of commitment, courage, and service to country.

It is also the story of steadfast support from forward-looking peers and superior officers who understood the historic importance of their effort and worked to secure their success. Among these was the commanding officer of Rosemary's first squadron, an African American commander who drew on the lessons of Black service members who integrated the US military to empower Rosemary in her own quest for equality.

Ultimately, though, it was the power of her own example—her character, dedication, and perseverance—and that of other pioneering navy women that enabled them to push the door wide and to hold it open for the generations that followed. The logic of the argument, as Rosemary described it in the *Washington Post* in 1997, was unimpeachable: Navy women should receive the same training as men and be allowed to gain sufficient experience to repay the country for that training. Segregation of any type, whether by race, gender, or any other measure, destroys unit cohesion. Inequality is an insult to the integrity of the chain of command. It is, quite simply, a matter of honor and respect.

From practically the very start, Rosemary was a presence in the public sphere as well as in military circles, at first drawing attention simply for being a woman pursuing a traditionally male path. But later, she capitalized on her prominence in the navy as a platform for speaking out against injustice and inequity that grew as military women became more numerous, more prominent, and more powerful.

She argued publicly that the Tailhook scandal of 1991, in which male navy pilots sexually abused military and civilian women in the halls of the Las Vegas Hilton, illustrated the harm inflicted by institutional discrimination that gives cover to individual assault.

"Sexual harassment will continue to be a problem in the military services as long as women are barred from combat duty—as long as we are considered institutionally inferior," she told the *Los Angeles Times* in 1992. "Just as in matters of race, separate is inherently unequal."

And just before retiring from active duty in 1997 and joining the University of Tennessee's Center for the Study of War and Society, where she specialized in military history and the juncture between war and conscience, she wrote in the *Washington Post*, "Integrating large numbers of high-quality female recruits into nontraditional fields made the All-Volunteer Force possible. . . . Combat exclusion policies do not protect women from coming home in body bags or becoming POWs. Rather, such arbitrary restrictions hurt combat readiness by limiting the flexibility of commanders to use all their soldiers, however needed, especially under fire. In terms of plain fairness, if American women are good enough to die for their country, they are good enough to fight."

Or, as she told *Glamour* magazine in 1982, "A machine gun is a great equalizer."

Until her diagnosis with ovarian cancer, the disease that took her life on January 24, 2019, at age sixty-five, Rosemary advised the navy on national defense policy and the continued integration of women into the armed forces. She served as an expert on military matters for a number of media outlets and mentored the young men and women in her classroom. Throughout, she remained a trailblazer, a scholar, and an advocate for talented young people wishing to serve.

Her leadership had a ripple effect that is still being felt today.

Each of the female pilots and crew members who volunteered to participate in the "Sabre 9" flyover that winter afternoon in Tennessee—Commander Stacy Uttecht, commanding officer of Strike Fighter Squadron (VFA) 32 and "Sabre 9" mission commander; Commander Leslie Mintz, executive officer, VFA-213; Lieutenant Commander Paige Blok, VFA-32; Lieutenant Commander Danielle Thiriot, VFA-106; Lieutenant Commander Jennifer Hesling, Naval Air Station Oceana; Lieutenant Emily Rixey, assigned to Strike Fighter Weapons School Atlantic; Lieutenant Christy Talisse, VFA-211; Lieutenant Amanda Lee, VFA-81; and Lieutenant Kelly Harris, VFA-213—knew her history.

Some had read her words or heard her speak. Several had met her. All were well aware of the debt they owed this groundbreaking aviator. All knew that without her and the other five female navy pilots who were the first to win Wings of Gold, they might not be where they are, flying the navy's first missing woman formation flyover, making history of their own, in her honor.

As Blok posted on Twitter: "I told my parents my dreams of becoming a fighter pilot at age 8. I'm blessed to serve & regard the pioneering women of Naval Aviation as foundational in making my dream possible. I met CAPT Rosemary Mariner; she's a beacon of leadership."

Describing the flyover squad in a video released by the navy, Thiriot said, "We have Top Gun graduates, we've got a commanding officer, an executive officer and combat veterans. . . . None of us are firsts, and she was a first. . . . The fact that none of us are first is really a testament to her."

"When I come into the ready room right now," said Lee, "I'm a pilot first, a person second, and my gender isn't really an issue. It's people like Captain Mariner that have paved that way for us."

And Mintz put it succinctly: "I wouldn't be standing here where I am today if it weren't for her and the other first female naval aviators."

That is their legacy. This is their story.

PART I
1903–1972

CHAPTER ONE

Essential but Expendable—A
Brief History of Early Military Aviation

ON OCTOBER 20, 1942, SIX WOMEN FLIERS EMBARKED ON THE FIRST all-female piloting mission in US military history, delivering Piper L-4 Grasshopper and Fairchild PT-19 trainers from factories to air bases across the United States. They were members of the Women's Auxiliary Ferrying Squadron (WAFS), a group of handpicked female pilots recruited to take over for men called to service in World War II. Soon to be merged with the Women's Flying Training Detachment and reconstituted as the Women Airforce Service Pilots (WASP), these skilled, dedicated female fliers and more than one thousand others just like them would ultimately fly more than 60 million miles in seventy-seven types of aircraft, every sort of military plane the United States could produce.

The idea of utilizing women as ferry pilots for the army had been floated several years before, but with America not yet engaged in the war, it was rejected. "The use of women pilots," wrote General Henry "Hap" Arnold in 1941, "serves no military purpose."

After Pearl Harbor, however, with war raging and all able-bodied male pilots being sent overseas, what had been theory became harsh reality. American factories were churning out fighters, bombers, and trainers at a rate of about one an hour; someone had to fly them to where they were needed. Arnold just needed prodding from some of his colonels; from air racer and test pilot Nancy Love Harkness; and from women's world speed record holder Jacqueline Cochran, who had led dozens of female American aviators in performing similar, stellar service for the British Air Transport Auxiliary, to realize he had a large, available contingent of capable pilots right under his nose. He only needed to open the cockpit door.

Though there were always far fewer female than male pilots, "lady pilots" or "girl fliers" were nothing new. Women had been flying since the dawn of aviation: A Frenchwoman, Jeanne Labrosse, soloed a hot-air balloon in 1798, and in 1908, another, Therese Peltier, was the first woman to solo an airplane. Still another, Baroness Raymonde de Laroche, became the first licensed female pilot, in 1910, followed the next year by American Harriet Quimby. Quimby would be the first woman to fly the English Channel and, in 1912, one of the first to die in an airplane accident. In this, she joined a long line of unfortunate aviation pioneers. Among them were US Army Lieutenant Thomas Selfridge, the first passenger to die in a plane crash, in a 1908 accident that severely injured pilot Orville Wright; and the first naval aviation fatality, Ensign William Billingsley, killed in 1912 for lack of a seat belt.

Aviation in those early days was dangerous. Just getting airborne and staying there, let alone controlling pitch and direction, posed vexing problems for every aircraft designer in France, Germany, Britain, and the United States. All too frequently, takeoffs in wood-and-fabric flying machines resulted in violent accidents that damaged both plane and pilot. The Wright Brothers' first flight at Kitty Hawk in December 1903 had been a 120-second hop straight ahead; their fourth flight of the day ended in a crash. Controlled, sustained flight was an ideal difficult to attain.

Concerned about their patents, the Wrights worked largely in secret on a wing-warping system that they hoped would solve the problem of directional control. Even as they improved their technology and refined their technique—flying an aircraft for the first time in a complete circle in 1904, for example—they kept their innovations under wraps. So much so that when they finally began demonstrating takeoffs and landings and flying circuits before audiences in Dayton, Ohio, in 1905, the general public, some French aircraft designers, and even the editors of *Scientific American* magazine didn't believe it.

The US Army was skeptical as well. That same year, the Wrights had tried to engage the military as a prime market for their airplanes, but their sales pitch was dismissed with a curt "No thanks," as "their machine had not yet been brought to a state of practical operation."

But within two years, the army became convinced of the airplane's military potential. At the end of 1907, the Signal Corps' new Aeronautical Division put out a request for proposals for a heavier-than-air flying machine, "designed to carry two persons having a combined weight of about 350 pounds, also sufficient fuel for a flight of 125 miles," having "a speed of at least 40 miles an hour in still air" and capable of being "quickly and easily assembled and taken apart and packed for transportation in army wagons. It should be capable of being assembled and put in operating condition in about an hour." In addition, it should be "sufficiently simple in its construction and operation to permit an intelligent man to become proficient in its use within a reasonable length of time."

Not to be outdone, the navy decided it, too, needed aerial capability. The Wrights' army contract, signed in February 1908, required a number of trials to be held throughout the year. Those tests, and the delivery of the world's first military aircraft to Fort Myer, Virginia, in summer 1909, drew navy observers interested in the potential of aerial scouts for use in naval warfare (despite Selfridge's death during one of the trials). After watching the Wright Military Flyer in action, one observer, Lieutenant George S. Sweet, wrote, "The Navy must have that! It will be most important to us."

He meant a Wright airplane. But it turned out that for the navy, the Wrights' rival Glenn Curtiss was their guy.

Constantly in litigation with the brothers over patents for aircraft design, Curtiss held the world speed record with a biplane that employed ailerons rather than wing-warping for directional control. With the Wrights apparently having cornered the market on sales to the army, Curtiss—who in May 1908 co-founded the Aerial Experiment Association with, among others, Alexander Graham Bell—looked to the navy as a potential buyer for the seaplane he wanted to build.

Curtiss decided he needed to put on a bit of a show for the navy brass.

In the summer of 1910, he dropped the first dummy bombs from an airplane over a lake near his home in Upstate New York. As a crude demonstration of the vulnerability of ships to aerial bombardment, it got the navy's attention. He also piloted the first aircraft ever to have a gun fired from it in flight.

Then, a few months later, Curtiss had one of his civilian exhibition pilots demonstrate that it was possible to take off from a ship—an experiment Wilbur Wright had been asked to perform but turned down as too dangerous. As the USS *Birmingham* sat at anchor at Hampton Roads, Virginia, Eugene Ely taxied a Curtiss biplane down an 83-foot-long wooden platform affixed to the deck. Though the plane hit the water as Ely swooped down to pick up airspeed, he became airborne and flew for several miles before landing on a nearby beach.

Captain Washington Irving Chambers, tasked with exploring the potential value of naval aviation, wrote to the secretary of the navy: "Every cruiser should be equipped with planes. . . . I do not believe that the aeroplane will ever take the place of scouting cruisers, but I do believe that scouting cruisers will be made twice as valuable to the Navy, at small cost."

Two months after that, on January 18, 1911, Ely closed the loop by making the first landing on a ship. Piloting a Curtiss biplane with floats under the wings, he managed to snag one of a series of arresting cables on a wooden platform that covered half the quarterdeck and extended diagonally down over the stern of the USS *Pennsylvania*, at anchor in San Francisco harbor. Stopping 1,000 pounds of pilot and airplane traveling at 40 miles an hour within 30 feet, the arresting cables were a precursor to the system used on today's massive aircraft carriers, floating airports from which the United States projects its power around the world.

Said Captain C. F. Pond, commander of the *Pennsylvania*, "This is the most important landing of a bird since the dove flew back to the ark." Wrote the *San Francisco Examiner*:

Eugene Ely's success in San Francisco harbor yesterday was epoch-making. It changed in an instant the whole theory of naval warfare. In a single spectacular flight, Ely convinced the admiralties of the world that the aeroplane must be a necessary part of naval equipment in the future.

Heretofore the battleship has been limited to a range of vision bound by the horizon of the sea. An admiral of a fleet approaching a hostile shore had no means of learning the mysteries of the fortifications and batteries and big guns which he was on his way to attack.

Yesterday Eugene Ely in San Francisco harbor changed all that. He proved convincingly and finally that it is practical for a battleship to send a scout into the sky and that from the safe vantage of an altitude of thousands of feet the scout can sail over cities and fortifications and return easily to the cruiser's deck from which it started in his aerial reconnaissance.

Still, as impressive as Ely's feats were, some skepticism remained. Earlier that month, Secretary of the Navy George Von L. Meyer had written to Curtiss, "When you show me that it is feasible for an aeroplane to alight on the water alongside a battleship and be hoisted aboard without any false deck to receive it, I shall believe the airship of practical benefit to the Navy."

Having set up a training facility on San Diego's North Island to give military officers free flying lessons, Curtiss took up the challenge in Spanish Bight. On January 26, 1911, he performed three water takeoffs and landings in a biplane outfitted with pontoons instead of wheels, and a month later followed up with the exact demonstration Meyer had demanded. Maneuvering his floatplane next to the *Pennsylvania*, which had sailed down to San Diego, Curtiss and his aircraft were first hoisted on board by the ship's boat crane and then lowered back down again to take off from the water.

That sealed the deal.

On May 8, 1911, the navy obtained its first flying machine, an amphibious biplane with retractable landing gear called the A-1 Triad— for land, sea, and air—able to operate on land or water and capable of speeds of at least 45 miles an hour.

But unlike the Wrights, with their innovations on land airplanes, and Curtiss, with his experiments on seaplanes and flying boats, the military showed little imagination in adapting its new aerial fleet for uses beyond scouting. Although the next few years saw a US patent for an airborne torpedo and the first successful test of an aircraft launch by catapult from a ship, Rear Admiral Richard Wainwright rejected the idea for a Navy Office of Aeronautics in the belief that aerial warfare would soon become illegal under international law. And the army, inexplicably, declined to adopt inventor Isaac Lewis's design for a machine gun capable of being fired from the air. Lewis took his invention to Britain instead.

When World War I broke out on August 14, 1914, the US Army Aviation Division had just 12 officers, 54 enlisted men, and 6 usable aircraft. Its navy counterpart had 48 pilots, 238 enlisted men, and 54 air-craft. The British, French, and Germans, whose aircraft numbered in the hundreds, had military pilots; the United States had flying scouts. As the US Army was testing an aerial bomb-dropping device at North Island, the Germans were bombing Paris from the air (albeit in rudimentary fashion, with the pilot pitching explosives over the side of his airplane).

Innovations in aircraft design, materials, maneuverability, altitude, size, power, and firepower (including Lewis's now-British armaments) were happening in Europe, not the United States. The country that had given the world controlled, sustained flight was left behind.

As an internal US Army report stated: "The Army's total purchase of planes had been 39 up to the end of 1914 and 224 up to April 1917, but as yet these deliveries had not included any models designed entirely for military use. As of early 1917, no 'battle planes' had been built in the United States, and 'only a handful of Americans had ever seen one.'"

According to another report: "The entrance of the United States into the war in April 1917 . . . found the country almost totally unprepared in aeronautical experience, equipment and personnel . . . the Aviation Sec-tion of the Signal Corps had no accurate knowledge of the equipment of a military airplane. No airplane in America up to 1917 had ever mounted a machine gun, and aviation personnel had practically no knowledge of radiotelegraphy and telephony, photography, bombing equipment, lights for night flying, aviators' clothing, compasses used in flying or other avi-ation instruments well known to the aviators of Germany, England, and France."

American aircraft weren't prepared for war. But American aviators were. Even before the United States officially entered the fray, American pilots were signing up to fly for France, honing their aviation skills and learning aerial combat under French command as members of the Lafayette Escadrille. And when the United States did finally declare war, the Escadrille pilots were there to greet their fellow US Air Service fliers and school them in the nuances of formation flying and combat operations (all in French-manufactured aircraft). Meanwhile, American naval aviators—a term formalized in 1915—were spotting and bombing submarines, destroying mines, conducting scout patrols, and escorting convoys in Britain, France, Belgium, Italy, and the Azores, flying primarily French airplanes.

By the end of the war, the US Army Air Service had 7,726 officers and 70,769 enlisted men in its ranks, and US Navy / Marine Corps aviation units counted 6,998 officers and 32,873 enlisted. Among increasingly advanced aircraft, Curtiss's flying boats in particular were hailed for their technological innovations and long range. Even as the United States stepped down from its war footing, aviation had become a military priority, with the establishment of the Navy Bureau of Aeronautics in 1921; the first demonstrated carrier takeoffs and landings—without unwieldy retrofitted platforms—in 1922; and the development of sleeker aircraft with metal frames, more-powerful engines, and more-sophisticated armaments, including dive-bombers. The need for more-structured military flight training became a priority as well: in Texas for the army, and at Pensacola, Florida, for the navy.

What made a military pilot?

As Lieutenant S. H. Warner wrote in *Proceedings* magazine in June 1928, in an article titled "A Naval Aviator in the Making":

[T]here is no special type of man who can be pointed out as a potential aviator. Of course, there is the hero-aviator in the movies, who is always a smiling Adonis, but in actual practice, it is otherwise. One may be short and bow-legged, or tall and awkward; high-strung and vivacious, or dignified and proper. There is something else that is required, something psychological. Perhaps the type which comes

nearest to being a good aviator is the successful, all-around athlete. The same faculties which make for success in athletics are necessary attributes to an aviator. Presence of mind, confidence, aggressiveness, endurance, quick thought, sure judgment, and instantaneous action: all these, and more, are necessary.

It turned out that each of those qualities but one—maleness—was found in female pilots, too, a point that the army, though not the navy, reluctantly conceded during World War II.

With the German invasion of Czechoslovakia and Poland in 1939, a nation that had by and large ignored the renewed unrest in Europe was forced to refocus its attention across the sea and consider the lessons of the European war that had ended two decades before. Airpower had been a decisive factor in defeating the Germans in 1918; with former allies Britain and France newly declaring war on Germany, Washington recognized that the airplane would once again be an indispensable weapon—this time, with the United States as a key supplier.

American factories, particularly those producing commercial aircraft and automobiles, were reconfigured to churn out warplanes. Between 1939 and 1944, the US aircraft industry soared from forty-fourth in the world to first, increasing America's arsenal from about 2,500 military aircraft to 300,000. Even before the United States entered the war following the bombing of Pearl Harbor, the government was committed to turning out 50,000 airplanes a year; after Pearl Harbor, many of those fighters, bombers, and trainers were produced by women working assembly lines in place of men sent to fight overseas.

Once rolled out of the plants, those airplanes needed to be ferried to military bases for use in training young pilots, or overseas for action in Europe and the Pacific. But with male pilots gone to war, no able-bodied aviators of appropriate age for military service remained at home to ferry the planes, to act as test pilots, or to teach the men who would be needed to fly all of those fighters and bombers in combat.

As in the factories, women were the solution.

Like many young men, young women found the lure of the skies irresistible in the years after World War I. Flying cheap, obsolete surplus wooden military biplanes, they performed as stunt pilots, barnstormers, and wing walkers, even playing tennis or dancing in midair, before awestruck crowds who'd never seen an airplane before.

Charles Lindbergh got his start this way, selling $5 airplane rides before becoming the first human to fly solo, nonstop, across the Atlantic. Fellow World War I veteran Roscoe Turner promoted himself as a pilot, airplane racer, and entrepreneur by flying with his pet lion, Gilmore. Bessie Coleman, the first African American woman to earn a pilot's license—she learned to fly in France because no American would teach her—did daring stunts in her biplane, but only before integrated audiences, as she refused to perform for segregated crowds. Amelia Earhart, airplane sales representative Louise Thaden, and movie stunt pilot Florence "Pancho" Barnes set speed, endurance, and altitude records.

Women worked as flight instructors—if a female could fly, how hard could it be?—and demonstrated and sold aircraft for private manufacturers. They pursued careers as air-mail and airline pilots. Soon, they would be competing against men in long-distance airplane races, and winning.

In 1929, when Earhart, Thaden, Barnes, and other racers in the first transcontinental Women's Air Derby, aka the Powder Puff, decided to form an organization of women pilots, they invited every licensed American female aviator to join. There were 117 of them, and 99 signed up, giving the organization its name.

By the time Hap Arnold, overcoming deep-seated resistance and doubts, took up the challenge of creating the first official corps of women to fly for the US military, there were more than 3,000 licensed pilots to choose from. Nearly 25,000 more American women were willing to learn to fly and serve their country.

The 1,830 accepted applicants had to pay their own way to training, first in Houston and then in Sweetwater, Texas. Once there, they had to foot the bill for their uniforms (cobbled together, for the most part, from small-sized men's clothes) and for their room and board.

They had to be at least 5 feet, 4 inches tall and eighteen to thirty-five years old; have at least a high school diploma and a pilot's license, with a minimum of 35 hours logged; and be able to pass an army physical. For thirty weeks, they lived in military-style barracks and led a military-style life: marching, drilling, doing calisthenics, and undergoing physical fitness training—the same routine as male Army Air Corps pilots. The only difference was less-intense instruction in combat-focused skills like gunnery and formation flying.

Ground school was 560 hours studying weather, navigation, principles of flight, physics, math, aircraft systems and engines, communications, and code. Flight training was 210 hours in the air, learning to fly the army way.

The 1,074 WASP who won their wings starting in 1943 were then dispatched to 122 air bases around the country, where they not only delivered military planes ferried from the factories, but acted as test pilots and taught men to fly. They trained alongside male pilots in advanced aircraft, including some, like the B-26 and the B-29 bomber, that were notoriously difficult to handle (if a woman could fly it, it must be safe). And they were used for target practice—literally—towing targets for gunners to shoot at using live ammunition.

Throughout the ranks, many army men eventually came around to the idea, as Arnold had, that a skilled military pilot was a skilled military pilot, regardless of gender. But others believed women had no business flying warplanes. Some up the chain of command thought female pilots could be very useful performing desk jobs; one base commander told the female fliers they should "go home and knit socks for the troops." WASP taxiing in on delivery runs were frequently greeted by men gawking in disbelief. Male controllers were flummoxed by female voices calling for clearance to land. Often, the WASP had to find their own accommodations after dropping off an airplane; the base somehow didn't have any place for women to stay, and they sometimes were literally driven off the premises. Occasionally, suspicious things happened to their aircraft.

One member of WASP tried to start her engine only to find it stuffed with rags; another found her rudder cables had been partially cut. At least one died as the result of sabotage; after the fatal accident, sugar was found in the fuel tank of her plane at a base in North Carolina.

All told, thirty-eight WASP were killed in the line of duty. For them, there were no military honors, no flag-draped coffins, and no transportation home. Friends, family, and their sister WASP had to pay to ship the bodies to their final resting places.

Ultimately, in December 1944, with the war winding down and the men coming home, the WASP organization was disbanded. Congress had considered making the WASP an official part of the army—but no. Though they had served with distinction and died for their country, the Women Airforce Service Pilots were summarily dismissed, having to pay their own way home. An essential military asset was suddenly expendable.

At the graduation ceremony for the last class of WASP, Arnold told the assembled crowd that when the program began in 1941, he was not convinced that

a slip of a girl could fight the controls of a B-17 in heavy weather. . . . Now, in 1944 . . . it is on the record that women can fly as well as men. . . . Certainly we haven't been able to build an airplane you can't handle. From the AT-6s to B-29s, you have flown them around like veterans. One of the WASP has even test-flown our new jet plane.

You, and more than 900 of your sisters, have shown that you can fly wingtip to wingtip with your brothers. If ever there was doubt in anyone's mind that women can become skillful pilots, the WASP have dispelled that doubt. . . . I do not look upon the WASP and the job they have done in this war as a project or an experiment. A pioneering venture, yes. Solely an experiment, no. The WASP are an accomplishment.

The lessons of the WASP soon faded from memory, however. Famous in their day—some thirteen million Americans saw a July 1943 *Life* magazine cover story that began, "The time-honored belief that Army flying is for men has gone into the ash can"—the WASP were largely forgotten by the public, and by military brass who would soon be learning those lessons all over again. Not until several decades later were the WASP finally recognized for their service with military pensions, the Congressional Gold Medal, and the right to be buried at Arlington National Cemetery.

But Rosemary Mariner and her fellow female naval aviators remembered. For her in particular, the members of WASP were role models. "The WASPs are the ones who started it all for us. We are their intellectual heirs," she said in 1991.

Their story of military recruitment, grudging acceptance, and then insult and indignity was one she knew well. It was one she was intent not to repeat.

CHAPTER TWO

Equal Means Equal

For Admiral Elmo R. Zumwalt Jr., it was the right thing to do. It was also a potential solution to a serious personnel problem.

A native Californian, born into a family of physicians—both his parents were doctors—Zumwalt was drawn toward a medical career but found his calling in the military. He enrolled at the Naval Academy in Annapolis in 1939 and skipped his final year, along with the rest of the class of 1943, to join the fight against the Axis powers. He served on destroyers, was awarded a Bronze Star, and led the occupation of Shanghai. Post–World War II, there was a navy ROTC teaching post, more sea duty, and a stint at the Naval War College, where a paper he wrote on Soviet affairs drew the attention of Paul Nitze, then assistant secretary of defense.

Zumwalt's appointment as Nitze's top aide, a post he held during the Cuban Missile Crisis, marked the start of a meteoric rise. In 1965 he was named the youngest rear admiral in US history, at age forty-four, jumping ahead of some 130 other officers. And just five years later, after his opposition to the Vietnam War put him in the good graces of President Richard Nixon—even as Zumwalt commanded a flotilla of one thousand Swift boats patrolling the Mekong Delta's muddy waters—he was appointed chief of naval operations, cutting a line thirty-three senior officers long. Again, he was the youngest in history, not yet fifty years old.

Zumwalt's primary, and immediate, challenge was a crisis of morale. In a country rocked by the civil rights movement, the youth counterculture, and the sexual revolution, societal strictures were giving way throughout civilian life. But the navy remained hidebound and rigid, and was losing recruits in droves. The reenlistment rate, normally around 35 percent, was down to 9.5.

Zumwalt's mission was to change how the US Navy did business. The method: what came to be known as Z-grams, a series of 121 communiqués sent from the very top of the chain of command directly to the fleet. The target: decades, if not centuries, of policies and traditions that held no place in Zumwalt's vision of a modern navy.

He wasted no time. Z-gram #2, dated July 14, 1970—just two weeks into his term as CNO—announced the formation of a study group of young officers and enlisted men, "to review any policies or practices which bear on retention and morale," with the goal of "improving the quality of Navy life in all respects and restoring the fun and zest of going to sea."

No quality-of-life issue, it seemed, was too small for a Z-gram. There were missives relaxing bans on civilian clothing, raising the check-cashing ceiling, allowing booze in some barracks, limiting the amount of time a sailor would have to stand in line—for anything—and setting up direct communications between navy wives and commanding officers ("the importance of the Navy wife as a member of the Navy team cannot be over emphasized"). Z-grams tackled shore-leave policies, the appropriateness of riding motorcycles, and a lack of lockers and wash facilities onshore. They lengthened commissary hours and instituted Programs for People, "a central point of contact . . . where all Navy people can turn with confidence on matters concerning conditions of service and personal affairs."

Effective with Z-gram #57 (November 10, 1970), "demeaning or abrasive regulations"—in navy parlance, "Mickey Mouse" or "chickenshit" regs—were out.

Zumwalt stood up for facial hair and, in true 1970s fashion, sideburns. ("I will not countenance the rights or privileges of any officers or enlisted men being abrogated in any way because they choose to grow sideburns or neatly trimmed beards or moustaches or because preferences in neat clothing styles are at variance with the taste of their seniors, nor will I countenance any personnel being in any way penalized during the time they are growing beards, moustaches or sideburns.")

He also addressed festering racial tensions head-on. Though the military had been officially desegregated by President Harry S Truman in 1947, "racism and sexism were still an integral part of the Navy tradition," Zumwalt wrote in December 1970. Not that the navy was unique in this; racial animus ran deep in all branches of the US military. But it was especially pernicious on navy ships and in billets onshore.

Discrimination tainted every aspect of navy life, from recruiting and training to promotions, even to the goods available in commissaries. As Zumwalt wrote in his autobiography, "The Navy systemically excluded, except for menial service, people with dark skins and non-European ancestries . . . the routine for assigning minority officers was to send them to dead-end billets so that their promotion beyond middle rank would be unlikely." IQ exams used for determining career paths were biased against African American test takers. Bigoted housing personnel blocked Black service members from finding homes for their families. Day in and day out, there was harassment, disrespect, discrimination, violence, and, of course, liberal use of the N-word.

Z-gram #66, "Equal Opportunity in the Navy," issued December 17, 1970, minced no words: "There is no black Navy, no white Navy—just one Navy—the United States Navy."

In it, Zumwalt called out ingrained racism, putting the onus on each base, station, squadron, and ship commander to appoint a special assistant for minority affairs who would investigate the depth of the problems under his command and report back up the chain, with a deadline less than a month away. He imposed measures to root out discrimination in housing and ordered that "special needs of minority groups are recognized and provided for" in terms of grooming products, foods, books, magazines, music, and barbers or beauticians.

Zumwalt further demanded that all personnel "seek out and eliminate those demeaning areas of discrimination that plague our minority shipmates. Ours must be a Navy family that recognizes no artificial barriers of race, color or religion."

As he reiterated in a speech to navy brass: "Equal means exactly that. Equal."

But "artificial barriers" weren't going to come down with just a written missive from the top. There was pushback—from white sailors and officers unhappy with increased enlistment of African Americans, and from conservative admirals and government officials convinced that Zumwalt's push for integration was destroying navy discipline. During the summer of 1972, race relations became increasingly fraught, flashpoints that would erupt several months later in brawls—some say riots—on the fleet oiler *Hassayampa* and the carriers *Kitty Hawk* and *Constellation*.

Zumwalt decided it was a good time to rock the boat even harder, with the release of Z-gram #116 in August 1972.

"Equal Rights and Opportunities for Women in the Navy" was intended as the beginning of a solution to a raft of looming challenges.

With the Vietnam War winding down, the navy could no longer count on enlistees choosing service at sea as a more-palatable alternative to jungle warfare. The impending end of the military draft meant the navy—already suffering from dismal recruitment and retention rates, unauthorized absences, and desertions—would soon have to find a way to attract volunteers. And with the expected passage of the Equal Rights Amendment, it was widely assumed that the Constitution would soon require expanded opportunities for women, something the navy—a seagoing force that barely allowed women on ships, limited them to certain types of jobs, restricted their advancement, and barred them from most positions of command—was thoroughly unprepared for.

Z-116 could allow the navy to draw on an untapped pool of personnel to fill jobs that would free up men for sea duty, prepare itself for the ERA, and begin meeting new societal demands of women no longer satisfied with the traditional career paths of secretary, teacher, or librarian.

It would just take updating regulations in place since 1948.

Public Law 625, also known as the Women's Armed Services Integration Act, and codified for navy personnel under Title 10 US Code Section 6015, was enacted after World War II to do away with women's auxiliaries and give women official military standing and expertise in case of national emergency. It authorized regular status for both enlisted women and officers in all branches, and opened up opportunities beyond nursing and secretarial jobs.

However, women were limited to 2 percent of enlistees; only one woman could be promoted to the rank of captain, and then only temporarily; just 10 percent of female officers could become commanders; women's promotion lists would be separate from men's; women under twenty-one who wanted to enlist needed parental permission, though the enlistment age was eighteen; military women could not claim their families as dependents unless they could prove they were their "chief support"; and the secretary of each branch had broad discretion in terminating the commission or enlistment of any woman.

And there was this, under Section 6015: Women "shall not be assigned to duty in aircraft while such aircraft are engaged in combat missions, nor shall they be assigned to duty on vessels of the Navy except hospital ships and naval transports."

As the House Naval Affairs Committee's powerful chairman, Carl Vinson, known as "the father of the two-ocean Navy," put it: "Just fix it so they can't go to sea."

Jean Ebbert and Marie-Beth Hall described what this meant in their book, *Crossed Currents: Navy Women from WWI to Tailhook*:

Allowing women to reach no permanent rank higher than commander . . . severely restricted not only individual advancement but also their impact on any but women's programs. Even the most senior woman in a service, as only a temporary captain . . . had neither entrée to nor influence on that service's highest decision-making councils. The provisions concerning authority and types of duty ensured that women would not serve in combat or exercise military authority over men. The separate promotion list meant that women would be competing for promotion only with women, not with men. The requirement for parental consent for women under the age of 21 to enlist reflected society's view that women needed parental guidance longer than men did, while the provision regarding husbands and children reflected its view that, unless proven otherwise, husbands rather than wives were breadwinners. Finally, the service secretaries' blanket authority to discharge any woman, officer or enlisted, facilitated the discharge of pregnant women or women who married men with dependent children.

Some of the groundwork for Z-116 was laid in 1967 with an amendment that lifted the 2 percent cap on enlistees and removed rank restrictions on women. Members of the Defense Advisory Committee on Women in the Services, or DACOWITS, had lobbied strongly for the changes. DACOWITS was a panel of civilian women created in 1951 to advise the Defense Department on issues of great import to female service personnel; its influential members carried the protocol rank of three-star general. Similarly, in 1971, Zumwalt consulted with two study groups looking into the retention of women and concluded that the navy was underutilizing its female talent.

This was his response, on August 7, 1972:

"Equal Rights and Opportunities for Women in the Navy"
 1. *There has been much discussion and debate with respect to equal opportunity for women in our country over the past few years. My position with respect to women in the Navy is that they have historically played a significant role in the accomplishment of our naval mission. However, I believe we can do far more than we have in the past in according women equal opportunity to contribute their extensive talents and to achieve full professional status. Moreover, the imminence of an all-volunteer force has heightened the importance of women as a vital personnel resource. I foresee that in the near future we may very well have authority to utilize officer and enlisted women on board ships. In view of this possibility we must be in a position to utilize women's talents to help us achieve the size Navy we need under an all-volunteer force environment and still maintain the sea shore rotation goals for all naval personnel towards which we have been working. To this end the secretary of the Navy and I have established a task force to look at all laws, regulations and policies that must be changed in order to eliminate any disadvantages to women resulting from either legal or attitudinal restrictions.*
 2. *As another step toward ensuring that women in the Navy will have equal opportunity to contribute their talents and*

background to accomplishment of our missions, we are taking the following actions:

a. *In addition to the enlisted ratings that have recently been opened, authorize limited entry of enlisted women into all ratings.*

b. *The ultimate goal, assignment of women to ships at sea, will be timed to coincide with full implementation of pending legislation. As an immediate step, a limited number of officer and enlisted women are being assigned to the ship's company of USS* Sanctuary *as a pilot program. This program will provide valuable planning information regarding the prospective increased utilization of women at sea.*

c. *Pending formal changes to Navy regulations suspend restrictions regarding women succeeding to command ashore and assign them accordingly.*

d. *Accept applications from women officers for the chaplain and civil engineer corps, thereby opening all staff corps to women.*

e. *Expand assignment of technically qualified unrestricted line women to restricted line billets and, at the time of legislative authorization, permit them to request designator changes.*

f. *Offer various paths of progression to flag rank [admiral] within the technical, managerial spectrum in essentially the same manner as we are contemplating for male officers.*

g. *Assign the detailing of unrestricted women officers to their cognizant grade detailers.*

h. *Increase opportunity for women's professional growth by:*

   (i) eliminating the pattern of assigning women exclusively to certain billets; and

   (ii) assigning qualified women to the full spectrum of challenging billets, including those of briefers, aides, detailers, placement/rating control officers, attachés, service college faculty members, executive assistants,

special assistants to CNO, MAAGs/missions, senior enlisted advisors, PEP, etc.

   i. Equalize selection criteria for naval training by:

     (i) opening midshipmen programs to women at all NROTC [Naval Reserve Officers Training Corps] campuses effective in FY-74, and

     (ii) considering women for selection to joint colleges (National War College / Industrial College of the Armed Forces).

   3. Finally, I enjoin all commanding officers and others in positions of authority to actively reflect the spirit and intent of this message in their own command regulations, policies and actions. Specifically, I expect each commanding officer to:

    a. Initiate similar equalization actions in matters within their purview to ensure that women are accorded full trust and responsibility to function in their assigned position or specialty.

    b. Be guided by standards of duty, performance and discipline which are truly equitable for both women and men.

   4. In summary, we all must actively work together in order that we may more equitably include women in our one-Navy concept.

—E. R. Zumwalt, Jr., admiral, US Navy, Chief of Naval Operations

Barely two months later, the navy expanded the list of "challenging billets" when Secretary John Warner announced the opening of naval flight training to women—an experiment in females doing a job that, until that point, had been reserved exclusively for men.

To be sure, the women enticed to sign up by Z-116 and Warner's announcement were by no means the first to answer the call to naval duty, or even the call of naval aviation. Women had served in the US Navy since 1908, when the so-called Sacred Twenty nurses were appointed by an act of Congress; some 11,000 women volunteered during World War

I, primarily doing clerical work. Though they were mustered out when the war ended in 1918, barely twenty years went by before women were again needed, as World War II loomed.

Over the objection of members of Congress and other (male) officials concerned about protecting women from the realities of war—apparently forgetting that many had already served with distinction—some 70,000 enlisted women and 20,000 officers joined a new reserve program called the Women Accepted for Volunteer Emergency Service (WAVES). Many members of WAVES performed administrative tasks, as women had done in the First World War. But others filled skilled technical jobs in logistics, training, medical services, and aviation, freeing men for service with the fleet.

Less by-the-book—as a relatively new unit, it was *writing* the book—the Bureau of Aeronautics was unbound by centuries of tradition and far more open to innovation than other parts of the navy. And with the new emphasis on airpower in wartime, the bureau had a huge need for personnel. At the beginning of World War II, the navy had estimated it would require 25,000 women to fill spots held by men needed for combat; by war's end, 26,000 had served in naval aviation alone, more than in any other bureau.

Among these were some 1,200 women—an estimated one-quarter of them pilots—who taught navigation skills to thousands of airmen between 1943 and 1945. Several dozen would serve as airborne navigators themselves.

Thanks to the efforts of Lieutenant Commander Joy Hancock of the Bureau of Aeronautics, twelve members of the WAVES reported to Naval Air Navigation School in Hollywood, Florida, along with eighty-eight men, in the summer of 1943. Hancock, a civilian pilot who served as a yeoman during World War I, pressured the brass in Washington to open this all-male field to women; later, as a captain, she would become director of the WAVES.

Perhaps selected because they possessed pilot's licenses or superior math skills, the dozen female navigator candidates studied meteorology, aerology (the atmosphere and how it is affected by weather), Morse code, the drawing of weather maps, and the use of octants and other navigation instruments. They learned dead reckoning—determining an aircraft's position by calculating speed, direction, and time since the previous position report—and radio navigation, using signals from radio beacons to find the aircraft's location. They plotted courses, accounting for wind speed and direction. And they became proficient, by comparing time and distance traveled against expected fuel consumption, in calculating the Point of No Return—after which there was no choice but to go on, as there wasn't enough fuel to make it back.

There was also physical conditioning and nighttime training in astronomy and celestial navigation based on the stars and constellations.

Any navigator candidate who didn't maintain a grade-point average of at least 3.2 out of 4 throughout the seventeen weeks of training was "bilged" out. Tests included the "dry swim," a grueling four-hour exercise requiring repeated calculations during a simulated flight between remote Pacific islands.

Halfway through the course of study, ground school gave way to aerial instruction for a total of 50 hours in twin-engine Beechcraft SNBs, navigating across the southeastern United States and back and forth to the Florida Keys, Cuba, and the Bahamas—all while toting custom-fitted parachutes.

The first twelve WAVES candidates also shouldered the burden of publicity; the novelty of females in aviation was an irresistible opportunity, and the women posed for lots of photos while standing next to aircraft, navigation instruments in hand.

With a new class of one hundred navigator candidates starting every two months, their ranks quickly grew, and while many of the female graduates ended up assigned to teaching duties on the ground, eighty or so eventually got to teach aerial navigation in flight, on both the East and West Coasts.

They instructed male navigators and conducted checkrides in multi-engine Martin PBM-2 flying boats and PBM-3 Mariner patrol bombers. On the ground, they administered four-hour tests in the Celestial Link flight simulator in preparation for the most dangerous type of flying: long-distance flights at night over water. Sitting outside the sim, they would feed Morse code signals with information on wind speed and direction—which was often very different from what the forecast had predicted—to the male trainee inside and monitor as he would "shoot" the stars with the octant, plot the new fix, and set a new course for the pilot while preparing ongoing position and weather reports.

For navigator instructors who remained in Florida, there were flights to and from Puerto Rico, Guantanamo Bay, and the Panama Canal Zone.

For those assigned to duty in San Diego, the main departure point for aircraft headed to the Pacific Theater, there were four- to eight-hour forays far out over the ocean in preparation for Trans-Pac—trans-Pacific flights to the war zone—usually in a Consolidated PB2Y-3 Coronado or Martin flying boat. Their secondary mission was to keep an eye out for Japanese submarines. Another duty was to teach celestial navigation to carrier-based pilots who, flying without benefit of a navigator, had to find their way to their targets and then back to their ship at its new position, since it was moving and wasn't where it had been when the pilot took off.

Although women were barred from combat zones, some WAVES navigators were assigned to Hawaii, which was technically part of the Pacific Theater. And that opened up opportunities for the women to officially serve as aircrew, as a way to gain personal experience for teaching Trans-Pac. This made the WAVES navigators the first American female military aircrew members, as the WASP were technically civil servants.

They were also the first women to wear navy wings, a distinctive air navigator insignia approved in March 1945 that bore a compass rose in the center, over crossed anchors. Ensign Madeline Burks, quoted in *Aviation History*, said, "We found we had to carry a copy of the orders authorizing our wings on us at all times because senior officers might stop us and point out that we . . . weren't allowed to wear our boyfriend's wings on our uniform. Well, seeing our orders would sort them out pretty fast!"

Anecdotal evidence suggests that some of the WAVES navigators who held pilot's licenses may have unofficially piloted some flights as well. Other enlisted women and officers trained as metalsmiths, aircraft mechanics, parachute riggers, electronics technicians, air traffic controllers, and plane captains, ground crew members responsible for ensuring an aircraft is fit to fly. They became experts in photo interpretation, aircraft recognition, gunnery, and communications procedures.

The question of why women couldn't be actual navy pilots was put before all Bureau of Aeronautics personnel in 1942, even before the WASP took wing for the army, in a letter in *BuAer News Letter* No. 176 on August 15, 1942. Asked fourteen-year-old Ann O'Hara of Minneapolis: "Why can't girls win wings as well as boys?"

According to an article in the July 1977 issue of *Naval Aviation News*, "In answering the letter, one of the navy's veteran pilots confessed that there was no reason why women shouldn't fly as well as men. He wondered, though, if they could patrol 20 hours at a stretch on instruments over the foggy Atlantic, or land on the heaving deck of a converted merchantman carrier; if they could peel off on a dive-bombing attack against a Japanese cruiser, as he wished he could right then. He then admitted, reluctantly, that women could probably do all these things and eventually might."

The article went on to quote "an old-timer, a diehard male chief aviation machinist's mate," about his wartime service with a group of female aircraft mechanics at Naval Air Station Whiting Field: "I didn't want women mechs but I had to take them. I was wrong. I have nearly 200 women manning this line and it's the best line we've ever had."

After the war, navy women were expected to go back home, as they did after World War I and as the WASP were forced to do in 1944. But for many women, the navy held the potential for a fulfilling career. The Women's Armed Services Integration Act did away with the WAVES in name but gave them formal status. Despite the navy's limitations, women were assigned overseas; were involuntarily recalled to service during the Korean War; gained the opportunity for (limited) sea duty aboard transport ships for military dependents; and rotated through billets in administration, training, communications, personnel, intelligence, legal, aerology, and planning, so as to become "experts in the operation of the shore establishment." In assigning those positions, the chief of naval personnel noted in 1954, female officers were "not precluded from serving as non-pilot aviation officers or other specialist categories."

Later, responding to the pressures of the Vietnam War, the navy opened its ROTC scholarship program to women in February 1972. No more than sixty women would be admitted, however, and those with children were ineligible. Though they were expected to take the same courses as men—engineering, data processing, calculus, physics, and the naval sciences, to learn all aspects of naval warfare, management, and operations—while the men did summer sea duty, the women were limited to shore commands.

Women wishing to enlist in the navy had to meet higher mental standards than men, and, unlike their male counterparts, were subjected to grilling by recruiters, "to ensure that no pattern of promiscuous or indiscreet sexual morality is evidenced in a woman applicant's background." Any woman who'd ever had a terminated pregnancy or given up a child for adoption was automatically rejected. Women with children under eighteen had to leave the service, until an air force captain sued in 1970 to challenge a regulation forcing her to give up her son in order to stay on active duty.

While a military wife was automatically assumed to be her husband's dependent, a husband could not receive benefits as a military spouse unless he was physically or mentally incapable of working and could prove that his wife provided more than one-half of the family's financial support. (The Supreme Court struck down those rules in 1973 in a reverse sex discrimination case argued by future justice Ruth Bader Ginsburg.) Women who got pregnant were out unless the chief of naval personnel granted a special exception on a case-by-case basis.

For female prospective officers, too, there was a separate, more-limited path to navy service. Theirs began at Women's Officer School (WOS) in Newport, Rhode Island—as opposed to the standard (male) Officer Candidate School program in Newport or, for pilots, Aviation Officer Candidate School in Pensacola. WOS was heavy on bookwork and protocol but offered far less physical training and little to no shipboard experience to budding officers in the United States' seafaring military branch. Derided as the sort of place where, Rosemary Mariner told the Los Angeles Times, candidates were taught that it "was undignified for female officers to sit atop barstools," WOS was designed for women destined for clerical or administrative duties, not for the new breed of officers Zumwalt seemed to be inviting in.

Certainly not for Barbara Allen Rainey, the first woman to win the naval aviator's Wings of Gold and to qualify in a navy jet. Or for the military's first two female helicopter pilots, Joellen Drag Oslund (who also challenged the status quo in federal court) and Ana Maria Scott. Or for Judy Neuffer Bruner, the first woman to solo a navy aircraft and the first female Hurricane Hunter. Or for Jane Skiles O'Dea, the navy's first female flight instructor, the first woman to fly huge C-130 cargo planes, and the first naval aviator to have a baby.

Or for Rosemary Bryant Merims Conatser Mariner, the first woman to fly a tactical jet; the first to command an aviation squadron; one of the first to serve on an aircraft carrier and qualify as a surface warfare officer; and a nationally recognized advocate and mentor for generations of navy women and men.

Part II
The 1970s

CHAPTER THREE

The Word Goes Out

BARBARA ANN ALLEN WAS A LIEUTENANT (JUNIOR GRADE) IN THE US
Naval Reserve, nearly two years into her commission. Lieutenant (j.g.)
Judith Ann Neuffer was a computer programmer stationed in San Diego.
Jane Millen Skiles was an officer candidate at Women's Officer School
in Newport, Rhode Island. Joellen Drag, a self-described "navy brat," had
recently graduated from college and was job-hunting when a friend in
the Reserve told her the navy was opening flight training to women and
suggested a visit to the local recruiter. Ana Maria Scott was a college
graduate seeking her path in life when her father told her about a news
article he'd seen. Purdue University student Rosemary Bryant Merims
found out from a newspaper clipping mailed by her mother; a TWA vice
president had recently told the aeronautics undergraduate that women
would never fly for the airlines.

When Navy Secretary John Warner announced in October 1972
that naval flight training was opening to women, it was an invitation, as
Ebbert and Hall wrote in *Crossed Currents*, to enter "an elite community
whose claim to being the cream of the crop was challenged only by sub-
mariners. Only those with superb mental and physical conditioning need
apply for flight training."

The first six female navy pilots to earn their Wings of Gold certainly
were athletic, as Lieutenant S. H. Warner had suggested a naval aviator
must be way back in 1928. They also, for the most part, had family traditions of military service and, not surprisingly, a common interest in aviation. Rosemary and Ana Maria were already licensed pilots when they

signed on. Jane's father had been a naval aviator and often took her flying, although, as she told an interviewer in 2017, "little girls didn't dream of being pilots in the sixties." Judy's dad had taught her to fly a Piper Cub, and she soloed at sixteen, though she hadn't earned her pilot certificate. Barb had some limited flight time, perhaps 5 hours in her logbook. Only Joellen had no flight experience other than as a passenger.

Beyond that, the six shared the mental toughness, fortitude, and determination to stand up against pushback: from family members and a country opposed to the Vietnam War and increasingly hostile toward the military; from defenders of rigid gender roles; and later, from flight instructors, commanding officers, and other navy personnel who thought women had no business piloting military aircraft. Perhaps most important, they all had the courage to embark on an adventure that would challenge decades of tradition, and to shoulder the responsibility of proving to the country—again—that women have what it takes to fly.

BARBARA ANN ALLEN RAINEY, BETHESDA, MARYLAND

Born at Bethesda Naval Hospital in August 1948, the daughter of a naval officer, Barb was the first woman to earn naval aviator's Wings of Gold and to qualify as a navy jet pilot. She grew up in California and was an outstanding high school and college athlete. After graduating Phi Beta Kappa from Whittier College with a bachelor's degree in physical education, and facing a scarcity of teaching jobs, she joined the Naval Reserve to follow as closely as she could the path of her brother, a marine helicopter pilot who served in Vietnam. She was the first of the six to be commissioned an ensign, on December 18, 1970, and was promoted to lieutenant (j.g.) in March of 1972.

Though the military offered a choice of career paths, the issue for Barb, as for so many civilian women, was opportunity. The options for navy women outside the medical field were fairly restricted; without a nursing degree, she was largely limited to working in administration or communications. So when word of Warner's announcement came down while Barb was serving as a communications watch officer on the staff of the Supreme Allied Command, Atlantic, in Norfolk, Virginia, she jumped at the chance.

Slightly more than two years later, on February 22, 1974, her father, retired commander Bill R. Allen, pinned Wings of Gold on the United States' first female naval aviator, at Naval Air Station Corpus Christi, Texas.

JUDITH ANN NEUFFER BRUNER, WOOSTER, OHIO

Judy Neuffer, the first woman to solo a navy aircraft, grew up around aviation. Her father, an Army Air Corps flier during World War II, managed a small airport in Orrville, Ohio, and Judy, born three years after the war ended, in June 1948, spent her summers at the field. She answered the phone, did odd jobs, and, during quiet spells, flew with her dad in his Piper Cub. She soloed at sixteen, and once, during high school, an airline pilot came for Career Day and told her she might someday be a stewardess but never a pilot, even though she was the only other person in the room who had ever flown.

But aviation was expensive, and her professional interests lay elsewhere.

"I grew up with *Star Trek*, wanting to be a scientist, work for NASA, and find life out there," she says. The military wasn't part of those plans—certainly not the navy, for a girl who lived hundreds of miles from the ocean and had seen Lake Erie maybe once. But after three years of taking out loans and working multiple jobs to put herself through Ohio State, Judy was ready to listen when an army recruiter came to her dorm with an offer to pay for her senior year if she enlisted.

Judy wasn't necessarily interested in the army, so she asked a navy recruiter if he could match that deal. He couldn't, but the program sounded interesting enough that she signed up anyway. Summer between her junior and senior years was spent at Women's Officer School in Newport for half of basic training. In June 1970, at the end of her senior year—which she paid for herself—she received her bachelor's degree in computer science at graduation ceremonies in the morning and was sworn in as an ensign in the afternoon.

It was a two-year stint, and she thought maybe she'd see a little of the world before continuing her education and pursuing the scientific path she wanted. She was still at her first duty station, working as a computer programmer at Fleet Combat Direction Systems Support Activity at Point Loma—"a landlocked Ohio girl in San Diego, not flying, but in San Diego, with a balcony overlooking the bay"—when the word went out about flight training. That invitation rekindled Judy's interest in aviation.

"I knew I liked flying, I knew I could fly, and thought, let me apply and see what happens," Judy says. She wasn't trying to be a pioneer, she said in an interview with *Naval Aviation News*. "I would say that I was at the right place at the right time."

But a pioneer she was—on January 10, 1973, in a grand ceremony at the Pentagon, Warner himself signed the orders authorizing twenty-four-year-old Lieutenant (j.g.) Judith Neuffer as the first woman officially assigned to US military flight training. "This is a great day for the navy," he told assembled members of the press, posing with Judy and other officers with an oversize set of wings trotted out for the occasion. And because of that, after earning her wings for real on February 27, 1974, the *Star Trek* fan from small-town Ohio got to see the world, as well as the literal eye of the storm as the nation's first female Hurricane Hunter—and, later, to forge a most impressive career at NASA.

JANE SKILES O'DEA, AMES, IOWA

For Jane Skiles, daughter of a naval aviator and a US Naval Reserve Supply Corps officer in the WAVES, who both served in World War II, the military was in the family's DNA. So was grit, the sort of toughness that taught her to stand up to neighborhood bullies and empowered her to pursue a nontraditional career as a military aviator.

Born in 1950, she was drawn to aviation, but given the tenor of the times, flying was not a job for a female. "It wasn't something I had dreamed of as a schoolgirl," she told *Stars and Stripes* in a 1975 interview, though her father gave her her first flight in a Ford Tri-Motor, and they often flew together in his Beechcraft Bonanza. When she was in high school, she asked to work the ramp, fueling and parking aircraft at the local airport where he kept his plane. But receptionist was the only job open to a girl.

Jane graduated from Iowa State in 1972 with degrees in political science and music—she started playing violin at age seven—and considered a career in law, inspired by a female cousin who was an attorney. Then, a friend of her father's told her the navy was considering opening flight training to women. Her interest piqued, she saw a recruiter and signed up. Jane was in the midst of officer candidate training in Newport when it became official, and she immediately applied, seeing a no-lose opportunity.

Aviation offered a chance to follow in her father's footsteps, and, "I figured if I wasn't selected, I'd get out of Iowa for a few years and finance law school through the GI Bill," she said in an interview. Her mom was behind her 100 percent; her dad was skeptical.

But from the very beginning, she was changing minds.

"One of my favorite memories was flying a cross-country flight into my former employer's airfield in Des Moines, Iowa," she told Linda Maloney in *Military Fly Moms: Sharing Memories, Building Legacies.* "I taxied to the parking ramp in my dirty, greasy S-2. My former employer was there to greet me and shake my hand. He rolled out the red carpet usually reserved for wealthy Learjet owners. What a sweet moment for a girl who was told she couldn't fuel airplanes on his line!"

Jane was winged on April 5, 1974, her proud father, Paul, pinning his own Wings of Gold on his daughter—the first naval aviator to do so. It was the first time she had ever seen him wear his dress blues. Lieutenant (j.g.) Jane Skiles would become the first woman to fly the C-130 Hercules—"Janey" splashed across the front of her flower-adorned flight helmet—and the first navy woman to qualify as a flight instructor. She was also one of the first female naval aviators to carrier-qualify; to achieve command and to make captain; the first to serve overseas; and the first-ever pregnant navy pilot.

JOELLEN DRAG OSLUND, CASTRO VALLEY, CALIFORNIA

Joellen Drag wanted to be a professional horse show jumper.

Growing up at a time when girls' sports programs were pretty much nonexistent and women were not expected to be physically fit, Joellen found outlets in solo sports. She and her sisters rode horses, and she taught swimming, horseback riding, and skiing.

But when Joellen graduated from Cal State Hayward in December 1972 at age twenty-two with a political science degree, the options seemed far more limited. She'd had little mentorship in college, and there were few obvious paths beyond traditional women's jobs: teacher, nurse, librarian, secretary.

But she was dating a guy in the Naval Reserve, and he showed her a notice about Warner's announcement. After some back-and-forth, she went to see a recruiter; like Judy, she says she was in the right place at the right time—"and I had enough chutzpah to think I could do it." Also, "It looked better—and paid more—than a legislative internship in Sacramento."

The recruiter hadn't heard about the experiment and at first didn't believe the navy wanted women to fly. But when Joellen returned the next day, she got a much warmer welcome, and after passing a written exam and posing for publicity photos, she was in.

On January 10, 1973, the same day Judy Neuffer became the navy's first female flight cadet, retired commander Theodore Drag affirmed his daughter's "groundbreaking choice" by administering the oath of enlistment at Naval Air Station Alameda, California. They stood next to a Beechcraft T-34 Mentor trainer, with Joellen's mother, Mary, a former US Marine Corps sergeant, looking on. Joellen was the first female civilian student naval aviator recruit.

She also hadn't flown before. Like many of the male student pilots, but unlike the other women, she had no idea what flying was about before she strapped herself into the T-34 at Pensacola. That made her the subject of a double experiment: "They wanted to see if raw talent could get you through."

But the first time she flew a helicopter, she "found a home." Part of the reason, she says, is that some of the same skills you need when you ride horses competitively translate to flying helos; the feel and the feedback are similar. Like "Janey," she decorated her flight helmet with flowers. "The navy," she says, "didn't quite know what to make of us anyway."

After being winged on April 19, 1974, Ensign Joellen Drag became the US military's first female helicopter pilot—and immediately encountered an unexpected roadblock. Section 6015, banning women from combat, put any ship that could in theory engage in combat at any time off-limits to navy women. Flying to and from ships, however, was a primary job for navy helo pilots; Joellen was being evaluated by the same standards as her male colleagues for work she wasn't allowed to do. The law was depriving her of the flight time she needed to advance, and depriving the navy of a qualified pilot.

After watching multiple pleas for equal opportunity vanish up the chain of command, Joellen joined a federal class-action lawsuit challenging the combat restriction, and in 1978, Judge John Sirica ruled in favor of the plaintiffs, opening the door to shipboard duty for women—at least, to a degree.

Joellen was the first female pilot assigned aboard a navy ship and, while serving on active duty and in the Reserve, the first navy woman combat search-and-rescue helicopter aircraft commander, logging seven rescues of aircraft accidents: six in the open ocean, and one in steep mountainous terrain. And later, after retiring as a captain, she and her husband, Captain Dwayne Oslund, were outspoken advocates for military women and their rights.

ANA MARIA SCOTT, WILLIAMSPORT, PENNSYLVANIA

The only one of the six not from a military family, Ana Maria Scott was born on the East Coast—but her passion for aviation was born on the West. Her family moved from Pennsylvania to the San Francisco Bay area when she was a teenager, and when she was sixteen, her boyfriend and a pilot friend of his took her for a night flight.

"It took my breath away," she says, and she asked her parents for flying lessons. Her mom was hesitant; her dad said, "Go for it!"

After college, having earned her private pilot certificate and a degree in political science at the University of California at Santa Barbara, Ana Maria returned east to rejoin her family at their new home in McLean, Virginia. Being fluent in Spanish, she pondered a career in the diplomatic corps, but she was somewhat at a loss about her path in life. That's when her father told her about an article he'd read announcing that the navy was looking for women to fly. Ana Maria sought out a recruiter in Washington, DC, and signed on, a month after Warner's announcement, at age twenty-two. The benefits extended beyond the chance to fly: Equal opportunity, equal pay, and the potential for management experience made the navy an attractive option.

"Since I had my private pilot license, they just took me without a problem," Ana Maria says. She reported to WOS with the other civilian candidates on January 23, 1973. Slightly more than a year later, on May 20, 1974, Ensign Ana Maria Scott won her Wings of Gold. She would become the US military's second female helicopter pilot, with the goal, like Joellen Drag, of landing on combat ships and flying search-and-rescue. She flew VIPs and surreptitiously made some history of her own before leaving the military and flying all over the world as a pilot for FedEx.

ROSEMARY BRYANT MERIMS CONATSER MARINER, SAN DIEGO, CALIFORNIA

The last of the six to earn her Wings of Gold was perhaps the most driven, the most outspoken, and the most determined, as Texas Woman's University professor Katherine Sharp Landdeck told CNN, to kick open doors, put in a doorstop, and tell others behind her to go through.

She was also the only one clearly focused on aviation as a career.

Rosemary Bryant Merims Conatser Mariner was born in Harlingen, Texas, in 1956, the daughter of an air force captain who died in a crash while ferrying a transport plane near Atlanta when she was three years old. Five years later, her mother, a World War II navy nurse, moved Rosemary and her two sisters to the San Diego area with their stepfather. Aviation was literally in the air, and one of Rosemary's favorite pastimes when babysitting for her sisters was to bring them to watch jets take off and land at Naval Air Station Miramar.

Captivated by the aviation adventures so vividly brought to life in the books of Ernest K. Gann, Rosemary decided by ninth grade that she was going to become an airline pilot. She cleaned houses and washed airplanes to pay for flying lessons, and received her private pilot certificate while still in high school, at age seventeen, in 1970—the year Barb was commissioned. It was the first of many achievements to draw the attention of the press, with local papers describing Rosemary as a combination of Wonder Woman and Calamity Jane.

She went on to earn her commercial pilot's license, instrument rating, and flight instructor certificates. By the time she joined the military, she was already a multiengine instrument flight instructor with 620 hours in her logbook.

Most of that flight training happened at Purdue University, where Rosemary enrolled in the professional pilot program and would rack up the first of many firsts—the first female graduate of the aviation technology department. Being the only woman in a program with about twenty guys "was an eye-opener for me," she said. "It was good preparation for what I was going to encounter in the navy."

Back in the 1930s, Purdue had hired Amelia Earhart as an in-house expert on women in aviation; for Rosemary, university faculty members became the first in a long line of supporters and mentors who recognized her exceptional commitment, talent, and leadership, and helped her on her way to making military aviation history.

As one former classmate posted in the funeral home's online guestbook shortly after her death in January 2019, "At Purdue, we knew Rosemary as Rosie Merims. It was a short walk from the Harrison Hall dorm to the Purdue airport. Rosemary would invite friends to fly with her whenever she was logging flight hours. Her personality was engaging, but she was not one to seek the spotlight. She simply pursued her love of flying and did not see any reason for roadblocks. . . . Of all the great pilots from Purdue, it seems that Amelia Earhart and Captain Rosemary Mariner would be at the top of the list of female pilots."

It all happened in a hurry: Her mother mailed her a newspaper clipping about Warner's announcement soon after that discouraging encounter with the airline executive, and Rosemary wasn't about to let the opportunity get away. Talking with a recruiter who said she could make the cut if she graduated by January 1973, she scrambled to finish her degree in just two and a half years. She tested out of her remaining classes, aided by professors and university administrators—including a female dean who had served in the navy during World War II—and earned her bachelor's degree a month before that deadline, in December 1972. "I spent Christmas vacation writing papers and studying for exams," she told the Associated Press. "[I] also spent a lot of time trying to chase down professors."

Two weeks later, she was on her way to Newport amid a storm of publicity about the new prospective female navy fliers. "It was exciting," Rosemary told the authors of *Ladybirds*. "There is nothing like watching [*The Tonight Show with*] *Johnny Carson* and hearing yourself mentioned in the monologue. I was nineteen years old, and on top of the world."

Reported the *Daily Herald* of Jasper, Indiana: "The pert, longhaired brunet [*sic*], who has been flying since she was sixteen, says she not only plans to make the Navy her career but also wouldn't mind becoming an admiral or an astronaut in the process. Miss Merims, a native of San Diego, Calif., was sworn in [in] a brief ceremony at Sky Harbor Airport [in Indianapolis] this morning. Miss Merims then climbed into a two-place prop-driven Naval training plane and, with Lt. Cmdr. Glenn Fant Jr. who inducted, took off for a short flight. Fant said he probably was the only man in the Navy who had kissed his co-pilot before a flight."

It was the first step in the trailblazing career of a naval officer whom Deborah G. Douglas, in *American Women and Flight since 1940*, called, "Arguably the most historically significant woman in American aviation since Amelia Earhart and Jacqueline Cochran."

Commissioned officer or college student, the women who signed up for what a recruitment film described as the navy's most ambitious program for females hoped it would open a door to a whole new world of possibility. For them, it was an unprecedented chance to gain experience largely unavailable to women; to serve their country; to follow family tradition; to find a better, more exciting job. And, of course, to forge potential careers as military pilots.

Whether that's what Warner and Zumwalt had in mind is far less certain.

Unlike Hap Arnold, who had proclaimed the WASP a "pioneering venture," not "solely an experiment," an unclassified September 1972 navy document titled "Public Affairs Guidance Pertaining to Flight Training for Women" stated explicitly: "This is an experimental program." Warner publicly explained several weeks later that it was a test to open up flying of transports, helicopters, "and other types of aviation for those girls that are up to it."

An official announcement distributed navy-wide from the chief of naval operations on November 2, 1972, titled "Eligibility for Flight Training for Navy Women" and referencing Z-116, spelled out

specific actions being taken to ensure equal opportunity for and increased utilization of Navy women in pursuit of our one-Navy concept. In furtherance of this aim, the Navy is initiating a trial program to train women as Naval Aviators. While we are limited by legal constraints in the assignment of women to combat missions, there are many assignments for which women may qualify.

We are seeking applicants from active-duty women officers and officer candidates. Applications should be submitted . . . citing this msg as authority. Flight physical results and AQT [Aviation Qualification Test] / FAR [Flight Aptitude Rating] scores must follow ASAP. . . . Eight candidates will be selected by the end of calendar year 1972. After these women have completed approximately 18 months' training and served for a period of about 6 months in flying billets, the program will be evaluated and a final decision made on numbers to enter the program on a continuing basis. Commanding officers are requested to disseminate widely the contents of this message and ensure that interested personnel are provided ample opportunity to apply.

The rationale was to engender equal opportunity before the ERA made it mandatory and to bolster a flying corps depleted not only by the impending end of the draft and the Vietnam War, but by competition from higher-paying airline jobs that didn't carry the risk of being shot down.

As Warner told NBC News' John Cochran on *Face the Nation*: "Admiral Zumwalt and I have come out with a new policy on women . . . we're opening up the rates; we're bringing them into the NROTC [Naval Reserve Officers Training Corps] program, and recently I announced that we were going to open them up to naval aviation. Why shouldn't they be able to fly in the same manner as the men? They're able to do it. It's a great opportunity. I believe in the immediate future . . . that the Armed Forces of the United States will be one of the greatest, if not the greatest, training areas open to young men and women. Why shouldn't they be given all the opportunities to improve themselves, and if they don't wish to make it a career, go back and become leaders in their society?"

"Don't wish to make it a career" is what many expected would happen.

Men completing navy flight training had three options: helicopters, propeller planes, or jets. For the women, the choices would be helos or transport planes; sexy jets were strictly off-limits. Navy brass would see how "those girls" would do and reevaluate in six months; other women wishing to fly navy would have to wait. Meaning that once they completed their training and were sent out to their first billets, the first six female naval aviators would be alone, with no other women pilots coming up behind them to bolster their numbers and provide support in a sea of men who didn't necessarily want them there.

This may have made the experiment palatable to the Old Guard—the "We've always (or never) done it that way" crowd—but it gave the navy little incentive for long-term, or even short-term, planning to accommodate women in the pilot corps. Where they would sleep and even whether there were appropriate bathroom facilities would be a common and persistent issue. Pushback from navy wives to the eighty women billeted on the noncombatant hospital ship USS *Sanctuary* in an experimental program under Z-116 did not bode well for female fliers stationed at primarily male air bases. And whatever happened, they were committed for six years.

The navy, says Joellen, did not expect them to persist. "They thought it would be cute to have us around for a few years and that we'd do six years, find a husband, and go away, and they could say, 'We tried.' To their amazement and horror, we decided to stick with it."

For the first six who made it through, Joellen says, "it was just throw them in, stir the pot, see how they do. They didn't have a career path, didn't think about what they would do with the second assignment. They didn't even have the right equipment. They had nothing sized to fit women. They didn't have uniforms with pants; we were still in skirts. . . . I was in my squadron for a year before I got my first uniform with slacks. Prior to that, when I had duty watch, I had to walk the flight line in heels and a straight skirt."

In the April 1973 issue of its official magazine, *All Hands*, the navy introduced the program this way: "If you have accepted the idea of women serving on board ships—and a surprisingly large number of Navymen have welcomed the idea—then you shouldn't have much trouble with the thought that women will soon be flying the Navy's planes."

Initially, twenty-six women applied, all commissioned officers or WOS officer candidates. "They weren't overwhelmed with applicants," says John Rainey, Barb's husband. "There weren't so many jumping for the opportunity to be under that much pressure and scrutiny" that they rightly feared was coming.

Of the twenty-six, only four passed the initial exams—eyesight (20/20 uncorrected), general intelligence (ostensibly a predictor of performance in the academic phase of flight training), personal and medical histories, hand–eye coordination, mechanical reasoning (if a flywheel in the picture is turning one way, which way is the other one turning?), spatial perception (if the horizon in the picture is tilted, which way is the airplane banking?).

"If you hadn't had some type of exposure to tools before, you were at a disadvantage," said Jane to *Stars and Stripes*. She had learned about tools and how they functioned in her father's carpentry workshop. "The lack of exposure to mechanical things, compared with a man in the testing, was a distinct disadvantage."

So recruiters sought additional applicants. Four civilians were accepted and would report to Pensacola for flight training after completing WOS and earning their commissions. Of the eight who ultimately made the cut, one officer and one officer candidate dropped out. There were also two alternates, but because Zumwalt wanted to compare the women's attrition rate with the men's, they were not allowed to begin their training until 1975, after navy brass had reevaluated the experiment and decided to continue. They earned their wings a year later.

The circus started even before the first of the women arrived at Pensacola. Joellen was sworn in as an officer candidate on the same day Warner signed Judy's flight training orders at the Pentagon, and together, the two events on January 10, 1973, made national news. One newspaper story about Joellen taking the oath, receiving a kiss from her father, and stating that she hoped to qualify to land on an aircraft carrier and fly jets was headlined, "Girl Flier Gets Kiss, Wants Combat, Too." United Press International described her as "the newly enlisted woman, who had her blonde hair in bangs and wore boots," and reflected on what prospective love interests might think about her flying. ("The men I go out with think it's fantastic. They want me to take them up in a plane," she said.) Illustrating the story was a picture of Joellen wearing high-heeled boots and a miniskirt, leaning against a T-34, captioned "The shape of things to come."

At the Pentagon, the Associated Press described a "Hollywood-like ceremony publicizing Warner's announcement that eight women had been chosen to begin training to be pilots of Navy transport planes or helicopters" and introducing Judy as their representative. The report said the "pretty, 24-year-old brunette" would "like to be considered" for astronaut training "if the opportunity came along," to which Warner replied, "I would so recommend." Various newspaper headlines on the story included "Navy Flight Cadet Is a She (The First)" (*Philadelphia Inquirer*) and "Gal Seeks Those Navy Wings" (New Brunswick, New Jersey, *Home News*).

The *New York Times* account was written in fairly straightforward style, quoting Judy as saying, "I'm thrilled, I'm going to give it everything I have." The story mentioned the combat exclusion but countered that Judy had "no desire to be a combat pilot anyway." It did note, however, that for the women, "There will be no prohibition against their carrying feminine gear such as makeup in the capacious pockets of their flight suits, should they desire." The writer added that "a man pilot is allowed to carry personal objects" as well.

Video of the ceremony shows Judy holding up a model of a C-130 and chatting with Warner as other military brass look on.

Barb received her training orders several weeks after Judy, and the two arrived at Pensacola a few days early. Scarcely had they set foot on base when, "looking more like models for the trim Navy blue uniforms," they were summoned to meet the press, the Gannett News Service reported on March 2, 1973. They "answered newsmen's questions quietly and blushed into a phalanx of television cameras," seated "at a camellia-strewn table" as they "tugged at their narrow skirts."

Soon, there would be photo shoots, game-show appearances, newspaper interviews, magazine profiles, and still more photo opportunities. There would be covert and overt resistance; legal roadblocks and mentors who offered sage advice and helped clear the way; routine training flights hijacked for purposes of publicity; and relationships with navy men that could turn very dark indeed.

As for Zumwalt, Warner's announcement couldn't have come at a more inopportune time.

He was already no favorite of the thirty-three or so superior officers he had leapfrogged to become chief of naval operations, and in fall 1972, with racial unrest permeating the ranks, a group of disapproving retired admirals tried to take Zumwalt down with the help of some equally disapproving members of Congress. The congressional hearing that followed put his entire approach to modernizing the navy on trial, on grounds that integration, among other reforms, was destroying military discipline. As he wrote in his autobiography, his Z-grams were portrayed as "the root of permissiveness that was poisoning the Navy."

Zumwalt's defense was that race relations would have been far worse had it not been for his leadership in battling ingrained prejudice, and he beat back the challenge to his authority and legacy with help from supporters in the White House. He retired the following year, in July 1974, and went on to write several books, dabble in business and politics, and advocate for bone marrow donation after his son, Elmo Zumwalt III, died of cancer from exposure to Agent Orange under his father's command in Vietnam. Among all of Zumwalt's accomplishments, the decision to open navy flight training to women didn't particularly stand out in his view—in his memoir, *On Watch*, it takes up all of one sentence. But it profoundly affected the lives of the female aviators for whom Z-gram #116 and its aftermath opened the door.

Zumwalt, Joellen says, was probably one of the most forward thinkers the navy has ever had. "One regret," she says, "is that I never got the opportunity to shake his hand and say thank you."

And Rosemary, who earned her Wings of Gold just two weeks before Zumwalt retired, wrote this about him in the *Washington Post* after his death in 1990: "This remarkable man changed my life and untold others forever. More important, he changed the Navy, and hence the nation, for the better."

CHAPTER FOUR

Women's Officer Training
(Not Quite the Same as Men's)

FOR THE NAVY'S NEW PROSPECTIVE FEMALE FLIERS, AS FOR ALL STUDENT naval aviators, the path to earning Wings of Gold began at Naval Aviation Training Command, Pensacola, Florida. Over the course of twelve to eighteen months, depending on training location, weather, aircraft availability, individual progress, and the like, newly minted officers could go from zero hours logged to piloting the most sophisticated aircraft the United States could produce.

Step 1: *Physical and mental testing*—including flight physical exams, conducted over three days at the Naval Aerospace Medical Institute.

Step 2: *Environmental indoctrination*—three weeks of aviation ground school, including meteorology, aerodynamics, rules and regulations, engineering, internal components and aircraft systems, navigation, and flight physiology; also, water survival exercises and land survival training in the field.

Step 3: *Primary flight training*—done in the Beechcraft T-34B Mentor trainer, a single-engine propeller airplane with a nosewheel, retractable landing gear, and front-and-back seating—the military equivalent of a Beech Bonanza. For about six weeks, student naval aviators learned how to take off and land, fly straight and level, turn, stall the aircraft (the wings, not the engine) and recover, perform basic maneuvers, navigate from point to point, and so on. Then, after the first solo—always a landmark event in any pilot's life . . .

Step 4: *Basic flight training*—including formation flying (the first step toward learning to land on an aircraft carrier), aerobatics, night flying, and flying by reference to instruments alone in low visibility and bad weather, for approximately twenty-two weeks in the North American T-28 Trojan, another single-engine trainer with retractable tricycle gear and front-and-back seating. Also, lots more ground school.

Step 5: *Advanced flight training*—done at various naval air stations, over the course of fifteen weeks or so, depending on which of the three types of aircraft the aviator was assigned to upon completion of basic instruction, according to grades, aptitude, the pilot's interest (to some degree), and the navy's needs at the time. There were big propeller-driven airplanes, helicopters, and jets—the sexiest option of all, where the pilot got to climb up a ladder and close the cockpit canopy rather than walking up a staircase and shutting a door.

But in 1973, only men got to fly jets. For the women, the choice was multiengine training in the T-S2A version of the Grumman S-2 Tracker, in preparation for flying huge prop planes like the P-3 Orion or the C-130; or the TH-57 Sea Ranger as an introduction to rotary flying and the TH-IL Huey for instrument and formation helicopter training.

Step 6: *Being winged*—earning Wings of Gold as official naval aviators.

Step 7: *Assignment to operational squadrons*—for training in the specific aircraft the naval aviators would fly on active duty for the next four and a half years.

But first, for the original female naval aviators, there was Women's Officer School.

Established in 1949 to centralize the somewhat ad hoc women's training programs set up on college campuses for the WAVES during World War II, WOS was located in Newport along with other navy facilities, including (men's) Officer Candidate School and the Naval War College. For the women, the basic course of study was similar to the men's. But rather than learning skills needed for service at sea—including navigation, essential for aviators as well as sailors—the women had a shore-based curriculum, with a focus on history, tradition, and administration. This was presumably fine for women in the unrestricted, or general, line, designated as 1100, who would be working primarily in offices. But for prospective naval aviators in the restricted, or specialized, line, with a 1310 designation, it was woefully insufficient.

As Ebbert and Hall described in *Crossed Currents*: "The trainees studied naval tradition, history, customs, organization, administration and correspondence, and they learned to recognize different kinds of Navy aircraft and ships. . . . They learned to drill. . . . They also stood watch and took turns as platoon leaders and company commanders. The most significant carryover from the WAVE years was the unremitting emphasis on ladylike behavior."

It was, Captain Rosemary Mariner (ret.) told an audience at the Smithsonian Air and Space Museum in 2011, "what us young whipper-snappers uncharitably called the WAV-Y Navy."

For Rosemary, it was the barstool remark that stood out. For retired captain Mary Lyons, it was cosmetics. In an oral history about her time at WOS in the early 1970s, she recalled: "On one occasion, our male counterparts were driving Yard Patrol boats around Aquidneck Island, Rhode Island, while my class listened to a representative from Max Factor instruct us on the proper wearing of makeup."

WOS, says Joellen Oslund, was "sixteen weeks of wasted time." She reported for duty in Newport on January 23, 1973—three days before the military draft ended—with Ana Maria Scott, Rosemary Merims, and Jo Anne Hellman of Zephyr Cove, Nevada, who had just married a navy recruiter and dropped out before flight training began. The prospective naval aviators and forty or so other female officer candidates spent lots of time learning about the Bureau of Personnel Management (BUPERS) manual, drilling, marching, and running. As the curriculum was designed for women not going to the fleet, it was "very broad and general in terms of navy hierarchy and supporting them," Judy Bruner says. "It got me into uniform and gave me discipline for a way of life I was going to have for the next twenty-eight years, rather than teaching pertinent skills for flying."

Rosemary wasn't nearly as kind.

"I hated it," she told the *Los Angeles Times*. "Nothing I was taught applied to the real Navy. What they were dealing with was a woman's Navy, and that is not the real Navy." She was dedicated and focused on her goals, recalled one retired lieutenant commander: "Rosemary and I were members of the same OCS class in Newport, Rhode Island. At the time the idea of women flying in the navy was revolutionary. She was one of the youngest people in the class, but I remember that she also had more private flying hours than people much, much older. She was funny and bright and clear-headed about what she wanted to achieve. Achieve it she did."

The clash between the two navies would be a persistent theme, one that struck Jane Skiles at the very beginning of her naval career. As trainees in the unrestricted line, she recalls, female officer candidates had to wear skirts and heels, even when marching in the snow. She was midway through WOS when word about flight training came down, and she switched gears to apply for the aviation experiment. As Jane told an interviewer in 2017: "The commander, a pioneer in her own right, was excited for me but cautioned me to be careful, saying, 'The Navy does not reward pioneers.' She was right."

Had they been allowed to enter Aviation Officer Candidate School (AOCS) in Pensacola, which opened to women in 1976, the first female naval aviators would have been steeped in aviation culture from day one. From reveille until lights out, the conversation there revolved around airplanes, with the focus on shaping up prospective pilots to fly. Drill instructors might call a marching formation to a halt and command, "At ease, eyes up" so the student naval aviators could watch the Blue Angels streak by. A candidate who neglected to perform some task might find a drill instructor yelling in his (or her) ear: "Are you going to forget to put your landing gear down?!" Visits to the National Naval Aviation Museum, right on the premises, provided tremendous motivation. Classwork devoted to navy regulations, administration, and the like, the primary feature of WOS, was condensed in favor of studies of aerodynamics, aerial navigation, aircraft engines, and other flight-related subjects. AOCS students got six to eight weeks of ground school; the women got a three-week version after they arrived at Pensacola.

Not only was this valuable aviation training unavailable at WOS, but even basic navy skills—ship handling, for example—were not imparted equally, as Z-116 implied they should be.

Retired captain Mary Louise Griffin, one of the female naval aviator alternates who finally started flight training in the second group, in 1975, and was in the last separate WOS class before it was integrated with the men's program, recalls that the men

had a simulator, a small room with a mockup of a bridge, some con-
trols, and rudimentary displays showing direction and so on. The guys
spent lots of time there learning ship handling. The women's class
came along, and our commanding officer asked if her girls could do
that. Captain Julia DiLorenzo was our CO, a go-getter, pushing for
women to do anything and everything she could get for them. They
gave us a compact crash course. Also, the men practiced ship handling
in what was called YP, Yard Patrol, 40- to 45-foot-long mini-
destroyers. They had a dozen or so, and the women got to take them out
in Narragansett Bay one day.

Typically, a ship that size is run by the senior enlisted person, and
there were six- or seven-person teams. We spent a week learning how
to conduct ourselves on the bridge, terminology, a crash course in driv-
ing a ship. I was the battalion commander, in the lead vessel. We did
our first three and a half weeks without uniforms, in dresses—civilian
clothes—which was disconcerting to people in the shipyard.

Newport is the headquarters of the destroyer force of the Atlantic
Fleet, and as we went out, this little formation of YPs going from
the piers to the bay, a destroyer was coming in from out at sea. The
tradition, which we had learned in communications class, is that the

junior, smaller vessel always salutes the senior vessel. On the destroyer, the three-star admiral who ran the fleet was there . . . and we didn't even have our commissions yet.

We whipped out the book, got the signal flags, and raised them to render honors to the destroyer. The closing speed is not real fast, but you've got to get moving, so we ran up the flags and manned the rail. In our case, we woman-ed the rail in our civilian clothes, facing the ship and saluting. If social media had existed, it would have all been on YouTube. It was hilarious! The ship sees our honors and returns honors—they're on the rail because they're coming into port—and return salute to a ship full of women out of uniform.

So we tootle around in our little formation, come back and dock, and march back to quarters, and here comes a Navy message that they were very impressed.

With fewer resources and more restrictions than their male counterparts—another persistent theme—the women managed to meet their military obligations and do their duty. But they had to improvise, be more creative, and work harder.

For Barb and Judy, who'd gone through WOS as 1100 unrestricted line officer candidates and were at their first billets when flight training opened up, the shortcomings that Rosemary and the other prospective pilots found so grating weren't an issue. But when they arrived at Pensacola, it quickly became clear just how unprepared they were.

On March 2, 1973, five weeks after the four civilian recruits reported to Women's Officer School and two days after the Pensacola press conference, the first prospective female naval aviators—Lieutenant (j.g.) Judith Ann Neuffer; Lieutenant (j.g.) Barbara Ann Allen; Ensign Kathleen Lou McNary of Plainfield, Illinois; and Ensign Jane Millen Skiles—began their flight training.

First came three days of indoctrination and psychological and physical testing, followed by weeks of intense instruction in physical fitness and survival training. Every exercise was designed to test physical and mental will, as well as equip potential pilots for the risks and catastrophic occurrences associated with flying. Those who could not pass the tests early on would surely not be up to future challenges.

All students, men and women, had to do a mile-and-a-half cross-country run, tread water for thirty minutes, and swim a mile in a pool wearing a (man-sized) flight suit. Some of the flight suits were so large, the crotch stretched down to the women's knees; one member of a later class did her mile swim in a 44 long.

They had to master exiting the Dilbert Dunker, a giant red contraption that simulated crash-landing in the water. As a student sat inside, it plummeted into the pool and then flipped upside down, testing the pilot's ability to escape.

Water entry practice involved strapping on a parachute harness and helmet, being pushed off a platform 10 feet or so above the water, and being dragged along by a boat. This was to simulate ejecting from an aircraft, landing in the sea, and being pulled by the wind in the chute. The only way to stop it was to undo the harness while in motion; a pilot who couldn't release a wet parachute would eventually be dragged under by the weight and likely drown.

There was ejection seat training, which involved sitting in a chair on a rail and being thrust skyward. This simulated ejecting from a tactical aircraft, but at a slower speed.

There were push-ups, pull-ups, and chin-ups; building stamina was important, no matter what aircraft a student would ultimately train to fly.

To prepare for changes in air and atmospheric pressure at altitude, groups of students entered a hypobaric chamber, where they were slowly and deliberately deprived of oxygen. This was so they could experience what hypoxia feels like should they lose their air supply in flight—and learn what to do about it. Then, "explosive decompression" was initiated, to simulate a midair catastrophe.

And then there was the obstacle course, 600 yards of tire trap, hurdles, low crawl, Jacob's ladder, horizontal ladder, maze, sand to slog through, and two walls to scale, one 15 feet high with ropes, and another 8 feet tall, to scramble over. Trainees had to run the course multiple times, all while being guided—sometimes goaded—by marine drill sergeants, and all to be completed in a matter of minutes. The women had slightly longer, maybe twenty seconds or so.

Even for many of the men, the walls could pose a huge challenge. For the WOS women, possessing less upper-body strength to begin with and having graduated from an officer training course with far less emphasis on physical conditioning, these were enormous, literal obstacles in their path.

"When we reported to Pensacola, the hardest thing there was the obstacle course," Jane says. "We all had trouble with the big wall; the only one who got over was Barb. She was very athletic, a PE major." Jane was a very strong swimmer and "did great in the pool. We had to strap up with everything, flip upside down, and had to get out, then do a mile swim in our flight gear." As for survival training in the woods, "I thought I was going to freeze to death." (Judy brought a metallic blanket because she knew they'd be sleeping on the ground. The guys pooh-poohed her—but that night in the tent, "there were five or six lined up like pencils under my blanket.")

"When Barb and Judy went through OCS, women . . . weren't really prepared for the obstacle course," says John Rainey, a 1972 Naval Academy graduate who trained at Pensacola at the same time as his future wife. "When we went through the obstacle course, if we could get over the 8-foot wall—jump, grab hold of the top, and pull yourself over—the 15-foot wall had a rope . . . a female with no prior training didn't have the upper-body strength to get over the walls, so they ended up in refresher physical training. From their OCS and background, they were poorly served."

In fact, the question of physical fitness standards for the women seems to have been its own mini-experiment. The navy's *Public Affairs Guidance* of September 1972 stated: "The physical requirements are the same as for men . . . the minimum height is 64 inches and minimum weight is 107 pounds. Height requirements are necessary to permit pilots to reach flight controls. . . . The flight training program is recognized as being very strenuous physically. This is purposely done to build physical stamina to withstand the rigors of flying and to develop discipline and a competitive spirit. The physical standards are being reviewed by flight surgeons to ensure realistic requirements for female aviation candidates."

In a memo from the chief of naval operations dated January 16, 1973, titled "Women Naval Aviator Trial Program," the navy's Bureau of Medicine and Surgery was asked to provide "specific guidance for data collection required to evaluate the physiological and psychological aspects of this program, with emphasis on the physical fitness requirements."

Unable to meet all the men's standards, the women were given a progressive exercise schedule: pull-ups, push-ups, sit-ups, bike, rowing, and weight lifting on Mondays, Wednesdays, and Fridays, with running on Tuesdays and Thursdays to build strength and stamina.

But was all that really necessary to qualify as a navy pilot? Were those skills pertinent to handling an aircraft?

From Judy's later experience flying the P-3, the answer was—no, not really.

One of the tests for a P-3 pilot was called a boost-out. This involved disabling the hydraulics on the controls to see if the pilot could muscle through, like a driver has to when the power steering goes out. "I hold the record for most boost-out time in the P-3," she says, because whenever an aircraft commander flew with her for the first time, he wanted to test whether she could handle herself in the airplane. The catch, though, was that the procedure for a boost-out wasn't to manhandle the controls; it was to get the copilot on the controls along with the pilot. It was far more about technique and cooperation than brute strength.

Navy brass soon realized that most of the WOS crew weren't going to get over the obstacle-course walls without help; not long after, that requirement was eliminated for them altogether, and some of the other physical standards were changed. "It's probably one of the only times they let the women proceed when we didn't necessarily meet the requirements," Judy says. Those failures would have been grounds to kick out a male student, she notes, "but if they had used them for the women, they would have lost the entire group."

"The physical test we had to go through obviously had been set up for men," Barb told the *Los Angeles Times*, "mainly because there haven't been any women in it. The Navy got upset when they found we couldn't do it, so they set up a work schedule to show themselves that we could do the work to handle an airplane."

According to a story in the *Christian Science Monitor* on August 13, 1973, Barb, Judy, and Jane "are said to be doing well except that they have not been able to meet Navy flying standards for arm strength. That is, they could not meet the standards for push-ups and chin-ups or scale an eight-foot obstacle course by pulling themselves over. While it has been assumed hitherto that this kind of strength is required to pull a plane out of a spin or open a canopy during a spin, the Navy is trying to redefine minimum strengths required for these tasks and to complete the course. Three other girls . . . knew they were going to need greater arm strength and built themselves up nearer the usual requirements while at Officer Training School."

Ana Maria, who was in the second group of "girls," had the impression that they "always had the best instructors. People wanted us to get through." Conquering the obstacle course was particularly satisfying. "One of the trainers started running with me," she says. "He ran with me halfway through and pulled me along. I was really grateful to him and really pleased that I managed that in the time limit." The training at times was difficult, "but there was always lots of help and positive reinforcement."

Joellen, for one, didn't see what all the fuss was about. "For guys, it's all about the upper-body strength, you know, 'We're stronger than you,' and the truth of the matter is that's not what it takes 99 percent of the time," she said during a 2013 panel discussion on women in combat. "I was fortunate; I had a lot of upper-body strength that I got mostly through riding horses and shoveling what comes out the back end, and I have to say that served me well in the military, that particular skill, on so many levels. But it really wasn't an issue except in the minds of the people who opened the flight program to women."

Joellen, Ana Maria, and Rosemary, who were commissioned on May 16, 1973, and reported to Pensacola a few weeks later, "didn't get to enjoy the initial circus that took place," says John. With no reporters and photographers following them around, says Ana Maria, they were able to focus on what they needed to do. But Barb, Judy, and Jane bore the full brunt of the navy's publicity offensive.

Barb and Judy were brought down to Pensacola early not to get a jump on their training, but for PAOs—public affairs opportunities (aka photo ops). They posed for endless pictures: standing in the sand next to the wall on the obstacle course, wearing their dress blues with heels, white gloves, and purses; on the flight line, sporting custom-made, unusually form-fitting, Blue Angels–style flight suits that someone up the chain had commissioned for them, though they hadn't had even a single lesson in a navy aircraft.

It didn't go over well.

"A lot of people didn't want women there," says John, "so to have them show up and pose against airplanes wearing flight suits normally worn by the premier flight demonstration unit in the world was unearned."

Barb, for one, recognized the bad optics of those publicity shots and the scorn they earned, and packed that flight suit away. It didn't come out again until she had her official portrait painted when she won her Wings of Gold.

"Early on, we were a photo opportunity," says Judy. "Even after I got out to my first squadron, they put me on TV shows. They sent me to New York to be on *To Tell the Truth* and *What's My Line?*" But as an aviator, she needed to stay focused and concentrate on her training, rather than think about how her mere presence was shaking things up. "I was working too hard just trying to do the best I could, to prove I had a right to be there."

One photographer asked Jane to pose in a bathing suit. "Do they take pictures of male flight students in bathing suits?" the ensign asked in response. But she wondered, the *Pensacola Journal* reported, "whether or not the Navy was admitting them as 'tokens' of their sex. 'We're hoping it's an honest opening of fields, but only time will tell.'"

An excerpt from an evaluation of the first female student naval aviators a month into their training, April 2, 1973, suggests a good-faith effort:

These students are average to slightly below average academically, partially due to their lack of a basic background in engineering and principles of mechanics. Their motivation is better than average, and this, together with their diligent application, resulted in a respectable class standing upon completion of their work. With continued application, they should do well in future academic work and, as their fund of mechanical knowledge increases, better performance can be expected.

Their biggest handicap, physically, was in upper body strength and running stamina. None of them satisfactorily completed the obstacle course, cross-country course, shuttle-run or chin-up requirements based on male student standards. All were above average in swimming ability, possessing exceptional confidence in the water.

Only where upper body strength was necessary did they have trouble in the sea survival situation; however, no serious problems were encountered in entering rafts or in parachute release. Their interest, imagination and motivation made them distinct assets in the land survival situation; in possible future survival situations, these students should encounter little problems and can be expected to do as well or better than men.

All four women were well accepted by their fellow students and were integrated into regular class work smoothly and with no difficulty. When given leadership responsibility, they performed competently and were well accepted by their male classmates. The instructor reaction was consistently favorable. They spoke highly of these students' diligence, motivation and spirit.

The women were soon split up, each in a separate squadron with twenty or so male student aviators, for ground school and introductory flight training. They weren't part of a class per se; wherever the individuals were in their training, the next phase would start on a Monday, with graduation on Fridays. Then, on to the next stage, to begin the first Monday after arrival at the new post.

The first stop was Saufley Field, a training airport just west of Pensacola.

"We started out at Saufley, divided up right from the start into various squadrons," Judy says. "We never saw each other because we were in different training groups. We saw each other in BOQ [bachelor officer quarters] at night, but that was about it. I started through initial flight

58

training at Saufley, soloed the T-34, then went on to the second phase at a navy base a few miles north of Pensacola, Whiting, flying the T-28, and completed my training there. When we were all at Whiting, again, we were put in separate squadrons and never saw each other. We lost one of the group at Saufley."

A prospective naval aviator could separate from the military for any number of reasons: DOR (drop on request), physical injury, academic failure, or misconduct. He or she could be found not to be officer material (for a DUI or other violation of standards of behavior) or Not Aeronautically Adaptable (airsick, unable to handle inverted flight), or fail a flight test. Each flight was graded on fifteen to twenty-five parameters, depending on the expectations for the trainee and the difficulty of the lesson. The grading started with ground preparation and ended with securing the aircraft after the training mission was over. Students could fly a textbook set of maneuvers and fail a flight for cutting off another aircraft while positioning to land. And always, they were judged on their head work—the ability to focus and function under pressure. It was all about attention to detail and inner strength. Could they stay calm and follow procedures during the worst crisis? How well could they handle bad weather, or rough seas, or loss of an engine?

"We were very closely watched during flight training," Jane told *Stars and Stripes*, "much more than the men." Being first, they knew that everything they did would reflect on the program and weigh on its future.

Adding to that pressure: Somehow, when the women were around, the cameras always seemed to come out. As Judy says, "It was hard to blend in when we were always being followed by photographers."

For publicity purposes, the navy wanted pictures of the women engaged in all the basic elements of instruction—leaping into the water, getting out of the Dilbert Dunker, doing survival training in the woods. Judy volunteered for the Dilbert Dunker photo shoot because she knew there'd be a snake in the survival pictures. "Everyone hated the Dilbert Dunker, even the guys, but it was better than having to hold a snake." (Barb ended up holding it.) "They made the woman take a bite," says Judy. "None of the guys would touch it. It didn't taste all that bad. Tasted like chicken."

When Judy taxied out for her first solo in the T-34 on May 10, 1973—the first time a woman soloed a navy aircraft—it brought the entire field to a standstill. The historic event was captured in pictures and on film and was included in a 1974 promotional and recruitment video titled *Ladies Wear the Blue.* Judy is shown tucking her hair into her flight helmet, taxiing, and taking off. There's air-to-air footage of her T-34 in flight, then a brief shot of her shaking hands with her skipper and her flight instructor after a successful landing, all backed by a triumphal musical score.

This is followed by a post-flight interview with Judy, her hair in a 1970s flip style. "It was a very good feeling to know that I had actually taken that plane off and brought it back home all on my own. It was definitely a feeling of satisfaction, a feeling of having gotten over one hurdle, and I think it helped to, sort of, build a little confidence too, that we are in the program, we can fly the plane, and we are able to cope with the pressures and rigorous training that we're involved in."

There are also brief clips of Jane, standing on a platform, helmet on, preparing to plummet into the water and release her parachute harness while being dragged along; and of Barb, kneeling on the wing of her T-34, checking the fuel.

The (female) narrator then intones: "Our navy's strength lies in the fact that individuals are given the chance to show what they can do."

Not surprisingly, there was some resentment among male students and superior officers who didn't have camera crews following them around.

"Was there lots of pushback? Yes, but it varied," Judy says. "It was something I anticipated, so for the most part I didn't ignore it, but I didn't let it eat up a lot of my energy trying to deal with it. It would vary, at all levels, from commanding officers to fellow students, depending on where I happened to be. For the most part, the male students were very focused on trying to get through flight training themselves, so there wasn't necessarily lots of obvious, overt pushback, but there were those who'd make it clear that we didn't belong there. Also, everywhere I went, I was able to find a little bit of support, maybe just one or two persons, somebody giving a little bit of encouragement, and I tended to focus on that. I knew

I wouldn't be able to change the minds of these other folks. . . . I focused on doing what I was asked to do."

The resistance, says John, began at the top, and it started early, with Judy and Barb's photo-op introduction to their commanding officer. During their initial interview, "he said he didn't want them there. That was their welcome to flight school in Pensacola. They took pictures at the meeting, but he told them they shouldn't be there."

That attitude trickled down the ranks. The guys, John says, knew the women were coming; he, for one, was "surprised and offended" that a female—his future wife—could keep pace with him, sit-up for sit-up. For John, that shock soon gave way to admiration. Their first time in a classroom together, someone started grilling the students about their athleticism, and Barb's hand was one of the few that stayed up through a barrage of questions: Who played sports in high school? In college? Who lettered in a varsity sport in college? In two sports? Later, the two would bond over sports; he didn't have a TV, but she did, and they'd get together at her place to watch UCLA basketball and other events.

Many other trainees, though, couldn't get past the notion of women in navy flight training. Soon after instruction began, some of the men started griping that they thought the women were getting preferential treatment.

"We were just starting at Saufley, and at one point the skipper called us into his office—we all probably had a few hours of flight time with our instructors—and he said the male students were complaining that the women students got the best instructors," says Judy.

He said, "We are going to change your instructors." When we arrived, they had told us how important it was to develop a rapport with your initial instructor because he was the one who'd get you to your first solo. So here they were, halfway through, and they were changing all the instructors. As it turned out, there were four of us with four instructors, and when the dust settled, we had the same four instructors, but we were different pairs now. I got Barbara Rainey's, she got mine, and so on. This was a very challenging time, as we had tried to establish some kind of relationships with the crews and instructors in the beginning, and we had to do it all over again. Shortly after that, we lost one member of the first group of four. She went ahead and dropped out. Then there were three: Barb, Jane, and myself.

Says John, "I don't know what it accomplished except some amount of turmoil to add to the scrutiny and stress they were already under. The guys didn't encounter that."

One thing it did accomplish was to set a 25 percent attrition rate for the female naval aviators, slightly higher than the men's, and a number that stayed consistent when one of the four women who had been recruited as civilians quit before flight training even began. Of course, this was out of a pool of just eight people, a statistically insignificant proportion by any measure. But it added to the pressure of a program whose success was to be evaluated after only six months, a life-or-death decision that would determine whether women would continue in the aviation corps, or the experiment would end practically before it began.

On the other hand, that external pressure unexpectedly made even men who didn't want the women in their squadrons eager to claim them as their own.

From Saufley, it was on to Whiting Field, northeast of Pensacola. This was where a life-defining decision would be made: what type of aircraft the naval aviators would fly. Each flight would be graded; together, those grades determined whether the pilots would go jet, multiengine propeller airplane, or helicopter. For all the grumbling about the women's supposed preferential treatment, it wouldn't have made any difference, as the jet pipeline—the top pick for any naval aviator—was off-limits for the women. They were relegated to support squadrons, along with the lowest-performing male pilots, rather than receiving fleet orders to fly sophisticated military jets. Rosemary, for one, would have qualified for jets based on her grades. But for the women, grades were not the determining factor. For them, the choice was preordained.

Not only couldn't the women fly jets, but just two of the first three would be allowed to fly props. The third would have to go into the less-desirable helicopter pipeline.

Judy, the first to solo at Saufley and complete her training, was the first to go to Whiting. She requested the prop pipeline and got it. Jane finished next and also got props. Meaning Barb, who wanted props as well, had to go helo. Yet somehow, all three ended up going to Naval Air Station Corpus Christi for multiengine training in the prop pipeline. And Barb got there first.

The reason was another external force, but this time it had nothing to do with the navy. It was love.

"Barb was initially supposed to go helo and Judy go multi," says John. "The people going multi were all in VT-3 [Training Squadron 3] in Whiting, and the people going helo were in VT-2 or VT-6, smaller squadrons. If you were going multi, part of the curriculum at the end at VT-3 was a four-plane formation, because you needed to be able to fly four-plane to land on a carrier. Ordinarily, you did four-plane at VT-3 and then went to VT-5 at Saufley and did field carrier landing practice"—a series of touch-and-go landings and takeoffs at an airfield to simulate landing on a carrier, flying the T-28.

"Since Barb was going helo in VT-2," John continues, "she didn't have four-plane. But by then—we were not engaged yet, but we knew we probably would be—so she put in to switch from helo to multi" so they would more likely be stationed near each other. "It was approved, so she went from VT-2 without the four-plane to VT-5 to do field carrier landing practice, and they said she could do four-plane later."

By skipping four-plane at Whiting, Barb got to VT-5 early, which put her on track to get to Corpus and multiengine training ahead of schedule. This put Judy, the most senior of the six women, behind Barb.

The race was on. Who would win her Wings of Gold first and become Female Naval Aviator No. 1?

At Corpus, John and Barb were assigned to squadron VT-31 for more ground school and flight instruction in the T-S2A twin-engine prop trainer. Judy, who arrived a few weeks later, was assigned to VT-28. She quickly caught up to Barb, and soon, both had gotten way ahead of the guys. They were good—but they were also being pushed, says John. "Each CO wanted to claim he had the first female naval aviator, so they were beating the heck out of them."

While the standard for advanced trainees was one or two flights or flight simulator sessions a day, for Barb, he says, "it got to be beyond ridiculous"—she was doing two sim sessions every day and sometimes two sims and a flight. "Word was that Barb and her instructor could take an airplane away from anyone. If her plane broke, they could take one from anyone else who had a good airplane to get her flights out." The men never had that kind of priority.

"One day, Barb was embarrassed because she took two airplanes away from the same student and instructor," John recalls. "The guys probably weren't happy about that—but they knew what was going on, the pressure, and the race that was on."

Judy says she didn't feel the instructors were pushing them through, but she'd heard rumors about it, and about male pilots being bumped. "There were lots of unkind statements about this 'race' that the women weren't trying to race," she says, "but it was perceived as such. If we were bumping men from flights, if I were a guy, I would have been frustrated, too."

Fortunately, she had a mentor, a naval aviator who had been her skipper at her first billet in San Diego. Judy was a computer programmer then, but she and her mentor had talked about the flying she'd done as a girl back in Ohio, and when flight training opened to women, he encouraged her to apply. More than that, he took her out in an S-3 from North Island for her very first flight in a navy aircraft. As her career progressed, they stayed in occasional contact, and when the competition with Barb was burning up their squadrons, she turned to him for advice.

"There were, toward the end, all kinds of comments, really inappropriate remarks about the race between these two women," Judy says. "I talked to him about that, because even though I tried to let it all go, it was bothersome. He said to stay focused, know what your goal is. Don't let it get you off track. It was good advice. It helped keep me centered and focused on the task at hand. Because there were enough senior officers along the way who made a point that if it had been their decision"—rather than Zumwalt's and Warner's—"women would not be in flight training."

Barb and Judy essentially finished at the same time, and it might have been possible for them to be co-firsts. But the brass decided that wasn't going to happen. Someone had to be No. 1.

And so, on February 22, 1974, with 230 hours of flight time in her logbook, Lieutenant (j.g.) Barbara Ann Allen became history's first female navy pilot, at Naval Air Station Corpus Christi. Five days later, on February 27, 1974, Lieutenant (j.g.) Judith Ann Neuffer, the first woman accepted for navy flight training, was winged at Corpus as Female Naval Aviator No. 2—her description in the promotional video of her historic solo flight. (The admiral in charge was so opposed to the idea of women flying in the navy that he refused to conduct the ceremony; someone else had to be brought in to officiate.)

They were followed, less than two months later, by Ensign Jane Skiles, on April 5, 1974. And on April 19, 1974, Ensign Joellen Drag, the US military's first female helicopter pilot, was winged at Naval Air Station Whiting Field. Being in the second group, training played out a bit differently for her than it had for the first three. While there were some articles in the paper about the "tall, blue-eyed blonde with fetching bangs," there wasn't too much publicity. "It was better to fly under the radar, do the job, and not create controversy," Joellen says.

At the time, many of the flight instructors at Pensacola were selectively retained graduates—SERGRADS—newly winged navy pilots who, instead of shipping off to a squadron to fly fighters, were given a choice: Teach flying or go home. "The guys they met as instructors," says John, "were not the happiest people in the world."

Did they treat the women differently from the men?

"About the same, I'd judge," Joellen told the *Los Angeles Times*. "An instructor in the back seat doesn't figure you as a girl very long. All he can see is your helmet and the back of your neck, and all he can hear is your shaky voice, which sounds like any other shaky voice on the intercom. Instructors vary, of course. There are good ones and then there are the screamers who figure to have been in training work too long. If you're cocky, they can make it tough on you, but I was cautious—and too ignorant to be scared."

The most difficult part for her, as for many pilots, was instrument training—learning to control her T-28 solely by referencing the altimeter, airspeed indicator, attitude indicator, and other dials in the cockpit, rather than the horizon outside. The part she enjoyed the most was aerobatics, doing loops, rolls, spins, wingovers, and Immelmann turns. "I never got sick," she told the *Times,* "not even during unusual-attitude work when I was required to duck my head in the cockpit while the instructor kicked the plane into some crazy position. Then it was up to me to bring it out smoothly."

Joellen didn't really have a preference for type of aircraft, but when she was assigned to helicopter training—not surprising, since Barb, Judy, and Jane all did fixed-wing—she was thrilled. As a horseback rider, she somehow found helos "more intuitive, and I loved that type of flying. It was exciting." The biggest difference in transitioning from props to helos: "It's kind of scary . . . when you're used to worrying about keeping your airspeed up, to look down and find you're flying at zero knots—hovering, that is."

Helos also seemed, potentially, a better way to go in terms of deployment. In that, she was right: After her federal lawsuit opened more opportunities for female aviators, the helo pilots got to deploy more quickly than the fixed-wing types. But it didn't happen quite soon enough for Joellen.

With three of the women already pursuing advanced airplane training, the remaining two were on track for helos as well, and Ensign Ana Maria Scott earned her wings as the navy's second female helicopter pilot at Whiting on May 20, 1974. "I was pleased as punch," she says. "That I was even doing this was so amazing to me." Though she later became aware that the jet guys looked down on helo pilots, she didn't care. The transition from fixed-wing was not difficult at all, and she thoroughly enjoyed the different maneuvers, "rotation, autorotation, getting a good look at the scenery below, traveling so slowly from place to place, so you could see and examine and enjoy it."

But Rosemary, having married an ensign she met in flight school and now using her husband's name, was another story.

"Rosie was supposed to go to helo, but she had a degree from Purdue, she was a hard charger, and she had no intention of letting herself be put into helos," Joellen says. She had great grades, pushed back, and got herself into props, and on June 17, 1974, Ensign Rosemary Conatser earned her Wings of Gold at NAS Corpus Christi. And then, at her first billet, got into the pipeline for jet training.

The first group of female naval aviators having won their wings, the program was suspended for evaluation. But for the six, regardless of the outcome, their navy career had begun.

Chapter Five

No Place to Land

Their wings won, the nation's first female naval aviators dispersed to their first billets.

Lieutenant (j.g.) Barbara Ann Allen—VR-30 (Fleet Tactical Support Squadron), Alameda, California

Lieutenant (j.g.) Judith Ann Neuffer—VW-4 (Airborne Early Warning Squadron), Jacksonville, Florida

Ensign Jane Skiles—VR-24 (Navy Transport Squadron), Naval Station (NAVSTA) Rota, Spain

Ensign Joellen Drag—HC-3 (Helicopter Combat Support Squadron), San Diego

Ensign Ana Maria Scott—HC-6, Norfolk, Virginia

Ensign Rosemary Conatser—VC-2 (Fleet Composite Squadron), Naval Air Station Oceana, Virginia Beach

Wherever they went, whatever they did, publicity followed.

Here's a sampling of the coverage they received:

Associated Press, July 23, 1974: "A Navy pilot with long hair showed up for duty at the Oceana Naval Air Station on Monday, and most sailors here were delighted. That's because the new pilot is Ens. Rosemary Merims Conatser, the first female naval aviator assigned to the East Coast.

Interviewed Monday during her first duty day, she displayed her Navy wings proudly and talked about the romance of flying." Reported MilitaryNews.com: "[Ens. Rosemary B.] Conatser became the first female pilot to report to NAS Oceana. . . . Her arrival was a media sensation, with television stations and newspapers from around Virginia interviewing the 21-year-old Conatser.

"The entire center of the August 1, 1974, *Jet Observer* [NAS Oceana monthly magazine] was devoted to her arrival, including photos and media interviews. The story described her as 'the attractive and petite 5 ft. 4 in. pilot,' who had to deal with the problem of flight suits being too large."

Associated Press, September 1974: "Little Rock AFB—Jane Skiles, 24, has become the first female to undergo training to fly the C-130E Hercules aircraft. One of the first women to be trained as Navy pilots, she is a student in the 16th Tactical Airlift Training Squadron at Little Rock Air Force Base. After her graduation from training, Ens. Skiles will go to Rota, Spain, to fly C-130s for the Navy. She learned to fly the T-34 and S-2 aircraft before she was sent to the 16th, the only training unit in the armed forces for the C-130E Hercules transport aircraft."

Women didn't fly in the air force, and the brass at first didn't want to train one in their airplane. But they soon saw the benefits of publicity for the world's only C-130 school. On the day of Jane's checkride, the Associated Press reported on August 7, 1974, a dozen reporters, photographers, and TV camera crews were waiting for her as she taxied out. "You've got to be kidding!" Jane told her instructor, who told reporters that after the third landing during her first lesson, "I never touched the stick. She was able to land it . . . hands off by an instructor, which is kind of unusual. You're not usually able to let a student go that quickly."

Reported *The Drop Zone*, a Little Rock AFB publication, in a retrospective dated July 22, 2005: Her checkride in "the Herk" "was an otherwise routine flight to Jackson, Miss., but the crowds of people present at base operations when the aircraft taxied in demonstrated it was anything but routine to visiting press, dignitaries and ordinary sightseers. 'I didn't expect anything like this,' she later said."

All Hands, April 1975: "Helicopter Combat Support Squadron Six recently had its newest aviator report aboard, Ensign Anna Marie [*sic*] Fuqua. The petite, brown-haired, 24-year-old pilot arrived . . . determined to fit right in with her male counterparts. . . . Anna Marie reported to HS-1 for replacement air group training in Jacksonville, Fla., where she learned to fly the H-3 helicopter. She finished her training in September 1974 and took leave. . . . During this leave period, Anna Marie was married to LT Harry Fuqua, who is also a naval aviator. . . . ENS Fuqua hopes that someday she will be allowed to land on combatant type ships and that perhaps she can get involved in ASW [antisubmarine warfare] work. Until then, she busies herself with her scheduling and training job in HC-6."

Two years later, *Legion* magazine reported: "One week out of the month, Ana Maria is on 24-hour alert. She is personnel officer for her squadron, and she flies the Admiral to the Pentagon each week. . . . Several other women had preceded Ana Maria through flight school, so she didn't experience discrimination that might have been present in earlier classes. This past July 4th holiday, she was selected to fly Admiral Kidd, former Vice President Rockefeller and former Secretary of State Henry Kissinger from Washington to New York for the Bicentennial 'Operation Sail.'"

All Hands, April 1975: "In these days of female pioneers, Lieutenant Barbara Allen Rainey has earned the distinction of being the Navy's First Woman of Aviation. Less than a year after completing Flight School at Corpus Christi, Tex., and becoming the Navy's first female aviator, LT Rainey has set another precedent by becoming the first of her sex in the Navy to qualify as a jet pilot. She is attached to Fleet Tactical Support Squadron Thirty (VR-30) at Naval Air Station Alameda, Calif., and will be flying the T-39 jets by which that squadron transports ferry pilots and also uses for special VIP flights. When LT Rainey first arrived at her present duty station she chose to fly the C-1s [Grumman C-1A Traders] and the sleek, six-passenger, two-pilot T-39s [jet-powered North American Sabreliners]. Comparing the T-39s to the large C-9s which VR-30 also flies, LT Rainey says, 'It's the difference between a limousine and a sports car. I much prefer the sports car feeling I get flying these beautiful planes.'"

All Hands, April 1975: "'Sometimes the men in the control towers can't believe their ears when they hear my voice over the radio.' Ensign Joellen Drag, a woman in a world of men, is one of the Navy's first women helicopter copilots. The men in the control towers had better get used to it. . . . After Pensacola and its rigorous flight instruction, survival training, and hours and hours of practice, Joellen reported to the North Island Naval Air Station, San Diego, Calif., and helo training with Helicopter Support Squadron Three (HC-3). . . . Joellen is pleased she decided to take the rough road towards becoming a Navy pilot. 'My hours are long but I feel more professionally oriented than I would with a lot of jobs in the civilian world,' she said. 'Besides, I'm part of a team, not just a woman.'"

But being a woman made a huge difference. The caption on an Associated Press photo of Joellen that appeared in the *Atlanta Constitution* on May 24, 1974, told the story. Headlined "No Place to Land," it said: "Ens. Joellen Drag, 23, is training to become one of the Navy's first woman helicopter pilots. She's having a small problem, but the Navy says it will be solved. An old federal law prohibits women from landing aircraft on the deck of a combat ship. Meanwhile, she's confined to landing on a landing strip."

Of the ninety-eight pilots in her squadron, she was the only one not allowed to land on a ship—one of the primary functions of a navy helicopter support pilot. Even a task as basic as hovering her CH-46 Sea Knight to deliver the mail was off-limits to the navy's first female helo pilot under Section 6015, because the navy defined a combat ship as any vessel designated as having a combat mission, whether or not it was engaged in combat at that point in time. For that reason, "I could do hardly anything at my duty station in San Diego," she says. "Civilian women could go on ships, but I couldn't fly them out there. They went through contortions to keep military women off ships while allowing everyone else on."

As she said about that "old federal law" during a 2013 panel discussion on women in combat: "[Section] 6015 itself didn't need to be as restrictive as it was. It said that women couldn't be 'assigned to duty aboard ships.' Well, they took that to mean that if I went out to a ship that was anchored in San Diego Bay, that I wasn't allowed to hover over that ship. . . . So that's the kind of obstruction that occurs. It was news to all the men [in my helo squadron] that they were assigned to duty aboard that ship."

Her commanding officers went out of their way to make sure she got enough flight time, and she eventually logged the 300 hours needed to qualify as a helicopter aircraft commander. But it took her much longer than her male colleagues because her flight opportunities were severely limited. The restrictions also denied her the range of experience needed for promotion.

She couldn't go to sea on six- to eight-month resupply deployments to replenish ships in the Western Pacific with goods and gear, like the rest of her squadron. And she couldn't serve as officer in charge of the twenty-five or so enlisted and pilots on those deployments. Those missed leadership and career milestones eventually led her, several years later, to take her fight for equal opportunity to federal court—"my salvo in the battle," as she calls it, to overturn Section 6015.

Several of the others also found creative ways around the limits the navy placed on its first female aviators.

For Ana Maria, it came down to hiding in plain sight. Her CO at HC-6 was pleased to have her in Norfolk, aware that she was somewhat special and that a unique kind of publicity came with having her in the squadron. Flying the H-3 Sikorsky Sea King, she was a member of a small detachment attached to CINCLANTFLT—Commander-in Chief, US Atlantic Fleet. Two pilots were on alert at all times, carrying radios to notify them in case of national emergency. If a crisis occurred, they had to hightail it back to base, fly to CINCLANTFLT headquarters 10 miles away, pick up the admiral, and fly him to Langley, where he would board a plane that would serve as an airborne command center. She also flew VIPs to and from the Pentagon, departing in the morning for the ninety-minute flight, landing on the pad on the grounds, staying the day, and then flying back. Eventually, she became the division officer for fifty or so enlisted who provided maintenance for the H-3 VIP aircraft.

Ana Maria knew that, as a woman, she was taking up a billet that otherwise would have gone to a man who had spent two years overseas, and there was some resentment. "I had people tell me, but not in a negative way," she says. "I was staying. I accepted it and they accepted me." Though women were restricted to shore billets and barred from doing anything combat-related, "I had always wanted to do sea duty like the men," she says. "I wished to be on par with them." A new lieutenant commander in her detachment made that happen—sort of. "He was a good man and very pro-women's equality. So much so that he let me fly with him a couple of times when ship landings—destroyer and aircraft carrier—were required. This was done clandestinely, of course. I had to stay inside the helo with my visor down on board the ship/carrier." Only the two of them "ever knew I had disobeyed the law! It was a thrilling experience, and pretty amazing that he took this risk just so I could have a taste of 'being at sea.'"

For the fixed-wing pilots, flying cargo in the C-130 Hercules out of a transport squadron was the most likely billet after being winged. But Lieutenant Judy Neuffer made her way into the literal eye of the hurricane instead, battling blinding rain and waves, thick walls of clouds, powerful downdrafts, spiraling eddies, and winds topping 150 miles per hour inside some of the most intense storms in the world.

"I was going into a VR squadron flying C-130s, and made a few calls trying to figure out what support squadrons there were," she says. "I found a weather squadron in Jacksonville, flying P-3s, called the detailer, and asked, 'Could I go to Jacksonville?' They said okay."

The mission at VW-4 was weather surveillance and reconnaissance. And so the first woman to fly a navy aircraft became the first female Hurricane Hunter—and the first woman to fly the P-3. "At VW-4 in Jacksonville, there was a huge hangar with four squadrons," Judy says. "I was the only woman. I would walk down the hall, and guys would come out of offices and just stare."

But, "as far as life's experience, that set the stage for many lessons learned over the years," Judy says. "The first lesson being, it never hurts to ask. We were being told, 'This is what you're going to do'; I respectfully said, 'Yes, but can I do *this*?' Summers, I flew into hurricanes. I had sixteen hurricane penetrations. Winters, we flew North Atlantic winter storms, about twelve hours of nonstop turbulence. At least in a hurricane, going through the eyewall is pretty intense, but then you get to settle down a little. You normally make three eye penetrations per flight. I got to do some terrific flying. At that time, the navy and the air force were both flying into storms. Once the storm got close to land, there would be aircraft on-site twenty-four hours a day, seven days a week. The Weather Service would say, 'Go in high- or low-level,' depending on data, storm makeup, and so on. It seemed like the Navy always ended up with low-level night flights, so I had lots of interesting flying at 1,000 feet. Not combat, but a pretty wild ride."

Her skipper called it "the toughest noncombat flying job in the world."

During one penetration, a bird embedded itself in the leading edge of one of the P-3's wings. Yes, Judy says, "birds fly in the eye of the hurricane. It was a few feet from the engine intake." A little bit more, and "it would have been a very different ride."

After the Hurricane Hunters were decommissioned in April 1975, Judy went to VXN-8, an oceanographic research squadron at Naval Air Station Patuxent River, in Maryland. "I consider myself to be very lucky on every duty assignment I had," she says. "In VXN-8, I flew around the world a couple of times. I set foot on every continent except Antarctica, which I flew over twice. We would be out there carrying scientists in the back, sometimes NOAA scientists getting measurements. Depending on the mission, we would be at 20- or 30,000 feet, or 1,000 feet, flying across. Normally, if flying from Argentina to South Africa, we would be at altitude, but if the mission was checking thermal layers of the ocean or whatever, we would stage out of various places like Bermuda and would fly low-level flights." For one trip, a fourteen-hour flight on Thanksgiving, the crew had a full turkey dinner on board. "It's amazing what you can do in the galley of a P-3!" Judy observes.

"It was absolutely amazing duty in that I got to see the world," she says. "And I made aircraft commander in VXN-8."

For Rosemary as well, the path out of the transport prop plane pipeline involved an unusual request—and a yes from above. Even while in Women's Officer School, she had made no bones about her intentions, as she noted in the April 1973 edition of *All Hands*: "The only thing I'd like to be given is the chance to fly the F-4 Phantom."

Two years later, at NAS Oceana, where Rosemary was flying the Grumman S-2 Tracker, a twin-engine antisubmarine warfare prop plane, her commanding officer found himself needing more jet pilots than he had. That CO, Commander Raymond A. Lambert, was a groundbreaking naval officer in his own right. As the first Black squadron commander at Oceana, he had battled racial discrimination from his first days as a naval aviator. Lambert ran a request for Rosemary to attend jet transition classes up the chain of command, and even though women were legally barred from flying jets, an admiral gave the go-ahead. When Lambert told this to a reporter from the *Norfolk Journal & Guide*, he was "smiling like a proud new father." The June 21, 1975, story was accompanied by a photo of Lambert and Rosemary with the caption "Pair of Navy 'Firsts.'"

Barely a month later, Rosemary was in the news again, this time as a contestant in the annual All-Women Transcontinental Air Race, also known as the Powder Puff Derby, which continues today as the Air Race Classic. The navy thought it would be good publicity to enter a team, so, Rosemary, a budding jet pilot, was matched up with Joellen, a helicopter pilot, to fly a 2,590-mile course from Riverside, California, to Boyne Falls, Michigan, in a Cessna 172—a single-engine general aviation airplane with a cruising speed of about 100 knots, or 115 miles per hour. Says Joellen, "I wanted to go low and Rosie wanted to go at altitude—in a 172, it didn't work for either." Reported the *El Paso Times*: "They are now working out flight strategy, getting used to their plane . . . and figuring ways to keep baggage to an absolute minimum. 'I don't think we will be sharing a toothbrush,' laughed Lt. Drag, 'but weight is almost that critical.'"

Their team was sponsored by the Naval Aviation Museum in Pensacola, with the 172 provided by the NAS North Island Flying Club. One columnist reported that the two lieutenants would donate any winnings to the museum's building and aircraft restoration fund. He also noted that while the checkpoint at Phoenix was not mandatory for the racers, the navy had made it "semi-compulsory" for its team, to introduce Arizona air race fans to its female aviators.

A California columnist, meanwhile, griped about the two being housed at a nearby air force base rather than at the race headquarters hotel in Riverside. On the last leg, Joellen says, "They told us to look for a ski resort, so us two California girls expected to see a mountain with ski lifts. Instead, there was a hill with a rope tow—it took us three times before we recognized what we were looking at." They completed the course in 19.5 hours over four days, averaging 128 mph and beating their handicap by a very respectable 7 mph.

The race completed, Rosemary turned to jet transition training. She was already familiar with the A-4 Skyhawk from her day-to-day exposure at Oceana and from talking with the jet pilots in her squadron, including her husband, Ensign Douglas Hugh Conatser. Jet transition instruction at Training Squadron VT-21 at Naval Air Station Kingsville, Texas, would make it official.

For transitioning aviators, as opposed to those sorted into the jet pipeline from the start, the syllabus was a mini-version of advanced jet training. Ground school and aerial instruction were the same: familiarization, basic and radio instruments, formation flying, tactical formation, and weapon delivery.

Still, unlike the male pilots—including future commander Tommy Mariner, who would marry Rosemary several years later, after she and her first husband divorced—Rosemary was not allowed to complete the final stage of transition training. While the men carrier-qualified in their jets, she was done. For Rosemary, as for Joellen, ships were off-limits.

Still, the new year brought the nation's first female tactical fighter jet pilot back to Oceana, with Rosemary flying the A-4E/L Skyhawk. The most difficult part of transitioning to jets, she told *Virginian-Pilot* on January 30, 1976: "It's faster; therefore, you have to think faster."

In a wire service report, *The Record* wrote on February 1, 1976: "Plane Lady—The first American woman ever to solo in a military jet fighter favors the Equal Rights Amendment and hopes it will permit women to fly combat missions. Lt. (j.g.) Rosemary Conatser made military history this week by flying an A-4 Skyhawk from Oceana Naval Air Station in Virginia Beach, Virginia. The 5-foot-, 4-inch lieutenant, who just scraped by the height requirement for jet training, has flown planes for six years and received naval fighter training three years ago."

The St. Louis *Post Dispatch*, though, reported the same day: " 'I'm not a women's libber in the radical sense,' Lt. (j.g.) Rosemary Conatser said Thursday after making history by flying solo in an A-4 Skyhawk from Oceana Naval Air Station in Virginia Beach, Virginia. 'I had always been intrigued by flying, and somewhere along the line I got it in my mind that I could do it, even though I am a girl,' she said. 'I'm doing this as a professional goal.' "

By year's end, Rosemary had notched another milestone, as the first woman to fly a front-line light attack jet aircraft, the A-7E Corsair II.

Wrote one of her instructors on an online memorial website a few days before her funeral: "Rosemary arrived at the Fleet Replacement Squadron (FRS) for an abbreviated syllabus in the A-7E, a single-engine, single seat light attack jet. At the time, it was state of the art, with a heads-up display, inertial navigation and multi-mode radar. The ready room was obviously all-male, and there was a fair amount of grumbling about her even being there. I was the schedules officer, and the CO made it clear that this was not to become an issue, so I put myself on to fly with her on her first (and *the* first-ever female) flight in our two-seat trainer, the TA-7C. Walking out to the flight line, it was clear that she was uncomfortable, but also that she was equally determined. Suffice it to say that she flew the A-7 like she had thousands of hours in it. It was easy to 'get behind' this complicated jet, and even seasoned commanders coming back for refresher training often did so. Not Rosemary. She flew with great confidence and was smooth, but aggressive in all the maneuvers, including aerobatics. Back in the landing pattern, she looked ready to Hit the Boat [land on an aircraft carrier], keeping the big jet on speed and with the Ball [of the landing guidance system] in the center. I was impressed and told her so, along with all my fellow instructors."

Rosemary was assigned to VA-174, an attack squadron based at Cecil Field in Jacksonville—and again, the publicity machine began to churn.

During her first flight in the A-7E, her commanding officer, Vietnam War hero and future senator John McCain, had her recalled to the base so reporters could get the story of the nation's first female jet fighter pilot. "McCain made her land so they could make their 4 o'clock deadlines," Tommy Mariner told the *Washington Post*. "She was mad as she could be because she just wanted to take that jet out and have fun."

McCain included her achievement in the "Chronology of Historical Events" in his annual report to the chief of naval operations, titled "Command History of Attack Squadron ONE SEVEN FOUR for Calendar Year 1976."

As the Associated Press reported in the *St. Petersburg Times* on December 14, 1976,

> *The wheels of Navy plane 437 touched down on the Cecil Field runway. Immediately, the pilot gunned the throttle and the fighter was airborne again. It was like thousands of touch-and-go landings. Except this time, the pilot was Lt. (j.g.) Rosemary Conatser, the first woman to qualify in the A-7 Corsair II jet.*
>
> *After her final landing on her qualification test flight, fellow fliers gathered in the ready room and gave her the Navy's traditional "Well done." Along with seven other Navy pilots, Mrs. Conatser began further qualifying Monday, making simulated aircraft carrier landings in the attack aircraft.*
>
> *Some pilots have said a woman isn't strong enough to cope with hydraulic failure, which they say makes the Corsair about as maneuverable as a brick. Mrs. Conatser, 23, disagrees. "I've flown under similar conditions and I'm sure if I get scared enough I could handle anything," she said.*

Simulated carrier training, of course, was nothing new; doing short-field touch-and-goes on a runway to prepare for "going to the boat" was a standard part of the naval aviation curriculum. So was flying in four-plane formation to the training carrier *Lexington* to carrier-qualify—at least, it had been, until Barb, Judy, and Jane arrived at Pensacola.

"When they finished at Whiting, the normal curriculum was to go back to Saufley for carrier training, then on to Corpus," says Judy. "All navy aviators qualified on the carrier in flight training. That changed when the women got there because they wouldn't let us go on the carrier."

The curriculum had called for every student naval aviator to make at least two trips to the *Lex*, Training Carrier CVT-16, doing five landings, or traps, per trip. Guided in by the flight deck crew and a system of red, amber, and green lights, the pilot would line up with the 900-foot runway; if the middle, amber light—the meatball—was visible, the plane was on target. Once cleared to land, the pilot would come screaming in and try to snag one of four arresting cables with the plane's tailhook, as the ship pitched and rolled and the runway slewed back and forth. If successful, the cable would yank the airplane to a halt in about two seconds—all while at full power, in case the landing failed and the pilot needed to go around for another try. Log ten traps, and the aviator was a tailhooker—carrier-qualified.

This was never supposed to be part of the women's curriculum; the January 16, 1973, memo from the chief of naval operations on the "Women Naval Aviator Trial Program" stated: "The training will be conducted in accordance with current CNATRA [Chief of Naval Air Training] directives, with the exception of the carrier qualification requirement in the prop line, which will be eliminated."

But eight months later, on August 29, 1973, Lieutenant (j.g.) Judith A. Neuffer, Ensign Jane M. Skiles, and Ensign Rosemary B. Conatser sent a letter up the chain of command. The subject: "Change in Flight Training Syllabus; request for."

The current flight training syllabus for female Student Naval Aviators in the multi-engine propeller pipeline precludes flight instruction at TRARON FIVE. This instruction has historically been a normal prerequisite for designation as a Naval Aviator. Leading to initial carrier qualification, this phase of flight instruction is the culmination of the Basic Flight Training Syllabus and as such is the final evaluation of ability and performance prior to assignment for advanced instruction. The carrier qualification phase is the test that makes Naval Aviators truly unique with respect to their counterparts in the other services.

The uniqueness of the experience of "hitting the boat" has, no doubt, attracted many talented young men to the Naval Service; it is no less an attraction to aspiring female aviators. All flight and academic standards, to date, for female Student Naval Aviators have been the same as those required for males. Failure to carrier-qualify is a deviation from the normal path for designation as a Naval Aviator.

Female Naval Aviators desire to be considered professional Naval Aviators and desire to be evaluated with regard to ability and performance as professionals. Therefore it is requested that female Naval Aviators be given the test of uniqueness—that of carrier qualification.

In view of the above, it is requested that the syllabus for female Student Naval Aviators assigned to the multi-engine propeller pipeline be amended to permit carrier qualification.

The answer from the Chief of Naval Air Training in Corpus Christi, dated October 4, 1973, wasn't just a firm no:

Your request for a change of the multi-engine training syllabus for Female Student Naval Aviators (FSNA) to include basic carrier qualification is regretfully disapproved.

In an effort to reduce training time and costs, the Chief of Naval Air Training has been continually reviewing all aspects of flight training and reducing or eliminating training that is not related to follow-on flight tasks. In light of this analysis, CNATRA has forwarded a request for the elimination of basic carrier qualification from the basic prop syllabus. Carrier qualification would only be granted to those selected for carrier squadrons during advanced multi-engine training. Accordingly, even if it was desirous to honor your request, the basic carrier qualification training is being deleted from the basic prop syllabus. Further, the training for FSNAs is specifically set forth by the Chief of Naval Operations in his training guidance message, enclosure (1), and carrier training was specifically exempted.

Your interest, performance and desire to be treated as equals is laudable, and your rationale for this request is appreciated. However, unfortunately, CNATRA does not have the authority to authorize the training requested, nor would it be prudent to forward a request for modification of enclosure 1 to grant such training to FSNAs.

Not only couldn't the women carrier-qualify, but now, most of the men couldn't, either. They were all sent to Corpus without attaining the singular achievement that set naval aviators apart.

"There was more irritation at the women when the rules changed," says Judy. "Qualifying on the carrier was a big deal for a navy pilot."

(Though unsuccessful, that letter set a pattern for future battles with navy brass and subsequent victories in overturning policy. "Letter writing became an important tool in our limited arsenal," Rosemary told an audience at the Smithsonian Air and Space Museum in 2011. "First, it got our request on record and made sure that the entire chain of command knew about the situation. They had to endorse the letter. If some middle manager was doing his own thing, contrary to navy policy, then top management learned about it. And we also learned that an advance copy to the most senior addressee was an important guarantee that our letter would not get lost.")

Carrier training stayed for pilots who were going to fly the S-2, but for those flying the P-3 or the C-130, it was eliminated as a waste of taxpayer funds. Barb ended up flying the C-1, basically the transport version of the S-2, so she would have been eligible for carrier qualification had she been a man. But under the broad definition of Section 6015, the *Lex* was a combat vessel, even though it was permanently assigned solely to carrier practice. "Combat" outweighed "training."

Without carrier qualification, the women were relegated to the second tier of navy pilots. In the minds of many, without that essential rite of passage, the women weren't really naval aviators at all. It would take six more years before the first woman was allowed to carrier-qualify.

Barb's shortened training regimen did provide an advantage for her family life, though. "There were so many restrictions on women that there weren't that many places they could be assigned that also had squadrons that were career-enhancing for a guy," says John. Being assigned to a transport squadron, as Barb initially was, "for a guy, was the kiss of death, though it was a highway to the airlines." But her billet at Alameda, flying the C-1 and the T-39 Sabreliner, put her just across San Francisco Bay from Moffett Field, where John was stationed. So, after they got married, in the base chapel at Long Beach Naval Station, they set up household in Fremont, in the middle (though he twice deployed for six-month stints in Japan, while her assignments were strictly stateside and shore-based). They were fortunate, as accommodating couples when both husband and wife were on active duty became an increasingly knotty problem for detailers tasked with placing them in their next assignments. When it's not possible to get the best billets for both at the same place, which career do you pursue? Whose should take precedence?

With new opportunities becoming available for women, the navy slowly steered closer to Zumwalt's ideal of equal opportunity. NROTC and certain billets on tugboats and other service vessels, as well as flight training for women in the army, were opened up in 1974. A second group of women was accepted for navy flight training in 1975, including the two original alternates. Navy Aviation Officer Candidate School would admit its first female trainees in 1976 (with the same physical standards for men and women), as would the air force's pilot training program and the service academies (though female midshipmen would still not be allowed to serve shipboard during summer breaks).

But while there is strength in numbers, there is also potential peril. At the outset, pushback was localized because there weren't enough women to form a critical mass; they simply weren't well known. But as their ranks started to increase, broader resistance began to mount.

The opposition was given voice in the September 1975 issue of *Proceedings* magazine, in a column titled "Nobody Asked Me, But . . . The Female Naval Aviator: A Free Ride?"

The recent designation of several women as naval aviators has been accompanied by much publicity and ballyhoo as sympathizers of women's liberation cite this feat as a major breakthrough in the battle

NO PLACE TO LAND

*against sex discrimination. Ironically, though, a closer examina-
tion of the "waviator" program reveals blatant sex favoritism and,
rather than a triumph for sex equality, has led to a classic case of sex
discrimination—against men. . . . Waviators receive equal pay and
opportunity but are not statutorily and physically able to produce the
equal qualification and performance! The result is separate and preferential treatment for the women in the program, solely on the basis
of their sex.*

The author dragged out all the Old Guard's greatest hits: The women
were skating because they lacked night carrier qualification and were
exempt from "extended cruises and the arduous sea duty" (opportunities
they would have jumped at, if given the chance); their presumed inability
to meet physical requirements at Pensacola; even the old rumors—it was
"no secret," he wrote, that their flight instructors were "handpicked, leaving the less talented, less experienced and occasional 'screamer' instructors
to the male studs."

He complained that "the ladies get a once-a-month grounding for
several days for 'upper respiratory infections' "—something Judy and
Rosemary said never happened—while neglecting to mention the after-
noons the men sometimes took off to compete in intramural softball and
basketball games. He griped about flight test grades not mattering for
the women, as their "good billets" had been "pre-selected"—an enviable
situation for a middling man, perhaps, but not for an ambitious woman
with something to prove.

And he concluded by calling it "an interesting experiment in equal
opportunity that didn't really provide equal opportunity," a statement
with which every one of the female naval aviators, barred from the most
rewarding assignments flying the most prestigious airplanes, would have
agreed.

It was hardly the navy man accepting the idea of women serving on
ships and flying navy planes. (Soon after, Rosemary told the Smithsonian
audience, she had to do her annual instrument checkflight with him—
and, it turned out, he was "actually a pretty nice guy." He was also, she
said, "right on target regarding the fundamental unfairness to men of the

combat exclusion laws. Unless women went to sea on the same basis as men, there could be no equality.")

Unfortunately, he put on paper what many guys were thinking. And some of them acted on that resentment in some frightening ways.

There were snide, demeaning, sexist comments, or the silent treatment. There was persistent sexual harassment—the flight instructor who'd flunk a woman on a flight test to pressure her to transfer into his squadron, the scheduler who offered preferable flight times if she'd sleep with him. A male pilot might key the microphone in his plane to block radio transmissions between a female aviator and the tower. One trainee threw a live, burning firecracker into the quarters of one of the women (the perpetrator apologized decades later). Some women preferred to find their own housing off base, feeling it was safer than BOQ, where everyone knew whose quarters were whose (the firecracker thrower had asked for and been handed the woman's key by the officer on duty, just in case her door was locked).

Predatory men read Warner's announcement as a declaration of open season on young women—not that the female fliers were the only victims, or the first. There were catcalls and unwanted attention, relationships that turned violent, and marriages that became abusive. There was sexual abuse, assault, and out-and-out rape, issues that would come to a head with the Tailhook scandal a decade or so later.

In too many cases, the women walked away, quietly quitting the service.

"We were babes in the woods about being manipulated by older men," says Joellen.

For some guys, it was, "Who do you think you are? Go be barefoot and pregnant," says Mary Louise Griffin. But for every one of those, there was another who said, "We got this." For them, the guiding principle in this brave new world was simple: Don't be a jerk. They didn't necessarily know what to do, but they were trying.

"There were always people not happy to have us around, but always some [who were] quietly supportive," says Judy.

For four-plane training at Saufley, the pilots were divided into groups that stayed together throughout that phase of instruction. Each formation team was designated with a color—Form Blue, Form Purple, and so on. Judy's, of course, was Form Pink. For its final qualification flight, the guys went out and bought pink scarves; afterward, all four posed for pictures wearing long pink scarves, and signed them as mementos.

Later in her career, flying overseas sometimes meant landing at bases that had no facilities for women. Once, Judy was flying from Japan with a minimal crew—pilot, copilot, engineer, tactical officer, observer—when they had to land in Korea to get out of the path of an oncoming typhoon. The base had no place for a woman to sleep, so Judy remained on the plane. When the rest of her all-male crew found out, they gave up their quarters to stay with her on the aircraft. Everyone rolled up under the flight stations. In the morning, the crew commandeered one of the men's bathrooms in the barracks and stood guard so Judy could shower.

Bathrooms, along with upper-body strength, were a persistent, emotionally charged issue.

For Joellen, the lack of toilets became a subject of amusement. The helicopters she flew, of course, had none; on rare long flights, the men could use an apparatus called a relief tube, but that wasn't something a woman could make work. On her third flight, the guys in her squadron presented her with a gift: an oxygen mask with a large tube and a sponge attached, their idea of a female version of the relief tube. "I actually thought it was a good idea at the time," she laughed. "The navy never followed up on it."

But for every attempt to accommodate, even if in awkward, crude fashion, there was in-your-face hostility; having to deal with physiological differences brought out the worst in some officers.

When Jane reported to her billet in Rota, where just one other woman was stationed, the CO told her point-blank that there was just one bathroom—and she was not allowed to use it. Actually, as she related in *Military Fly Moms*, there were two: one marked "Officers" and the other marked "Men." "I decided that since I was an officer, it was totally appropriate to use the one marked 'Officers.' After the first time I walked in on a couple of the officers (stalls had no doors), the commanding officer redesignated them 'Men' and 'Women.'"

Speaking up in defense of the women could put a man's career in jeopardy; staying silent was the much safer course. Fortunately for the female aviators determined to make the navy their career, there were officers up the chain of command willing to become not only mentors, but friends.

CHAPTER SIX

Lessons from Integration

COMMANDER RAYMOND LAMBERT KNEW WHAT IT WAS LIKE TO BE
alone in a squadron full of people who didn't look like him. He also knew
what it was like to be judged, and prejudged, and denied opportunity
because of those differences.

The first Black commander of a squadron at NAS Oceana, Lambert
joined the navy in 1956 in answer to a challenge of sorts: His cousin, an
enlisted navy man, had told him he'd never seen an African American
officer. Lambert gave up a job teaching high school chemistry in New
York City, his hometown, and signed on.

He won his navy wings in 1958 and flew in all three types of squadrons: attack, antisubmarine, and support. By 1972, the former college
fullback at North Carolina A&T was head of the new NROTC unit at
North Carolina Central University, one of only five among all historically
Black colleges and universities. Less than two years later, he was named
skipper at Fleet Composite Squadron 2. Under his command were 263
enlisted personnel and 32 officers.

One of them was Lieutenant (j.g.) Rosemary Conatser.

The two quickly formed a bond. Lambert believed nurturing the
growth of his junior officers was an essential part of his job, and he saw
clear parallels between the challenges faced by Blacks in the military and
those confronting the first female naval aviators. He took lessons from his
own experience to mentor Rosemary in how best to handle them.

"I remember the special problems I had when I was starting out as
a naval aviator," Lambert told the *Norfolk Journal & Guide* in 1975, just

before leaving Oceana to join the navy inspector general's staff at the Pentagon. He was the only officer below the rank of captain, and the only African American officer, to have received such an assignment.

Some people didn't want to fly with me because I was black, and those who were above me were concerned that my commanding officer might refuse me in their chain of command because of my race.

I won't deny there were problems, but I overcame them with encouragement from people above me. That's what I try to do. . . .

Lt. (j.g.) Rosemary Conatser is a hell of a good pilot. It's funny, because I had someone call me to find out if I wanted her in my squadron—just like it happened to me when I was starting out.

Rosemary and I will sit down and talk about some of the problems. I guess we have the rapport we do because we've both experienced forms of discrimination.

Rosemary shared her experiences with the Smithsonian audience:

Shortly after I reported, Skipper Lambert called me into his office for a career talk. The first thing he said was that I was going to have a tough time because I was short. Which I couldn't do anything about. And he was a very big man. He then pulled out his bottom desk drawer, and he showed me a list of every Black naval officer, including every Black Naval Aviator, on active duty, retired, from ensign to admiral. This was my introduction to how Black men networked extensively to protect their careers and each other.

Next, I was warned to reject all attempts to create a female ghetto, some kind of career path only for women that was separate from the rest of Naval Aviation. Under no circumstances should we accept a female chain of command which allowed the normal chain of command to avoid accountability.

He told me that the Navy's only Black three-star admiral at the time, Samuel Gravely, had warned his fellow flags that if the Navy ever attempted to create an all-female ship, he would break his silence and speak out against it. While Admiral Gravely had not personally

served on the Navy's Black ship in World War II, the USS Mason, he
understood the folly of segregation. The message was clear: Separate is
never equal.
  So over the years, these became my guiding principles when deal-
ing with the issue of gender integration. "Gender-neutral" became the
key phrase.

As she told the *Washington Post*, "It really helps to have someone tell
you what the ropes are like, what the culture is like, how to set a goal and
obtain it."

For Rosemary, one of those goals was the dream she had nurtured
since at least Women's Officer School—flying jets. And when the opportunity arose, in spite of official prohibitions, people up above were there
to help.

It so happened that VC-2 had twenty airplanes: seventeen jets
and three twenty-year-old, Vietnam-era props. Meaning there wasn't
so much demand for prop pilots, but plenty of work for jet jockeys. To
Rosemary and Lambert's way of thinking, there was no reason to keep a
capable pilot from doing a job that needed to be done.

"I went through a back doorway," Rosemary said. "The decision was
made to transition the junior-most prop pilots, of which I was one, and
the guys' orders for jet transition training came back in about two weeks.
My orders got lost. It took a crusty fighter pilot named Commander
Chuck McGrail, the head of the junior aviation officer assignment shop,
to make my jet transition happen. I finally received orders in mid-1975.
Well, the late Chuck McGrail, who later became a rear admiral, was a
whirlwind force in opening opportunities to the first women pilots. As
the head detailer, his motto was, 'It is easier to seek forgiveness than ask
permission.' And that was a winning tactic in the bureaucratic world of
naval personnel."

However the door was cracked, it would take continued, coordi-
nated effort to force it open. Z-gram or not, women were going to have
to fight every step of the way for advancement. Zumwalt was able to
put female aviators in navy aircraft with a simple message to the fleet,
but he couldn't change the US federal code, with all its constraints.

Congress was responsible for that, and that meant things needed to change politically.

Here, too, Lambert's personal experience and knowledge of history and military culture provided an invaluable roadmap.

"We started networking, as my mentor had taught us," Rosemary said in 2017 at the University of Tennessee at Knoxville, where she was a scholar in residence with the Center for the Study of War and Society. "We would get together, and if we thought something was unfair—they wouldn't let women land on a ship, for example—we would write a letter up the chain of command and put it on the record that we wanted that changed.

"That network became very important, especially when it came time to repeal laws."

Band together, marshal your forces, state your case, and keep making it for the record. Don't take no for an answer. Keep pushing for more of what should be possible. Hold the door open for those coming up behind you.

As Rosemary told Henry W. Holden and Captain Lori Griffith,

I have spent all my adult life in the macho world of military fighter pilots. Women who have spent some time in nontraditional, male-dominated fields probably understand how different that male world is.

Sometimes I feel like an immigrant, reflecting upon my life in the promised land. I have learned to speak the language well (including the four-letter words), have experienced success beyond my wildest dreams and totally assimilated the values of my new country. But I have also learned the standards of this culture and understand that I, and those of my generation, will always be foreigners. We are the ghetto dwellers, excluded from the mainstream, and told we should be thankful for all that has been "given" to us. For no reason other than an accident of birth, we are subjected to many restrictions fully sanctioned by the law. Our only hope for total integration lies in future generations.

But like that same immigrant, I do not regret my choices. In my own career, I have been very fortunate. I have seen many male officers support women, even some risking their careers to do so.

There were other principles as well—discipline, fairness, and leadership—that Lambert modeled every day as commander of a squadron where he was the only Black officer and just 10 percent of the enlisted personnel were African American. Rosemary would apply these practices in her own squadrons in the years to come.

"I don't like to come down too hard on those in my command," Lambert told the *Norfolk Journal & Guide*. "First I like to talk with them and find out what the problems are rather than jumping to conclusions. I demand discipline, but I also want good relations—a harmonious command."

He continued: "A commanding officer has a lot of authority—sometimes too much. He can alter a man's life with his decisions. I try to counsel, but, if someone in my command persists after several warnings, I take disciplinary action. The safety and welfare of those in my command are important elements in achieving a smooth operation."

Unfortunately, in many squadrons, the growing numbers of female officers and enlisted personnel—and the official restrictions placed on them—made smooth operations difficult to attain. In April 1977, *Naval Aviation News* reported there were 6,300 female naval officers out of 63,000, and 19,000 enlisted women out of a total of 520,000 navy personnel. This "dramatic increase" meant accommodations needed to be made; from available equipment to housing to bureaucratic impediments, turning a big ship like the navy in new directions would not be easy.

Since women couldn't perform sea duty, they were limited to shore billets. But as the standard career path for navy men cycled through both, placing women permanently in shore-based assignments took up slots that men would otherwise have occupied. Of the twenty-four rates open to enlisted women, each one was "analyzed by billet base to arrive at the number of women who can be accommodated without encroaching on the shore duty opportunities of their male counterparts."

Even if women wanted to serve, operationally there might not be enough places to put them. And sometimes, it was just easier to keep women out than to deal with logistical complications. As *Naval Aviation News* reported, "It was felt that a large female population could jeopardize squadron readiness to deploy as emergency requirements might dictate, because of the berthing and other problems at deploying sites."

Commander John M. Quarterman, skipper of Helicopter Mine Countermeasures Squadron HM-12 in Norfolk, told *Naval Aviation News* about difficulties in integrating female personnel. "We went from 11 to 44 women within three months. It's a problem. We can't put our heads in the sand and ignore it. We had no place to house them, a shortage of small helmets, and even the small sizes were too big for some of the new women. . . . Five of the women had to have Size 3 [shoes] or smaller. We finally found a manufacturer through an orthopedic shoe company in Boston. Even the smallest foul-weather jackets didn't fit some of the women."

Ill-fitting flight gear was an issue for smaller men as well as for women. "Lieutenant Commander J. C. Patee, aviation medicine safety officer . . . is involved in a project to modify the MA-2 torso harness to accommodate smaller frames," *Naval Aviation News* reported. "He coordinates efforts with representatives in the Naval Air Systems Command and Naval Weapons Center, China Lake. Unfortunately, such programs take time and, because such a small percentage of personnel is involved, it is expensive to have gear specially manufactured for so few."

Another type of gear—essential, but only for an even smaller percentage of personnel—was entirely lacking: maternity uniforms, a symbol of the changing role of military women, changes in the makeup of the military, and changes in the law.

Until 1972, pregnancy was cause for instant dismissal. A change in policy that year made separation less of a foregone conclusion, because women could now request a waiver. But granting one was entirely at the discretion of her commanding officer; a woman's continued service was subject to the whims of the brass. A World War I–era navy policy barring women who had custody of a minor from joining up had been overturned only a year earlier.

It would take a series of lawsuits by military women to bring policies, if not attitudes, in sync with the times.

Lieutenant Sharron Frontiero, US Air Force

Frontiero joined the air force in 1968 and married a military veteran the following year. The couple applied for the same family benefits, including housing, that were available to male military personnel. But they were denied—unless they could prove that Frontiero's husband, Joseph, was incapable of supporting his wife. She sued on the grounds of due process and equal protection. The Federal District Court in Alabama ruled against her, writing that continuing to treat married servicemen and -women differently would yield a "considerable saving of administrative expense and manpower." After an appeal argued by future Supreme Court justice Ruth Bader Ginsburg, the US Supreme Court overturned that decision, a victory for the plaintiff in a landmark reverse sex discrimination suit.

Judge Advocate Tommie Sue Smith, US Air Force

Smith, the mother of a four-year-old son, joined the air force in 1966 after surrendering custody as a condition of her service. Policy prevented her son from living with her for more than thirty days a year. She applied for a waiver and was denied. Smith enrolled him at a boarding school near the Washington, DC, base where she was working, but when she was transferred to the Philippines in 1969 and told to either go without him or leave the service, she sued. The air force changed its policy the next day.

Seaman Anna Flores, US Navy

Flores was engaged to a navy enlisted man when she became pregnant in 1970. She miscarried before they could marry, but her commanding officer sought to discharge her for fear of seeming to condone out-of-wedlock pregnancy. She sued for discrimination on the grounds that the navy imposed this moral code only on women, not on the men who got them pregnant. The American Civil Liberties Union brought the suit and was granted class-action status. The navy gave in and changed its policy before the District Court for the Northern District of Florida could rule.

Captain Susan Struck, US Air Force

Struck was an air force nurse serving in Vietnam in 1970 when she became pregnant. Told to end the pregnancy or be involuntarily discharged, she was sent to McChord Air Force Base in Tacoma, Washington, for an abortion, but she decided to have the baby and told her superior officers she would give the child up for adoption instead. The air force nonetheless sought to discharge her from the service. Struck sued—in another case argued by Ginsburg—and lost in the Ninth Circuit Court. The Supreme Court agreed to hear her appeal, but before that could happen, the air force reversed course and granted Struck a waiver.

Stephanie Crawford, US Marine Corps

Crawford was working in an administrative capacity for the marines when she discovered she was pregnant in 1970. She was immediately discharged "for the convenience of the government"—a policy that also called for the parents of a pregnant servicewoman to be informed of the reason for their daughter's discharge. When she applied for reenlistment, she was denied because she had a child. She sued, and the US Court of Appeals for the Second Circuit overturned a lower-court ruling on grounds that the marines were automatically equating pregnancy with permanent unfitness for duty, a violation of due process.

The conclusion drawn from these cases, or the conclusion that should have been drawn, was that military service is not incompatible with pregnancy and motherhood. If the armed forces were willing to accommodate a new influx of dedicated, capable women, it made no sense to discharge them at the very beginning of their careers—especially, in the case of naval aviators, pilots whose training cost taxpayers hundreds of thousands of dollars, if not more.

As Rosemary wrote in the introduction to *Military Fly Moms: Sharing Memories, Building Legacies*: "Of all the advancements made in the 20th century, nothing was more important to the viability of women making a career in the US armed forces than the ability to combine military service with parenthood—just as men did. This was the result of hard-fought policy and statutory battles in the courts, Congress and the

Pentagon. By 1976, all the military departments revised their policies so that pregnant women, including aviators, were no longer automatically discharged."

None of this, unfortunately, made life any easier for Lieutenant (j.g.) Jane Skiles O'Dea when she became the first US military pilot in history to conceive—and to have a baby—while on active duty.

As the only woman flying support for the Sixth Fleet in the Mediterranean Sea out of VR-24 in Rota, Spain—known as the Go-Go Airline—Jane attracted a fair amount of attention, though she tried to maintain a low profile. That tension was evident in a *Stars and Stripes* profile in March 1975, seven months after she arrived in Rota, which quoted the base public affairs officer as saying, "We've been keeping her hidden from the press until she has had a chance to settle in here. In the States, every time she landed there was somebody waiting with a camera."

The story was headlined "Navy's First Woman Flier Overseas—The Blue Yonder's Wild About Her," and referred to Jane, newly promoted to lieutenant (j.g.) as "the Go-Go Airline Girl."

She doesn't say it but you suspect there is some loneliness now in going through what she calls this "period of acceptance." "You have to grin and bear it sometimes," she said. "A man comes out of flight training with some credibility; I had none. Some resent what I'm doing. Pilots are such a close-knit group, it's difficult gaining acceptance." She feels her integration into the VR-24 detachment has been made easier by the integration of enlisted women into the unit. . . . "Now that I've been here long enough and proved myself competent," she said, "I've had no problem in working relationships. . . . I think I'm competent for my experience level and think I've earned their respect, and that my professional acceptance has been very good. That's the first step."

On the duty roster there's no deference to the lady, and that's the way she likes it. The crews who fly the C-130s out of Rota are not kept intact but are formed as names reach the top of the roster. She is carried as a copilot. "Eventually you fly with just about everybody," she said. "You also split the flying, so the copilot gets half the landings, takeoffs, etc." The job itself offers satisfactions beyond the exhilaration

of flight. "It's personally gratifying," she said of the mission of hauling
mail and hard-to-procure items needed by the fleet. "They're really
glad to see us coming."

She's not sure what the future holds for the Navy's women pilots.
"The six of us who are flying are in no-man's-land," she said. "Our
career paths are so different at this point in time. Right now we
cannot have a warfare specialty. I don't think the Navy knows quite
what to do with us." She explains that most of the male pilots have
already flown in a career specialty before being assigned here and will
return to their specialty when their tour here is complete. She says as
an example that many of the squadron's pilots have been in antisub-
marine warfare, flying the electronic-laden P-3 Orions on patrol. At
the present time Navy regulations prohibit women pilots from such
duty or even flying C-1 or C-2 on COD (carrier onboard delivery)
missions, hauling cargo from shore to the carriers.

With 250 to 300 flight hours under her belt, Jane told the reporter
she hoped to make the 1,500 hours needed to qualify for aircraft commander by the end of her time at Rota, and that if she were to start a
family, "A person wouldn't miss that much active duty. Besides, men get
time off from flying to help out when their wives are nearing childbirth,
so the difference in lost flying time wouldn't be all that much."

She put that to the test a year and a half later, sometime after she and
Tom O'Dea, an enlisted crew chief in charge of maintaining the C-1s at
Rota, got married in a ceremony at Gibraltar. They had met on a COD
flight and managed to skirt the rules about fraternization between officers and enlisted through a combination of Tom's likability and discretion
about public displays of affection.

"Pregnant, Iowan Gets Navy Flak," ran the front-page story in the
Des Moines Tribune on July 15, 1976: "Jane is six months pregnant, and
tickled. But, she has a few crusty military officers in a tizzy." It seemed
the squadron that told Jane she couldn't use the bathroom didn't want a
pregnant pilot around.

"After she became pregnant, Skiles ran into trouble with the Navy
brass," the *Des Moines Register Sun* reported. "Feeling perhaps that Skiles

might have delivered while flying somewhere over Europe, the brass tried to ground her immediately until after she had her baby. But Skiles was able to keep flying until about two months before the baby was due."

In her foreword to *Military Fly Moms*, Jane wrote, "The Navy leadership wasn't quite sure how to handle the situation. My commanding officer assumed that I would leave the Navy, but . . . [t]ogether, the Navy and I plowed this new ground. I am grateful to a very enlightened flight surgeon who made a politically risky decision and allowed me to fly until I believed it was imprudent for my health and the baby's health."

Another issue for Jane, reported the *Tribune*, "was the lack of toilet facilities for women in the C-130 cargo plane she flies. About the time she was grounded, she started catching flak about wearing civilian maternity clothes because she couldn't wear her issue uniform. . . . 'Understandably, some officers don't like for you to wear civilian clothes, but they have no choice. . . . It's right in the regulations. You can wear civilian clothes.' She had to buy men's white shirts and maternity trousers and alter them so they were similar to Navy-issue uniforms. 'My hope is the Navy would change women's uniforms,' she said. 'They're pretty far behind and impractical.'

"Her fellow pilots have accepted her pregnancy 'good-naturedly,' she said, even to the extent of advising her to name the baby after the C-130's nickname—'Hercules.' Once, she said, a pilot with whom she was flying listed the unborn child as a half-member of the crew."

Jane "pioneered the combination of motherhood and flying for the rest of us," Rosemary said in 2011. "Jane was flying the C-130 when carrying her first daughter, and she once told me it's a good thing that it had a very big cockpit. Her second daughter logged over 100 hours of T-34 flight time."

In *Proceedings* magazine, Jane described the pregnancy as "'a rather dark time in my life' as a result of hostile treatment she received." Even so, she and her husband saw no reason for her to quit. "I didn't feel I had to give up a career I had worked for," Jane told the *Tribune*. "Women have families in other career fields, so I decided to stay with it. Besides, it would be a cop-out. I have a contract to serve six years, and I've got two more years to go."

She moved to a desk job when she was grounded, and in November 1976, Lieutenant (j.g.) Jane Skiles O'Dea became the first US military pilot mom. Two weeks after that, she was promoted to lieutenant (s.g.), and she returned to flying status about a month later.

"They tried to get me to get out of the navy," she says. "I told them I wouldn't. And that was that." Maternity uniforms would become available to military women a year and a half later.

For another of the six original female naval aviators, though, pregnancy marked the end of active duty.

When Lieutenant Barbara Allen Rainey became pregnant in 1977, she considered taking maternity leave and then returning to her squadron at Alameda. But, as she told the *New York Times*, "there were other factors besides pregnancy that were making me reconsider a Navy career." Those issues, says her husband, John, were limitations on what she could do as a naval aviator. "If she stayed, and everything was evaluated fairly, there was no way a woman would get promoted because of the restrictions on them; they couldn't compete with the guys. If the guys were going to combat squadrons, doing what got the medals and awards, women didn't have that opportunity, so if a female naval aviator was being evaluated for promotion, if it was to be totally, objectively fair, the woman would never be promoted. But if she was promoted just because she was female, that wasn't right either."

As she told the Gannett News Service,

I think we (the first women students) were like most of the men first starting out—the objective is to learn to fly. Only later do you begin to realize that flying is only part of being a naval officer. Well, the patterns for male pilots to advance as naval officers are established. But with us, everything was play-it-by-ear, and it hasn't really worked out yet. . . . For men . . . the way to advancement is pretty well laid out. . . . For women . . . that just isn't true yet, and won't be true until they make opportunity really equal. . . .

Because of the limitations by law . . . Navy flying isn't a viable career for women. It's too limited. . . . Flying mail to a ship, for instance, meant you had to be assigned to the ship, and a pilot assigned

to a ship is a combat role, so I couldn't do it. . . . I had between 1,100
and 1,200 hours in the air and most of the men who had graduated
at the same time I did had 1,500 to 1,600 hours. I was falling behind.

Retired navy lieutenant commander Jerry Leugers, who arrived at
Alameda a year after Barb, remembers her as "very easygoing, lots of fun
to be around." VR-30 was all guys, except for her. Some of the higher-ups
"probably weren't happy she was there," but her peers "couldn't care less
that she was a woman."

When it came to work, though, it made a huge difference. Pilots who
flew the C-1 and T-39 Sabreliner, like Lieutenant (j.g.) Leugers, primarily shuttled back and forth between shore and ship, delivering parts, personnel, and mail. They did two-week detachments to San Diego, flying
out 100 miles off the coast to practice with the fleet squadrons—F-14s,
A-6s, A-7s, F-4s. But if a pilot couldn't go to a ship, there wasn't much
chance to fly. And Barb, the only female C-1 and T-39 driver, wasn't
allowed. In fact, she was all set to carrier-qualify in the C-1 when word
came down that a woman was not going to land on a carrier—the second
time in her career she was denied.

After two years at VR-30, Jerry had more flight time than Barb. He
made aircraft commander on the Sabreliner as a j.g. while Barb, a lieutenant, was still struggling to get the hours needed to qualify. When she
finally did make aircraft commander in the T-39, he was so far ahead that
he was the instructor who checked her out and signed her off.

So in November 1977, six months pregnant and feeling there was no
point in continuing such a restricted career, she was released from active
duty at her request and joined the Reserve as its first female pilot.

Reported the *New York Times*: "She won her Navy wings in 1974,
then qualified to fly jets. But she said she spent the next three years
watching her chances of promotion diminish. Mrs. Rainey, 29 years old,
resigned her lieutenant's commission earlier this month and joined her
husband, Lt. John Rainey, a flight instructor at Whiting Field near Pensacola. She expects their child in February."

CHAPTER SEVEN

Owens v. Brown

FOR TWO GLORIOUS DAYS IN 1974, INTERIOR COMMUNICATIONS ELEC-
trician Second Class Yona Owens was a full-fledged member of the
crew of the survey ship USNS *Michelson*. No men in her specialty were
available, and orders approving her for sea duty on the noncombat vessel
were signed and sealed.

Until they were rescinded by the navy's judge advocate general as
a violation of federal law. Under Section 6015, navy women were not
allowed to serve on ships—though civilian scientists, civilian technicians,
and army and air force women were all permitted to travel and work on
board.

Frustrated at the official restrictions that stymied her career hopes,
Owens had begun networking. A letter she published in the *Navy Times*
offering to share research she had done into women's rights in the military
yielded 312 requests for help. Yeoman Suzanne Holtman was a staffer in
a new personnel office for enlisted women. The two connected, and with
Photographer's Mate Natoka Peden (also a navy diver) and Seaman Val-
erie Sites, aided by the American Civil Liberties Union and the League
of Women Voters Educational Fund, they decided to file a class-action
lawsuit against the federal government, charging discrimination on behalf
of 21,870 navy women. The named defendants: Harold Brown, secretary
of defense, and W. Graham Claytor, secretary of the navy.

At the same time, Lieutenant (j.g.) Joellen Drag was chafing under
the limits that Section 6015 placed on her ability to do her job. She wasn't
allowed to hover her helicopter over a ship; civilian women could go on

ships, but she couldn't fly them there. Everything was stacked against her: Her San Diego squadron was geared toward building flight time and training pilots for deployment to the Western Pacific, but she was low in the pecking order in getting flight hours. There were always mechanical problems with the blades on the CH-46, so much of the fleet was frequently grounded, making it difficult for her to log hours and meet other qualifications needed to advance even in shore-based billets.

Joellen wasn't the only officer at San Diego who thought it was time to bring the rules up to date. While she was pursuing administrative remedies and writing letters up the chain of command asking to be allowed the same opportunities as her male peers, others were also questioning why Section 6015 still existed at a time when civilian women were claiming rights and making inroads in formerly male domains.

Among these was Lieutenant Suzanne Rhiddlehoover, who was studying at night to become an attorney. Also, Lieutenant Commander Kathleen Byerly, a Women's Officer School graduate who was the first female flag secretary and aide to a commander of an operational staff— and, coincidentally, one of twelve Women of the Year on the cover of *Time* magazine's January 5, 1976, issue, along with former first lady Betty Ford and tennis superstar Billie Jean King. The three officers asked Rhiddlehoover's constitutional law professor for help, and in the course of researching whether Section 6015 could be overturned, they discovered the class-action suit already in the works.

With her previous requests denied and her career stalling, Joellen sent one more letter, assisted by a JAG attorney at her wing and endorsed by her commanding officer:

4 March 1976
From: LTJG Joellen M. DRAG, USN, 547-86-5470/1310, Helicopter Combat
Support Squadron THREE, NAS North Island, San Diego, CA 92135
To: Secretary of the Navy
Via: (1) Commanding Officer, Helicopter Combat Support Squadron THREE

(2) Commander Anti-Submarine Warfare Wing, US Pacific Fleet

(3) Commander Naval Air Force, US Pacific Fleet

(4) Chief of Naval Personnel

(5) Chief of Naval Operations

Subj: *Request for duty in a flying status aboard United States Naval Vessel(s)*

Ref: *(a) 10 USC 6015*

(b) 10 USC 5590

(c) 10 USC 5573

(d) OPNAV P09B3 SNDL

(e) NWP 10-3(d) Navy terminology

(f) OPNAVINST 5720.2A

Encl: *(1) COMSC ltr Ser 20M 35 of 9 May 1975*

(2) Navy Times clipping of Dec 1975

(3) CINCPACFLTINST 5720.2H

(4) COMNAVAIRPACNOTE 5720 of 29 Dec 1975

1. *I wish to request duty in a flying status aboard US Naval vessels, primarily those with which my squadron now operates in the SOCAL area and in the Western Pacific. I am making this request so that my development and career as a Naval officer might keep pace with that of my contemporaries in this squadron. I am evaluated against them in my fitness reports, and accordingly feel that I must be allowed to compete with them in all areas on an equal basis.*

2. *This request includes many questions pertaining to the applicability, scope and validity of 10 USC 6015, reference (a). After twenty-eight years of virtually unchallenged existence, the time has come to cast some doubt on the continued viability of this law which is being used to prevent me and virtually every other woman in the Navy from realizing our potential. This statute precludes the assignment of certain classes of US Navy and US Marine Corps women to duty in combat aircraft on combat missions and US Naval vessels other than hospital ships and transports. It clearly does not apply to all military women and a literal reading casts doubt as to whether it even applies to all Navy women. In light of these doubts, I am requesting*

a re–evaluation of the legality and practicality of reference (a) when its only effect will be confusion at best and blatant discrimination at worst. If the statute is found to be still partially applicable to female Naval personnel, it must be specifically clarified as to which women it does apply and justification made as to why it should apply only to some Navy women and not all Navy women or even all military women.

Finally, even remaining within the strictest possible interpretation of reference (a) as it now stands, I am requesting permission to land aboard those vessels referred to as "transports" in references (a) and (d). HC-3, the squadron to which I am attached, routinely conducts training operations with these vessels and shipboard landing qualifications are required by this squadron in order for me to become Helicopter Aircraft Commander. Aircraft Commander qualification is the logical and necessary career step upwards for every Naval pilot, a step which will be delayed or even denied to me without shipboard landing qualifications.

3. In its entirety, reference (a) reads as follows:

"6015. Women members: duty; qualifications; restrictions The Secretary of the Navy may prescribe the manner in which women officers appointed under section 5590 of this title, women warrant officers, and enlisted women members of the Regular Navy and the Regular Marine Corps shall be trained and qualified for military duty. The Secretary may prescribe the kind of military duty to which such women may be assigned and the military authority which they may exercise. However, women may not be assigned to duty in aircraft that are engaged in combat missions nor may they be assigned to duty on vessels of the Navy other than hospital ships and transports. Aug. 10, 1956, c. 1041, 70A Stat. 375."

The last sentence is usually the line quoted to justify the exclusion of women from shipboard duty. However, the first sentence of the article obviously indicates that some women were intended to be exempt from the combat aircraft and sea duty restrictions. As set out in a note to the text, the limitation to "women officers appointed under section 5590" was originally inserted to avoid application of the 6015 to women officers in the Nurse Corps, Medical Corps, Dental Corps and Medical Service Corps. Today, however, it would also presumably preclude application of 6015 to women officers of the Judge Advocate General's Corps since they are also not appointed under article 5590.

Yet, all these women officers have been denied duty aboard ships on the basis of article 6015 restrictions. In addition, reference (b) refers only to women officers appointed to the Regular Navy and Regular Marine Corps and as such, article 6015 should logically not apply to women officers like myself who were originally appointed as members of the Naval Reserve or Marine Corps Reserve.

The problem is whether "women" in the third sentence means all women in the Navy or only those women specified in the first sentence. If it does refer only to those women in the first sentence, then the scope of the law is considerably narrower than is presently interpreted. Until last year, all women officers were commissioned as Reserves. They are, therefore, not appointed under reference (b), 10 USC 5590. The future graduates of the Naval Academy will be appointed under 10 USC 5573, reference (c), and as such, the sea duty limitations should not apply to them either.

4. Records of Congressional hearings used extensively in formulating the current interpretations of reference (a) imply that the drafters were attempting to keep all women off all ships. Specifically, Congressman Vinson stated: "I would not want to restrict [the prohibition] to combatant vessels. Put down serve in sea duty. . . . Just fix it so they cannot go to sea at all." (Hearings on S1641 before Subcommittee #3 of the House Armed Services Committee. 80th Congress, 2nd session 5711 (1948)). Despite Congressman Vinson's strong personal bias and his success at turning that bias into law, reference (a) does not quite "fix it" so that women cannot go to sea. Women enlisted under US Air Force, US Army and Coast Guard statutes and regulations are not restricted from serving on vessels at sea. Reference (a) does not apply to the women of other services and there are no comparable statutes for the other services. Even the Army Regulation that specifically deals with a separate women's Army Corps does not mention any restriction against women serving in combat. Women members of an Air Force instrumentation team attached to the Patrick Air Force Base Eastern Test Range are already serving aboard Military Sealift Command vessels, as shown by enclosures (1) and (2). The Commandant of the Coast Guard has stated that Coast Guard women will serve at sea. It seems absurd to think that [the] ultimate effect of 6015 will be to deny sea duty only to women in the sea-going military services.

5. The continued existence and current interpretation of 6015 is even more unreasonable in light of the fact that the Navy itself is already struggling with methods to work around the restrictions imposed by the statute. My squadron, HC-3, regularly airlifts female members of the Fleet Training Group, Pacific to aircraft carriers engaged in readiness exercises off the coast of California. The rationale for allowing these women to serve at sea aboard the largest combatant vessels in the Navy during combat-ready exercises is exceedingly tortuous to say the least. Reference (f) allows female military members to go aboard Navy vessels as "guests" of military members. CINCPAC-FLTINST 5720.2H, enclosure (3), and COMNAVAIRPACNOTE 5720 of 29 December 1975, enclosure (4), euphemistically refers to the periods at sea with women FLETRAGRUPAC members aboard as "orientation cruises." The notice specifies that their "guest" status is dependent, among other things upon providing their own transportation to and from the "point of embarkation." Even with a considerable stretch of one's imagination, it is difficult to classify the working women members of the FLETRAGRUPAC as guests. Their transportation to the HC-3 line, the "point of embarkation," is provided in the form of a Navy launch. They are in military uniform and perform in a duty status while aboard the ships. The final absurdity is that while OPNAVINST 5720.2G apparently creates a needed loophole for FLETRAGRU women personnel to serve aboard ship, it does not do the same for me. They are flown to the carriers at sea in HC-3 helicopters but I cannot fly them out there as a pilot. They remain aboard the ship for 8–10 hours a day but I cannot spend 15 minutes on the ship to land and disembark them as passengers.

6. *In addition to the loophole just mentioned, there are several other categories of women not covered by OPNAVINST 5720.2G. These include Department of the Navy civilian women and US Navy civilian technicians, and as such, there are no restrictions against women in these categories to prevent them from going to sea on Naval vessels. Other civilian women such as DOD employees not in the Department of the Navy and non-civil service personnel (e.g.: contract employees, Technical Representatives) are not even considered by these regulations. Women employees of the Customs Division of the Department of the Treasury sail with the USS ORISKANY. Again, reference (a) appears to preclude sea duty only to those women who most logically should be assigned to such duty. The great lengths to which a command will go to be able to work around 6015 in order to utilize needed trained personnel who happen to be women indicates that the useful life of 10 USC 6015, if it ever had one, is past.*

7. *10 USC 6015 does allow for the assignment of women to sea duty aboard hospital ships and transports of the US Navy. The decommissioning of the SANCTUARY marked the passing of the Navy's last hospital ship but there are still a number of Navy ships classed as transports. The NWP 10-3(D) Navy Terminology, reference (e), and OPNAV P09B3-107, The Standard Navy Distribution List, reference (d), list amphibious transports (LPAs) and Amphibious Transport Docks (LPDs), an Amphibious Transport Submarine (LPSS 574). [The] All Hands [issue] of January 1976 lists two ships as just plain transports of the Barrett class; the Barrett (T-AP196) and the UPSHUR (T-AP198).*

An obvious reading of 6015 would allow any and all women naval personnel to deploy aboard these vessels, one of which is a submarine. If these vessels are not the transports referred to in reference (a), then the definition of transport is so vague as to be utterly meaningless. If its interpretation can be changed by a stroke of the pen, then it is subject to abuse by those who would deny, either intentionally or unintentionally, the advance of equal opportunity and equal treatment in the Navy.

8. *The Navy is justifiably proud of its image as a leader among the services in the areas of equal opportunity and utilization of female personnel. Unfortunately, many of the steps already taken towards equality for women in the military will lead nowhere as long as 10 USC 6015 remains on the books and is strictly interpreted. All the advances made so far have greatly increased the servicewoman's benefits to equal those of men, but women's responsibilities, training, advancement opportunities and career patterns remain at a level far below that of their male counterparts. The gap is considerably beyond what might be justified by readiness and operational requirements. The Navy has critical "manpower" shortages in many ratings but ironically, many of these rates are the very ones closed to women because of reference (a) combat and sea duty restrictions.*

This situation becomes even more ironic when one considers the number of women leaving the Navy as unrated seamen and airmen because they cannot get training or schools in the ratings that are open to them. It is reasonable to say that part of the Navy's "manning" problems could be solved with women if the combat mission and sea duty restrictions would be lifted. The Department of Defense should see fit to resolve the inequities inherent in 10 USC 6015. It is as discriminatory on its face as the statute regarding women members' dependents which was found by the Supreme Court to be unconstitutional. Unfortunately, if the Department of Defense fails to act, the only remaining course of action for dedicated women is a judicial appeal.

9. *The previous arguments illustrate the following very real points of confusion regarding the scope, applicability and validity of 10 USC 6015:*

a. First, 10 USC 6015 does not apply to all Navy women. Even using the narrow construction employed by the Judge Advocate General in past interpretations and the fact that some women were intended to be excluded from its provisions, it is clear that the restrictions of reference (a) should not be applied to all Navy women. Specifically, its language excludes all women Reserve officers and Staff

Corps officers presently serving in the Navy. It will exclude Naval Academy graduates. What is the purpose of reference (a), if it excludes some US Navy and US Marine Corps women but not others?

b. 10 USC 6015 obviously does not apply to all servicewomen. What is the purpose of a law which excludes only women of the Navy and Marine Corps from duty aboard the ships of their own service but allows women from other services to be assigned?

c. There is no purpose to a law which has already failed of its initial intent. Women are already serving in limited areas aboard some US Navy and Military Sealift Command vessels and there is an increasing need for their assignments at sea and in potential combat situations. Navy units are finding it necessary to invent intricate word games to work around the restrictions of the statute. Why should fleet units be forced to operate at manning levels considerably below minimum effectiveness while the Navy continues to recruit and train increasing numbers of women which article 6015 restricts from full utilization in critical job ratings? Either the Navy must stop recruiting women (which is no longer a very feasible alternative) or it must eliminate all artificial restrictions.

10. In concluding, I will reiterate my request for sea duty. If article 6015 restrictions were lifted today, I would not expect to see all women assigned to sea and combat duty tomorrow. The changes in facilities will obviously take some time and the changes in the attitudes of men and women will take even longer. On the other hand, I do not think the military services can wait for attitudes to change before changing their policies. [The] 6015 prohibitions must be removed in order to promote long overdue changes. Until then, a liberal interpretation of reference (a) which would permit sea duty for myself and other eligible Navy women is the reasonable first step to insure reality of equal opportunity and treatment. Hopefully, the second step will not be far behind.

JOELLEN M. DRAG
LTJG, USN

The letter went up the chain of command—and vanished. Joellen says she suspects that one of the navy brass was dead set against the idea of female military pilots and that another, scarred by his experiences in Vietnam, couldn't square those horrific memories with the idea of women as prisoners of war. So the three female officers joined the four enlisted women in pursuing "the only remaining course of action ... a judicial appeal."

Lieutenant Rosemary Conatser was asked to be a plaintiff, but she didn't think it was a good idea. Convinced that working within the system would get women what they needed, she felt the chance of retaliation was too risky. Better to give the navy an opportunity to reform on its own.

"Suing the navy was not a career-enhancing thing to do," Rosemary said in her speech at the Smithsonian. "I was asked to join, but I chickened out. Things were going good for me, and I didn't want to upset the apple cart."

The suit was filed in US District Court in Washington, DC, on November 10, 1976.

"It needed to be done," says Joellen, "and I'm glad my name was on it and there was at least one aviator," because the ranks were growing. As the suit was making its way through the courts, the tally of female naval aviators reached thirteen—ten fixed-wing and three helo—with eight more in training.

Joellen didn't have to testify, and life at HC-3 went on as usual. Most of the men in the squadron weren't even aware there was a lawsuit, let alone that she was a named plaintiff.

But on July 27, 1978, US District Judge John Sirica, who had gained fame presiding over trials stemming from the Watergate scandal, ruled that Section 6015 was indeed unconstitutional, as it prevented navy women from "gaining access to a wide range of opportunities for the development of job skills and areas of technical expertise." His opinion addressed Joellen specifically, by name.

After qualifying as a helicopter pilot, plaintiff Drag was assigned to a support squadron whose primary function involves servicing vessels at sea with supplies. This duty typically requires a temporary assign-

ment to a supply ship and regular flights to and from cruising vessels. Yet because of Section 6015, plaintiff Drag is barred from this kind of duty, while equally qualified males are not. As her commanding officer noted to the Secretary of the Navy, plaintiff Drag 'is excluded from virtually all operational commitments routinely undertaken by her contemporaries' despite her 'demonstrated outstanding performance in all aspects of her assigned duties.' In addition, this same limitation on assignments also impairs plaintiff's ability to accumulate the flight time she needs to advance to higher ratings even as a shore-based aviation specialist. The reason is that helicopter pilots are required as a condition to advancement to qualify as aircraft commanders with 300 hours of flight time, a goal that is made especially difficult for women because of the scarcity of flight opportunities that are not precluded by the broad sweep of the statute.

The navy saw there was no argument left and declined to appeal.

In anticipation of an amended Section 6015, the navy had introduced its Women at Sea program a month before the ruling, calling for billeting 55 female officers and 375 enlisted women as crew members on 20 auxiliary and noncombatant ships. To prepare the crews, official guidelines suggested that to "actualize the highest potential of women, at-sea commands must emphasize to the entire ship's company" that "women are assets, not liabilities . . . women are different . . . and must be treated differently, not paternalistically or as inferiors or with favoritism . . . every person, man and woman, requires and deserves respect as a person" and that they should attend to "sensitivity of wives [regarding the] issue of women at sea . . . reasonable efforts [should be made] to avoid compromising situations, [along with] avoidance of encouraging excessive drinking . . . reasonable care in selecting movies for showing . . . [and making an] effort to maintain a generally high moral tone."

Only three-quarters of the target number of enlisted women signed up—but four times as many female officers volunteered as the program could handle. The women's arrival shipboard was greeted with responses ranging from a warm welcome to indifference from their male counterparts, and with a flurry of publicity. On one ship, the women's debut was re-created for photographers; the news conference that followed focused largely on bedrooms and bathrooms. Again.

Three months after Sirica's ruling, President Jimmy Carter signed the Fiscal Year 1979 Defense Authorization Bill, with its amended Section 6015. Navy brass had considered a repeal but decided that no, that was Congress's job. The amendment lifted the most grievous restrictions. But at the urging of Admiral James Holloway, Zumwalt's replacement as chief of naval operations, and Navy Secretary W. Graham Claytor, severe limitations remained.

For Joellen, the women had won the battle but lost the war.

The amended law allowed women to serve at sea, but only on hospital ships, transports, and certain other noncombat vessels. Women could also get Temporary Additional Duty assignments on combatant ships for up to 180 days—though deployments often lasted longer—if they were unlikely to have a combat mission during that time, and subject to approval. If a peaceful mission turned toward combat, the women would have to evacuate their posts. Surface warfare and some special operations training pipelines were opened to women, but because there weren't enough noncombat sea billets to accommodate them, the number who could actually select a warfare track was small.

Key for Joellen, though, was an order redefining the role of female aviators as a result of the amendment, dated April 18, 1979. This allowed them, for the first time, to land on ships at sea. Women pilots could finally carrier-qualify—though not in jets—and fly COD flights, bringing mail, equipment, and supplies.

In June 1979, Lieutenant Donna Lynn Spruill, a member of the second group of female naval aviators, became the first woman fixed-wing pilot to carrier-qualify, flying a C-1A Trader to the Norfolk-based *Independence* (though only, as Henry W. Holden and Captain Lori Griffith wrote in *Ladybirds*, after she had transferred "from the West Coast to the East Coast because a certain admiral wouldn't allow women aboard 'his' ships").

And for the first time in Joellen Drag's career—and in navy history— a female helo pilot would be assigned to duty aboard a US Navy ship.

The ship was the *Vancouver*, and the assignment was six days' sea duty during a military exercise 300 miles off the California coast. Flying out and landing—the only woman within miles—Joellen was tasked with retrieving remote-controlled target drones launched from the fifteen or twenty ships participating in the exercise. After waiting three days for the Russian trawlers that had been shadowing the exercise to move on, they sent out the drones. Measuring 8 to 10 feet long and looking like miniature orange airplanes, the drones simulated enemy aircraft for ships and planes to shoot at. Eventually, they would ditch in the ocean and the helos would fly over to retrieve them, one at a time. A crew member sitting in the doorway, dangling 10 feet above the ocean, would snag the drone using a long pole and then attach it to a cargo hook in the floor.

There were dangers, of course.

If the drone was at the wrong angle of attack, it could start flying on its own underneath the helo and cause serious damage. A chopper that hovered too low could suck ocean water spray into the engine intakes, collecting salt on the turbines and causing the craft to stall. That's what happened to the second helo in the exercise: The crew was unable to restart the engine, and the chopper flipped over in the sea. Having already recovered her target, Joellen flew over to rescue the second helo's five crew members and return them to the ship.

After recovering the rest of the targets and landing again, Joellen wandered toward sick bay to see if the other crew was all right. Suddenly, a sailor jumped out, saluted, and said, "I owe you an apology, ma'am." The sailors had been on the signal bridge when the helo went in the water, and they'd all bet that she was the pilot who'd been flying—they'd let the woman touch the controls, and she'd crashed. For the next three or four days, with the second helo crew grounded until the accident investigation was over, she and the other remaining male pilot had to do all the flying. More than once, hovering near the ship, she caught sailors taking pictures of the lady helo pilot recovering targets.

Still, in the face of this slow but steady progress, the political winds were starting to shift.

The Equal Rights Amendment failed to gain approval in enough states to become the law of the land. President Carter chose not to include women in registration for the draft. And the new chief of naval operations, Admiral Thomas Hayward, opposed the repeal of Section 6015. All "warnings of things to come," wrote Bernard D. Rotsker in *I Want You! The Evolution of the All-Volunteer Force.*

Some navy women resented having to shoulder new burdens, like standing watch, and performing other duties from which they had formerly been exempt. Some commanders took the new requirements for women's shipboard duty—such as separate berthing and bathroom facilities, a minimum of two women billeted, and approval from up the chain of command—as loopholes to be exploited, in order to delay or deny. So much so that Hayward sent down this directive in August 1979: "I want to make sure my philosophy is clear on this point. . . . Since my previous guidance may have been interpreted as suggesting restraint, as a policy, the following guidance is provided for clarification: Assignment of women to ships for temporary duty is authorized whenever required in the performance of military duties or in support of required training."

But there was a growing sense, wrote Jeanne Holm in *Women in the Military: An Unfinished Revolution*, that the expanding role of women could just be "a temporary condition that would pass with the demise of a misguided Carter administration." According to Holm, "It was no secret that, just below the surface of the military ranks at all levels, there persisted a deep well of resistance and even resentment toward women and their growing incursion into previously all-male preserves. Many . . . believed that military policy was being made by well-meaning amateurs, with little or no service experience, who were motivated more by political expediency and misguided desires for social equity than for national defense."

With Republican Ronald Reagan running for president on a platform of building a more-robust military; the Soviet invasion of Afghanistan; the Iran hostage crisis; and "a growing sense of awareness of the disparity between Soviet and American military growth," the national conversation was no longer focused as much on fairness, opportunity, equal rights, and the morality of the United States flexing its muscle as it was on new weapons and military readiness. "Supporters of women found not only that their items had been removed from the agenda, but also that new issues were sometimes formulated in ways that reversed previously won gains," Holm wrote.

For Joellen, the gains made were not enough.

Her second deployment was search and rescue at Naval Air Station Point Mugu, California, where there was little career development potential and few leadership opportunities. Though she had logged five rescues during the military exercises on the *Vancouver*, her next assignment would be more search-and-rescue duty—this time, in the Philippines, where she had lived as a child during one of her father's billets.

Joellen felt she was being warehoused—"It was not the stuff careers are made of," she says—so in November 1979, she resigned from active duty and joined the Reserve. She would fly the H-3 Sea King part-time out of support squadron HC-194 in San Diego for another five years, doing combat search and rescue (which she couldn't have done while on active duty), landing on ships—"a lot of fun flying"—before stepping back and following her husband, Lieutenant Commander Dwayne Oslund, to his various duty stations. (An item in the December 1980 edition of *Naval Aviation News* noted a history-making landing on the amphibious assault ship *Belleau Wood*, with copilot Lieutenant Joellen Oslund guided in by a landing signal officer who happened to be her husband of two years. It was also her first shipboard landing as a reservist.)

The Reserve provided leadership experience Joellen never could have gotten as a station pilot in the Philippines. She still managed to log about 100 hours a year, serving one weekend a month, doing mini-deployments in Nevada, flying two-week missions during active-duty joint exercises in Italy, and, finally, serving as navy liaison to FEMA in San Francisco. It was enough that she made captain before retiring in 1998. "I was sad that I couldn't stay on active duty," she says. "But things didn't change quickly enough."

Joellen was the first female pilot assigned aboard a navy ship and the first female navy combat search-and-rescue helicopter aircraft commander. She logged seven rescues: five off the *Vancouver*, one in steep mountainous terrain near Ventura, California, and one an A-4 pilot who ejected in the ocean off Miramar. She also served as a department head and as a commanding officer, and worked at the Pentagon.

While flying the H-3 provided opportunity and excitement for Lieutenant Ana Maria Scott, it seemed the navy might not be the best long-term career fit.

During Bicentennial celebrations in 1976, her VIP transport squadron was temporarily reassigned to the New York area, where Operation Sail was marking the two-hundredth anniversary of the founding of the United States. Her helo flew then-secretary of state Henry Kissinger, among other celebrities. "Pretty cool, although I didn't talk to him. It was simply amazing to be flying over NYC when it was decked to the hilt for this special celebration," she says.

At her next billet, HS-10 (Helicopter Antisubmarine Squadron) at NAS North Island, she served as legal officer and safety officer and worked in scheduling, in addition to maintaining her currency in day and night flying. She flew with pilots training in the H-3 and acted as a maintenance pilot, performing test flights on aircraft when they came out of the shop.

But after four years, it was clear to Ana Maria that an 8-to-4 daily routine was not for her. The strictures of a military career could not provide the independence she needed.

"I am definitely not the kind of person who enjoys routine," she says. "I like variety. I like to explore and to try and do different things. . . . For any high-level job, I would need to be 100 percent devoted to the work and to even commit to more than that. I needed to live and breathe navy. On the contrary, even though I always try to give my all to the work and to do my best, when the task is finished I like to have freedom to pursue other interests outside of work. . . . In any business, to get ahead, you have to say the right things, do all the right things to impress your superiors. . . . I don't want to be disrespectful to anybody, but sometimes I just don't want to follow the path everybody seems to be following."

Ana Maria put in her papers toward the end of 1979—and got a call from an admiral asking her to rethink her decision. It was flattering, but she'd already begun looking at the airlines. Most wanted only pilots with jet fixed-wing time—United said they'd hire her if she had a few hundred more hours—but FedEx was willing to bring in pilots with only helicopter time.

"Of course," she says, "being a woman and being military-trained was a huge plus."

Barb had already resigned from active duty two years before. A "Woman Aviator Assignment Chronology" dated October 1979 showed thirty female naval aviators (seven helo and twenty-three fixed-wing, including twelve in jet transition). An additional sixteen were in flight training. Three—lieutenants Joellen Drag Oslund, Barbara Allen Rainey, and Ana Maria Scott—had resigned or were in the process of doing so. Lieutenant Commander Judith Neuffer Bruner was no longer in a flying billet, assigned to Navy Personnel Command. Of the original six, only lieutenants Rosemary Conatser and Jane Skiles O'Dea were still flying on active duty.

"In hindsight," Judith Stiehm wrote in *Arms and the Enlisted Woman*, "antagonistic reactions to women's increased military role were not uncommon. What was uncommon before 1980, though, was any public expression of antagonism by high-ranking military or civilian authorities."

Which is exactly what the new administration's air force assistant secretary, Joseph Zengerle, demonstrated in a speech given on November 17, 1980, to members of DACOWITS: Of achievements by women in the military, he said, "The honeymoon is over."

PART III

THE 1980s

CHAPTER EIGHT

"The Honeymoon Is Over"

FOR WOMEN IN THE NAVY, INCLUDING ITS FEMALE AVIATORS, THE 1980S were, in the words of Lieutenant Joellen Drag Oslund, "two steps forward and one step back, two steps back and one step forward."

As she said during a 2013 panel discussion on women in combat: "If they could make a decision that obstructed the implementation of the law, then that's what they did, starting with the fact that as soon as 6015 was struck down . . . they promptly had a new version of it passed with the National Defense Authorization Act in 1979. That instituted the 180-day TAD thing [the six-month limit on women serving on ships] which we struggled with until 1991. And then there was the JAG interpretation of things. [Section] 6015 itself didn't need to be as restrictive as it was."

Air Force Assistant Secretary Joseph Zengerle's statement to members of DACOWITS that "the honeymoon is over" implied that military women had been handed their opportunities, rather than fighting for every advancement they had made—and that they should feel grateful for their hard-won victories. With mandatory draft registration reinstated (for men only) and renewed debate about women in combat, many of the old attitudes were reemerging. Zengerle's stated belief that national security and human rights, formerly on parallel tracks, were now on a collision course gave cover to traditionalists who favored old-time custom over newfangled regulations. It was exactly the dynamic Zumwalt's Z-grams had tried to reverse.

The army, for example, decided to slam the brakes on a planned increase in female recruitment, in what was known as "womanpause." Despite a decade or more of women performing "men's" duties, all the old questions came up again: women's strength, stamina, and agility; pregnancy and related medical issues; the difficulty in posting married military couples; care for dependent children in the event of emergency deployment; and the expense of creating facilities to accommodate women's needs, including day care. As Judith Stiehm put it, "They are all legitimate management concerns, but they are also complaints about the 'trouble' women create. Often the implicit message seemed to be: Let's go back to the good old days and ways."

In the navy, the lack of a defined career path for the growing ranks of women was felt even more sharply than before. Under Zumwalt, there had been clear guidance as to what equal opportunity should mean. But now, disagreements were erupting at the top and filtering down through the fleet. The new chief of naval operations, Admiral Thomas Hayward, and the new secretary of the navy, Edward Hidalgo, were contradicting each other in public on whether Section 6015 should be repealed. In the tug-of-war between the letter and the spirit of the law, it seemed the navy was doing the absolute minimum it could get away with in advancing the cause of women.

Yes, the first two female naval aviators were admitted to the US Navy Fighter Weapons School (aka Top Gun) in the early 1980s.

Yes, a woman, Lieutenant Pat Denkler, finally carrier-qualified in a jet (three years after the first woman aviator carrier-qualified in a propel-ler plane—and she had to switch oceans to do it).

Yes, the navy allowed women to serve temporarily on certain support ships in the Mediterranean, the Indian Ocean, and the Pacific.

Yes, the first women were admitted to navy test pilot school.

Yes, the aircraft carrier USS *Lexington* was reclassified as a noncom-batant ship to allow women to serve as crew.

Yes, the Naval Academy graduated its first coed classes. ("They say the definition of a radical feminist is a father who has a daughter at the Naval Academy," Rosemary Mariner told the *Washington Post*.)

Yes, the first two women were selected for flag rank (promotion to admiral).

Yes, outgoing president Jimmy Carter signed the Defense Officer Personnel Management Act, eliminating separate men's and women's promotion lists that had been in place since 1948.

But . . .

Many doubted that creating a single system for advancement would yield equal opportunities. With their limited career paths, how could women compete on the same footing as men? A full decade after Z-116, navy women were still overwhelmingly concentrated in administrative, medical, or dental jobs; they had no access to the variety of assignments required for future command.

While the navy projection for fiscal year 1983 was two thousand female surface warfare officers, the actual number was half that, because, good intentions aside, in practical terms there was just no place to put them.

While the jet pipeline was finally open to women, only five were allowed at a time—and they had extra hoops to jump through. Lieutenant Chrystal A. Lewis, a Naval Academy graduate, recalled her experience in the October 1986 issue of *Proceedings*: When she got her wings, "women could not go directly into the jets like men could. Women had to negotiate primary flight training and then go through props, get great grades and get winged before being allowed to submit requests for jets"— the path Rosemary Mariner and Raymond Lambert had pioneered. "Then, only two women a year were admitted into the jet community. If you finished at the right time, when a slot was ready . . . and you had the grades, maybe you'd get the slot." A photo caption accompanying the story read: "For a female aviator, becoming a tailhooker involves more hurdles than male aviators have to clear."

Joellen Drag Oslund had already resigned from active duty.

Barbara Ann Allen Rainey had already resigned from active duty.

Ana Maria Scott had already resigned her commission and left the navy.

Female Naval Aviator No. 14, Lieutenant Lucy Young, who earned her wings in 1977 and flew the A-4 tactical fighter jet, left active duty in 1983. Reported the *Washington Post*: "She said many women like her left the Navy within a few years because they were frustrated with the lack of opportunity. While her male counterparts were serving on aircraft carriers, Young was 'playing the bad guy' in mock missions to train combat pilots."

Even graduating first in jet school and winning awards for weapons operations were not enough to qualify a female pilot to fly with the fleet—and the enduring prohibition barring women from full tours of duty at sea denied them essential experience for moving up the chain of command.

As Lieutenant Commander Jane Skiles O'Dea said in a 1984 interview, "It's very discouraging to know the best you can play on is the junior varsity team no matter how good you are."

Perhaps adding to—and symptomatic of—the resistance was the scandal that erupted aboard the missile-tracking ship USS *Norton Sound*, the first ship in the Pacific participating in the Women at Sea integration program. In June 1980, around the end of the program's first year, the navy sent discharge letters to nineteen of the sixty-one enlisted women on board on grounds of homosexuality. Not that such charges were anything new, but this time, they were being leveled against some of the navy's first seagoing women—and they sued. The incident drew national attention and painted a picture of a vessel in chaos, with a stabbing, loansharking, the disappearance of a female crew member, drug dealing, and an onboard extortion racket run by a gang called the Dirty Dozen.

Fifteen of the accused sailors had the charges dropped, and after an administrative trial, two were acquitted. Wrote Judith Stiehm: "Some women saw it as a purposeful attempt to damage the Women at Sea program, and others saw it as intended to keep women from volunteering for the Navy at all."

A report released to Defense Secretary Caspar Weinberger in August 1987 showed just how frustrating, and threatening, life in the navy could be for a woman. A DACOWITS fact-finding panel visiting navy and marine corps installations in Hawaii, Japan, and the Philippines uncovered a pattern of "morally repugnant behavior" toward women, condoned by commanding officers. Investigators detailed multiple incidents of sexual harassment, verbal harassment, and discrimination—echoing a similar report the year before on women in the army and air force. One captain announced over his ship's PA system that female members of his crew were for sale. Base clubs featured sexually oriented entertainment. Senior officers, both male and female, demanded sexual favors from junior personnel. While many navy women felt shunted aside from jobs that would have given them experience needed for higher rank, the report found other female sailors assigned to jobs they had not been trained for—and then denied promotion for poor performance. The career path for general, or unrestricted, line officers, so clearly defined for men, was muddy for women. Complaints of harassment and discrimination fell on deaf ears.

"Leadership attitudes condone discriminate behavior, in part as a means of perpetuating the 'male mystique' that is traditionally associated with military forces," the report said. For the women, the signal was clear: "The leadership is seeking to force women out of the services."

DACOWITS vice chairman Judith Gibson testified before Congress:

> *I found a deep concern among Navy and Marine Corps women, officers in particular, about their prospects for viable careers in their respective services. Directly related to their perceptions of diminishing opportunities and limited promotions is the narrow interpretation by their services of USC Title 10, Section 6015. . . . I found, too, in both services that sexual harassment by men, and in some cases women, is a major problem.*
>
> *The situation is exacerbated by the belief of women in the Marine Corps, and to a greater extent Navy women, that the chain of command is uninterested and unresponsive to their attempts to address grievances or complaints. It condones and even encourages negative behavior toward women. . . . Many Marine and Navy women believe that they are not wanted in their respective services, that they have invaded what should be a male-only enclave. Morale is low. . . .*
>
> *Certainly there are military women who find their careers rich and rewarding and who have not had to deal with the burdens I have*

described. However, I believe that limited opportunities for military women as a result of restricted interpretation of combat exclusion laws and policies, and the sexual harassment they endure, are not unrelated.

"Rich and rewarding" and "limited opportunities" were apt descriptions of Judy Neuffer's trajectory for the rest of her navy career.

She made aircraft and mission commander as a lieutenant at VXN-8 at Pax River, in command of her P-3 and a crew of eleven or twelve. The acceptance she felt from that crew, she told *Naval Aviation News*, "made the difference between doing a job and loving a job." Still, she wished she had been allowed to land on a carrier, "the highlight of any Navy pilot's career . . . the one thing that really sets the Navy pilot apart from other pilots. . . . I regret not being given the opportunity to have an experience unlike any other in flying." And while she was without a doubt a member of the team—the guys even toned down their more-colorful language when she was around—being the only woman among all those men could be lonely. "Sometimes I really long to have a woman to go to lunch with or to talk woman things with. I just can't go to the wardroom and sit down to talk about woman things with the guys."

After two years, she shifted over to a nonflying billet at Navy Personnel Command as a detailer, assigning newly winged naval aviators to their first squadrons. As a detailer, she says, she sometimes had to help pilots navigate disappointing conflicts between their career goals and the navy's needs. It was never easy to tell eager aviators they were not going to be flying the aircraft of their dreams because the navy needed people in a different pipeline. And then, on to a second nonflying billet, this one at the Pentagon—where Judy was, as usual, virtually the only woman around.

It was the standard career path for naval aviators to rotate out of flying billets as they gained the varied experience needed for promotion. But the first woman to solo a navy aircraft would never fly for the navy again.

By the early 1980s, Judy had passed the ten-year mark in her naval career. She had married an enlisted man, Tom Bruner, and needed to decide whether to transfer into another squadron or to pursue her life-long interest in science and outer space. She couldn't fly patrol, because those jobs were off-limits to women, and the only squadron where she could fly P-3s was VXN-8, where she'd already been. She had applied to navy astronaut training several times and hoped to fly the space shuttle, but they wanted high-performance jet pilots, not P-3 drivers. So she resigned from active duty in June 1981 as a lieutenant commander, joined the Reserve, and applied for a computer programming job as a NASA contractor. If the navy wouldn't get her into the space program, maybe NASA would.

It had been a decade since she'd graduated from college, and she'd never used her computer science degree. But, she says, "I think the guy who hired me had been a navy pilot, and he figured if I could do that, I could do this." She worked at NASA during the week and for the navy on weekends. Her first job was writing ten thousand lines of code for the ground system that commanded the Hubble Space Telescope. And from there, she carved out a career at NASA that would last until 2016. She led data processing and science data branches. When a solar orbiting spacecraft lost communications, she was called in to lead the team that restored the spacecraft to routine operations. When the Wallops Flight Facility, NASA's launch range in Virginia, needed a new vision, she led the implementation team. She was director of safety assurance and of mission assurance at the Goddard Space Flight Center in Maryland.

Meanwhile, she held a string of command posts in the Reserve. Her first assignment was drilling two days a month and serving two weeks' active duty per year with Reserve Patrol Wing Atlantic, which oversaw patrol squadrons flying the P-3. But there, P-3s had a combat mission, which meant she wasn't allowed to fly them. Whenever the wing would deploy with a patrol squadron, she couldn't go, and because she was restricted in what she could do, her potential for advancement on the aviation side was limited. So after several years, she switched to the surface side, which opened up some opportunities. Her first year out of the wing, Commander Judith Neuffer Bruner was selected for her first command, a computer processing unit at the Navy Yard in Washington. It was the beginning of a string of postings in the DC area, including science and technology at the Office of Naval Research, navy logistics at the Pentagon—and three command tours.

One odd fact of life for naval aviators who want to move up the chain of command is that to do so, most must stop flying. While squadron members always have a desk job as well as a flying job, there are very few flying positions above the level of squadron CO. But there are hundreds of nonflying billets that require an aviation background, and even more in specialties not directly related to aviation.

At the same time, naval aviators who don't want a navy career get pilot training they don't have to pay for, complete their four-and-a-half-year commitment, and then go fly for the airlines. In the early 1980s, this constant churn caused a perpetual pilot shortage, one with dire consequences for the first female naval aviator.

Lieutenant Barbara Ann Allen Rainey, six months pregnant, had resigned from active duty in Alameda in November 1977, switched to the Reserve, and moved to Pensacola to join her husband, Lieutenant John Rainey, a flight instructor at NAS Whiting. After their daughter Cynthia was born, John resigned his commission and took a job flying for American Airlines. The family moved to Texas, and John joined a Reserve P-3 unit at NAS New Orleans, while Barb joined VR-53 and then VR-2470, fleet auxiliary squadrons at what was then Naval Air Station Dallas in Grand Prairie. She was the first female pilot in the Naval Reserve.

The rules on pregnant pilots tightened considerably after Cynthia's birth. Barb needed a waiver to fly into her second trimester to qualify in the four-engine Douglas R6D/C-118B Liftmaster—the military equivalent of the old DC-6—when she was pregnant with daughter Katherine, who was born in 1981.

Around the same time, the navy was looking into reactivating reservists as a way to solve its pilot shortage—there was chatter about bringing back a pregnant pilot—and soon after Katie's birth, Barb was recalled to active duty. John had recently been furloughed from the airline, and together, the two newly promoted lieutenant commanders signed on for three-year tours in October 1981.

Says John, "Barb missed flying, and it was an opportunity to deal with dedicated young people and teach them to fly." She was assigned to VT-3, a training squadron at Whiting, as a flight instructor.

Barb immediately bonded with another female flight instructor on the field, Lieutenant Patricia Welling, who had graduated from Aviation Officer Candidate School in the first class to admit women and was a member of the third group of female navy pilots to be winged. Barb, she says, was very down-to-earth, easy to know, and friendly. Patty was the daughter of a naval aviator, but what had impelled her to join the navy after college was a newspaper article she had seen about Barb when she was stationed at Alameda. Later on, when Patty was getting ready to resign from active duty and hunting for a Reserve unit in her native California, Barb would suggest that she look up a young lieutenant named Jerry Leugers at VR-30. Jerry and Patty married in 1984.

Patty and Barb instructed in the T-34C, the turbo version of the Beechcraft Mentor. The T-34C had air-conditioning, making flying in the Pensacola summer bearable. The days were long—three hops a day, briefing, flight, and debrief, then jump back in the plane with another student and do it all over again. All of the pilots wore parachutes for flight training, adding extra, awkward weight and straining their backs.

The fact that Patty and Barb were women didn't seem to be an issue. Safety, however, was.

The two had many conversations, as they changed into their flight suits in the locker room, about the hazards of being a flight instructor at Pensacola. The type of flying they were teaching was basic instruction, meaning visual flight rules only; students had to remain clear of clouds. But the Gulf Coast weather meant lots of cumulus clouds, those cotton-like puffs scattered across the sky. Students all had to share the same few clear patches of air to practice in. Once or twice, says Patty, she had a near-midair collision because of the volume of traffic. All those pilots dodging clouds as they tried to do their maneuvers while maintaining VFR made for some hazardous flying.

Adding to the danger were the conditions on the ground. There were a number of airfields in the area, but between them were miles of pine forest. If a pilot had a problem in the air and couldn't make it to a runway, there weren't many places to land.

Early in her navy career, Patty says, the trainees were told, "Look around you—some of you may not be alive by the end of your career."

On July 13, 1982, Barb and a student, Ensign Donald Knowlton, were practicing touch-and-goes at Middleton Field near Evergreen, Alabama. According to crash investigators, they were in the traffic pattern when the airplane banked sharply to avoid another aircraft, lost altitude, plowed into the ground, and burst into flames in a pine forest two miles from the airport. Both pilots were killed.

Barb was thirty-four years old.

Just four days before, student naval aviator Ensign Cary Jones, a Naval Academy graduate, had been killed in a midair crash over Cabaniss Field in Corpus Christi. In less than a week, the navy had suffered the first two fatalities among its women pilots. John Rainey was attending Jones's funeral when he got word about Barb.

Jones's parents were among the mourners at Barb's funeral a week later. Jerry Leugers was one of the pallbearers, having flown in with some other guys from Alameda on a C-9 to offer assistance. Patty heard the sad news while she was on her cross-country road trip home to California. For Jane, who had started instructing at Whiting eight months before Barb, the accident was devastating. They'd been close during training. "The hardest flight I ever flew was the one two days after she died," Jane says.

Lieutenant Commander Barbara Ann Allen Rainey, America's first female naval aviator, is buried at Arlington National Cemetery.

CHAPTER NINE

Down to the Sea in Ships

THE PATCH ON LIEUTENANT JANE SKILES O'DEA'S FLIGHT SUIT READ "High-Flyin' Lady."

The former "Go-Go Airline Girl," the only female pilot at VR-24 in Rota, Spain, had spent four years flying C-130s all over the Mediterranean, supplying logistics support for the Sixth Fleet and logging landings in Germany, England, France, Egypt, Israel, and Turkey. She participated in a minesweeping mission to clear the Suez Canal. After the USS *John F. Kennedy* and the USS *Belknap* collided in rough seas off the coast of Sicily, she flew a specially rigged Herk to medevac burn victims to the US military hospital in Wiesbaden, West Germany.

But in the face of a severe pilot shortage, the same one that would lure Barb Rainey back to active duty, Jane transferred stateside in 1978. After months of rigorous training, she became the navy's first female flight instructor, at VT-2—the "Doer Birds"—at Whiting Field.

She had hoped the transition would be publicity-free, avoiding the press attention too often showered on the original female naval aviators. But although Jane was no longer one of only six, she, and her family, remained topics of great public interest.

A local newspaper reported on the progress of her husband, Tom, a former navy enlisted man, in learning to maintain the lawn outside their house. The writer speculated about the chances that their eighteen-month-old daughter, Shannon, might someday become a third-generation Whiting flight instructor, following in the footsteps of her mother and grandfather. Three years later, in February 1981, *Naval Aviation News* reported that Jane, "civilian husband" Tom, Shannon, and younger daughter Kelly, who was born at Pensacola, "have made workable family arrangements to suit their lifestyle, demonstrating that a woman can combine a career in military flying with a family."

Jane's professional focus was on whether male student aviators might resent having a female instructor and how best to fulfill her mission of training what she called "the best pilots in the world." She taught flying in the T-34C, logging 100 hours while pregnant with Kelly and stopping in her sixth month only "because I was having a hard time reaching some of the buttons and switches." She headed a quality assurance team in charge of maintaining fifty aircraft, and, as a recruiting command staff member, taught prospective naval aviation recruiters to fly the distinctive T-34Bs, with "Fly Navy" emblazoned on their tails.

"I love instructing," she told *Naval Aviation News.* "I could become a professional flight instructor and be quite happy. It's hard work but very rewarding. I feel that, particularly in these years of a shortage of aviators, there's a great need for somebody to be doing the jobs women are doing. The Navy's hurting for pilots."

Still, something was missing. Two career-defining opportunities traditionally afforded to navy pilots—carrier qualification and sea duty—had been denied to the nation's first female naval aviators. Without that experience, how could they ever command an aviation squadron, or be promoted beyond captain and attain flag rank? Without carrier-qualifying, could they truly be considered naval aviators?

But in August 1980, the USS *Lexington*—the "Lady Lex," the storied World War II–era aircraft carrier where student naval aviators became tailhookers—was redesignated from CVT-16 (navy training carrier) to AVT-16 (auxiliary training carrier). With the change of one letter, women were suddenly permitted on board. Seven years after navy brass had declared it off-limits to most male pilots because three women asked to set their landing gear on deck, the *Lex* was suddenly the only aircraft carrier open to female crew members.

Two years later, both Jane O'Dea and Lieutenant Rosemary Conatser—soon to be Mariner—would come aboard.

For Rosemary, having set records and made national headlines during her first tour, at VC-2 at Oceana, her second billet marked a homecoming of sorts. The first woman to fly a US military tactical jet was going back to California, where she had fallen in love with aviation as a young girl. The location: what was at the time called Naval Air Facility China Lake, home to the Naval Weapons Center and VX-5 (Air Development Squadron) in the Mojave Desert, northeast of Los Angeles, where she would fly the A-7.

"I was an ensign at my first duty station (VX-5) when Rosemary got orders to the squadron to be the safety officer," wrote a retired female navy captain in an online memorial book. "There was a lot of resistance to having a female pilot in the squadron. Rosemary arrived, and I can only imagine some of the ridiculous garbage she had to put up with from some of those guys. And yet, she persisted. They grudgingly gave her their respect, as one of the best pilots in the squadron. She was a remarkable woman, and an incredible role model. As I went on to other positions in the Navy, sometimes when I was the first woman to hold that position, I remembered her powerful example. We would all do well to be more like her."

Wrote another former junior officer: "I served with Rosemary when I was an ensign and she was a lieutenant at VX-5. She came into the squadron with much opposition, and quickly proved herself to be an outstanding pilot. She was truly a role model for all women in the Navy. I will never forget her courage and her example."

One of those who noticed was a young lieutenant who had been in jet transition training at Kingsville at the same time as Rosemary. He had been aware of her presence there—it was hard not to be—but they hadn't really crossed paths. Now, Tommy Mariner, assigned to the China Lake Naval Weapons Center (NWC), had occasion to meet her face-to-face.

"She was a good-looking jet pilot that was feisty and intelligent," he said. "In naval aviation, she was a different character."

Their first date in the summer of 1977 took a little bit of contrivance on his part. "One day," Tommy said, "the master chief at the time said they got my airplane fixed and I could be on my way. I told them I would just go in the morning." Not having planned to stay the night, he wore borrowed clothes to dinner. She showed up in a "stunning" peasant dress with an off-white top.

Romance soon bloomed, and as he carved out his own career as a naval aviator, he would hitch his star to hers.

"I made the decision early on that her career was unique," Tommy said. "There was a lot of guys who could do what I did. But her path-forging career was one of a kind at the time."

He proposed a year later in his family's tobacco field in eastern Tennessee, and a year after that she said yes, by letter.

Rosemary and Tommy were married in 1980 at a chapel on the base. "There was VX-5 on the bride's side and NWC on the groom's side," he said.

As Raymond Lambert, her commanding officer at Oceana, had modeled and counseled, Rosemary led by example, always ready to learn from the aviators around her and treating others with respect. Her advice for female pilots dealing with less-than-supportive men: Drop the jerk, not the jet.

Those lessons made an impression; on Tommy, the effect was profound. "She grew me up," he said. "I was a different person. Rosemary changed me."

Husband and wife were together at China Lake for two years, but then duty called. Tommy was assigned to a post several hours away by car and soon after was off to sea. They tried to spend one weekend a month together when he was ashore; otherwise, the phone was all they had. "We spend a lot on travel and phone bills," she told United Press International at the time.

Back on that first date, he had asked her a simple question that yielded a deceptively complicated answer and instantly changed how he thought of her. "What's important to you?" he wanted to know. Her response: to be looked at as a person, he said—"not a woman, not a first anything, not a superstar."

"When people look at you as an exceptional person, they think that person can do it and nobody else can," he said. "Rosemary didn't want that. She wanted other people to be living their dreams, too."

As for herself, Tommy noted, "She wanted the same opportunities I had as a white male."

That, though, was easier said than done. He had a clear, long-established career path to follow. For her, progressing as an equal meant trying harder, pushing back, and finding ways around the rules that limited her advancement as a naval aviator.

She hadn't been allowed to carrier-qualify in advanced prop training at Pensacola, or during jet transition at Kingsville. She had to slip into jet training through a crack in the door. She couldn't go to sea and fly from carriers, as Tommy could. The A-7E Corsair II was a front-line attack aircraft, but she couldn't fly it in combat. Still, a research-and-development mission was permissible, so Rosemary fired guns, dropped bombs, and tested weapons systems over the Mojave as a project pilot in the A-7.

Serving in a tactical squadron gave her a sort of parallel track to the career path laid out for male naval aviators. She flew the same type of aircraft as pilots operating off carriers, and testing air-to-ground and air-to-sea weapons systems that would be used in combat promoted tactical thinking and strategy. Though she was not able to go on cruises with a squadron on a carrier for six- or nine-month tours (or longer), she could absorb the same lessons in responsibility, authority, and command that up-and-coming naval officers would learn aboard ship.

"Why do I want to go to a tactical squadron, to fly off a boat and perhaps be shot at? My reasons are the same as those that have always attracted men to Naval Air," she told *Naval Aviation News*. "It is because I have experienced the satisfaction of the first step—winning Gold Wings—and I want to continue to succeed at what is the most demanding form of aviation. I want to become a full professional in my chosen vocation. I began flying when I was fifteen and the sense of joy is as much with me now as on my first solo. It has taken different forms as I mature. What was once a quest for fun has developed into the desire to be a professional naval officer, learning to handle responsibility, with command in mind. If I have learned anything in my few years as a female in a male world, it is that the two are far more alike than not."

Similarities aside, there were fundamental differences that the navy still couldn't resist showing off.

As one navy captain posted in the memorial guestbook: "I . . . met her back in 1980 at an air show where the novelty of a woman in a flight suit, climbing down from the pilot seat of a tactical jet aircraft, got a lot of attention. She took it all in stride with an easy-going and friendly confidence."

She also caught the eye of the editors at *Glamour* magazine, who set up a photo shoot at the base for a feature naming her one of ten "Outstanding Working Women" of the year. The March 1982 article was titled "Success and the '80s Working Woman."

Rosemary Bryant Mariner, Aviator, United States Navy:
"Whether or not an individual goes into combat should reflect an individual's ability, not gender," says Lieutenant Commander Rosemary Mariner, who was among the first women to fly tactical jet fighters for the Navy and to test weapons for combat commands. "In modern warfare, the emphasis is not on physical strength, but on brain power in operating sophisticated weapons systems. A machine gun is a great equalizer." At 28, she earns $32,000 and has applied to test-pilot school, with an eye on the astronaut program. When she boards the USS Lexington next month, she will be the first female aviator assigned to an aircraft carrier. Major obstacles: "fighting to get training and the opportunities to do the job."

Nine years before, she had been one of three female naval aviators expressly denied permission to land on the *Lex*. Now, she had permission to come aboard.

One of the navy's youngest lieutenant commanders, male or female, Rosemary was assigned to working with radar on the *Lex*, not flying. But carrier-qualifying was still a dearly held goal. "Carrier aviation is the most glamorous and the most dangerous," she told United Press International in an interview in conjunction with the *Glamour* article. "It is also the most macho. Men fly the carrier planes and it is a place where tradition dies hard." Most of that machismo resided in the over-forty crowd, she said, and in younger men so insecure as to feel threatened by a successful woman. "But it is hard to find the macho spirit among the men we women in the Navy work with as peers, men who accept us as equals."

One encouraging sign, she told UPI, was the number of female pilots portrayed in the popular science fiction TV show *Battlestar Galactica*. "When television depicts women warriors to a whole generation of girls and boys, then you know you have an impact on society," she said. For herself, though, she didn't want to be seen as some sort of Amazon; "Flying the sophisticated equipment is more a matter of brains than brawn."

Rosemary qualified as a surface warfare officer, learning systems and operations and how to drive the ship. She was officer of the deck, in command of the bridge in the captain's stead. She served for two and a half years on the *Lex*, and finally, a decade after beginning her navy career, carrier-qualified. Eventually, she would rack up seventeen traps.

Of her fellow naval aviators, she said, "I have nothing but the highest respect for the men who fly off aircraft carriers on dark nights in pitching seas. I feel honored to have shared the camaraderie of their ready rooms. And I have seen the negative side of flying. I have been so scared, all alone at night in nasty weather, running out of fuel in a malfunctioning airplane, that I swore if I ever got down safely, I would never do this again! But six hours later I went up again."

Wrote an operations specialist in the memorial guestbook: "I knew the Captain when she was an LCDR on the USS *Lexington*. She inspired me to be tenacious in pursuing my Navy career."

For Jane O'Dea, duty on board the Lady Lex became a three-year stint as communications officer, officer of the deck, and a part-time carrier onboard delivery (COD) pilot. The timing was perfect. Her obligation to the navy was ending, and she was looking, like many of her male counterparts, to the airlines. But airline pilots were being furloughed, and the navy offered not only a retention bonus, but promotion to lieutenant commander and the chance, after a decade as a naval aviator, to carrier-qualify.

It was, she says, probably the highlight of her entire career: "It was really scary, but awesome." Nuggets—novice aviators—"don't know enough to be scared at the boat, but with 2,000 hours, I certainly did," Jane recalls. "Even so, it was incredible." Being catapulted off the bow of the ship was "terrifying . . . but one of the most thrilling rides of a lifetime."

Ten traps and she was good to go, ferrying mail and supplies from shore to ship in the C-1A. In fact, it was Jane's favorite aircraft and mission; flying the C-1A was both how she carrier-qualified and how she met her husband.

She was one of 10 female officers on board out of 120 officers and a crew of several thousand, bearing the unusual distinction of being a wife, a mom, and a naval officer at sea.

The navy magazine *Wifeline* reported in 1984:

As Lt. Cmdr. Jane O'Dea, Lexington's *communications officer, put it, "I feel I can have my cake and eat it too." The mother of two daughters, 7-year-old Shannon and 3-year-old Kelly, O'Dea requested* Lexington *because it is career-enhancing to be a woman on an aircraft carrier.*

"My husband, Tom, agreed that I should do what's best for my career," O'Dea said. Her husband is a high school teacher and manages nicely when she is away. "Although it's a tremendous strain on him, he's a great father and does an excellent job," she said. "I'm very fortunate."

Tom joined the officers' wives club, first for VT-2 and then for the *Lex.* "I participated as the other wives did," he says, pitching in to help officers' families with anything that came up. He was a trendsetter: Near the end of Jane's tour on the *Lex,* other men were getting involved as well, "and they were pressuring to change the name to 'spouse' instead of 'wife,'" he says. "I really didn't care."

At work, Jane was the dedicated, disciplined, uniformed naval officer and aviator. At home—when she was home, as the *Lex* deployed some twenty days a month—she was a combination of swim team mom and June Cleaver, the classic TV mother from *Leave It to Beaver.* She baked Christmas cookies, helped with homework, and built school science projects. She wasn't fully aware of how she transformed from one persona to the other until she went to a career day at her daughter's school. "I showed up decked out in full flight gear, including a combat knife strapped to my leg. I showed them the various tools of my trade, such as my helmet, oxygen mask, parachute, and kneeboard. I showed models of the airplanes that I flew. I shared the joys of flight, including taking off at first light to watch the sunrise. After my presentation, several of my daughter's friends who I knew from our swim team carpool came up to talk to me. They were in awe."

"O'Dea feels that being on a ship reinforces her role as a mother," reported *Wifeline*.

"The time apart makes us more appreciative of our time together. We have quality rather than quantity.

"My family is very important to me," she continued. "But I also need the self-satisfaction I get as an individual separate from my family. Don't get me wrong," O'Dea quickly added, "it's not easy to go. Sometimes I feel like my heart's being ripped out when it's time to say good-bye, but I never show it."

Still, there were professional frustrations. The *Lex* sailed on cruises of two to three weeks, from its home port in Pensacola to Corpus Christi or Jacksonville, and once to the shipyard in Philadelphia for refurbishment. It was a far cry from the months-long, open-sea deployments other carriers embarked on. Plus, there was still Section 6015. As *Florida Today* reported several months later:

The 34-year-old wife and mother of two from Des Moines, Iowa, said in a shipboard interview that she enjoys her career but is frustrated with a congressional mandate that prohibits women from performing combat duties. She said that limitation means she and other women pilots don't get the kind of experience, such as flying jet fighters, so critical for a naval aviator's career advancement.

"Within the Navy, my superiors have given me every opportunity that's available to me," O'Dea said. "What's limiting is the places

they can put me into." Her immediate goal is to become a squadron commander, but it would have to be something like a training or cargo squadron.

She would move on to serve as a TACAMO mission commander at VQ-4 (Fleet Air Reconnaissance Squadron), based at the time at Naval Air Station Patuxent River in Maryland. TACAMO—Take Charge and Move Out—meant ensuring unimpeded communications with the nation's strategic nuclear weapons arsenal, with aircraft on alert status twenty-four hours a day, 365 days a year. Jane and two other pilots would fly over the ocean for eighteen to twenty hours at a time, in a C-130 equipped with a bed in the cockpit and a place to sleep in the back, so they could trade off. They would release a trailing wire antenna several miles long and fly in circles until the weighted wire hung straight down, enabling communications with submarines.

"It was a great tour for the family," Jane says, "but Pax River was boring. We'd just go out and bore holes in the sky for hours at a time."

Before the decade was out, she would be promoted to commander and serve a stint at the Pentagon, where she was assigned to the Command, Control and Communications Systems Directorate of the Joint Chiefs of Staff, reporting to General Colin Powell.

Duty at sea and carrier qualification meant a huge career boost for Rosemary Mariner; it was experience essential for future command, although, she noted, "Everything I've done is really no big deal for a man." Still, for the 130 or so female naval aviators on active duty—only around 1 percent of all navy pilots—as well as for the 6,606 female officers and 42,258 enlisted women in 1985, the combat exclusion meant they would all eventually hit what was called the armor-plated ceiling.

Only 33 ships out of 527 were open to women, mostly repair or research vessels, or tenders—general support ships that operate at the fringes of the fleet. With the six-month rule still in effect, women couldn't go anywhere near a combat mission, or aboard any ship that might conceivably receive orders for a combat mission anytime in the next 180 days. While the navy touted its opportunities for advancement in rank and salary for women, Rosemary, now a commander, told the *Wall Street Journal*, "You can't confuse opportunity with equal opportunity. It's the kinds of commands and the kinds of jobs you get as a senior officer that are very important."

Even as a jet instructor and maintenance officer at Naval Air Station Kingsville, Texas, where she had done her jet transition training nine years before, she had prepared male pilots for missions she herself would not be allowed to fly.

And though retired Admiral Elmo Zumwalt, who had opened flight training and many other doors for women, warned, "We can no longer afford the luxury of discriminating against 50 percent of the population that has the kind of talent that is difficult to get," women across the fleet were still shunted into traditionally female careers and hitting professional walls.

Two-thirds of female navy personnel were either serving as nurses or performing administrative jobs. With men's and women's promotion lists combined, women doing desk jobs were forced to compete head-to-head against men alternating between shore and sea billets.

To try to compensate, the navy created a new, expanded career path for women stuck on desk duty: They could now become eligible for promotion by serving in a variety of non-command posts, in areas like intelligence, financial management, and computer science, rather than having to attain a position of authority as an executive or commanding officer in a training, recruiting, or personnel unit. This only reinforced the feeling among men that women were getting an unfair advantage by winning unearned promotions.

The biggest bottleneck was faced by the 175 or so female surface warfare officers, trained for duty at sea. For lieutenant commanders, having put in ten years of navy service, the next step had to be a billet as an executive officer on a ship—or their career was effectively over. The problem was, women could serve as an XO on just one ship, the USS *Norton Sound*, and that spot was not reserved for women; in 1985, the executive officer was a man.

Not surprisingly, many navy women called it quits.

As Lieutenant Deborah Barnhart told the *Wall Street Journal*: "To spend twenty years to get to be a captain of a tender isn't enough incentive."

Or, as Rosemary told the paper, "If I couldn't theoretically reach the top of the profession, how could I be anything but junior varsity?" Of particular frustration to the nation's first female tactical jet pilot was the navy's unwillingness to use her skills to their fullest. "Being paid to go out and fly is super," Rosemary said. "But the account comes due when we get attacked. . . . The reason you've got that uniform on is to defend your country."

That meant staying and fighting to break down barriers for the right to serve, as her heroines the WASP had done, to the best of her ability.

"I'd always been interested in history, and it was the injustice of it" that she wanted to change, Rosemary told the *Washington Post*. "I enjoyed the leadership part of the Navy, the airplane part of it. There was no other place you could fly those kinds of planes."

But being a naval aviator was about far more than just aviation, as she told the authors of *Ladybirds*: "The military is not a training ground for future airline pilots. If you want to be a Navy pilot, you better be willing to go to sea, and if necessary, go into combat; male and female."

It was about duty and discipline, respect, professionalism, and equality, lessons that she modeled for her squadron and that made a huge impression on those who served under her. Not just in California, but in billets that followed.

Wrote one aviation machinist mate in the memorial guestbook: "CDR Mariner set a course and met it. She mentored, encouraged and challenged those in service with her. She never rested on [her] laurels and wouldn't allow those around her to, either. As my Maintenance Officer in VT-23 at NAS Kingsville, she made me a better engine shop mechanic and flight line troubleshooter. Years later, she took the time to write a letter of recommendation to the FAA for my A&P [airplane mechanic] licenses. Her commitment to serving others has led to my 30th year at American Airlines."

And one male rear admiral, writing in the guestbook, attested to the power of those lessons.

"In 1984, then LCDR Mariner was my very first Maintenance Officer when I was the AME/PR Branch O in VT-23 at NAS Kingsville, TX," he wrote. "I remember her as being demanding but I learned a lot about the criticality of taking care of each other and our sailors. In 1995, I made the first CVN deployment where we fully integrated women. I remember thinking then, 'What's the big deal?' Rosemary shaped my thinking in many ways, and I sincerely thank her for that."

CHAPTER TEN

What's in a Name?

IN OCTOBER 1986, TWO SENATORS INTRODUCED A BIPARTISAN BILL confronting the exclusionary language of USC Title 10 head-on. It would allow army women to serve in combat support units and, for navy women limited by Section 6015, open up billets on ships in the Mobile Logistics Support Force designated for combat support—oilers, ammunition ships, stores ships, fleet ocean tugs, destroyer tenders, heavy repair ships, and salvage and rescue ships.

It was a direct policy challenge to the contention, as expressed by outgoing chief of naval operations Admiral James Watkins several months before, that women were taking desirable jobs away from navy men and female recruitment was harming military readiness. As the bill wended its way through Congress, the army sought to get out ahead by opening ten thousand combat support jobs to women. But the navy's response, in November 1986, was to rename the Mobile Logistics Support Force the Combat Logistics Force. In redesignating six types of ships as "combatant," not only were the supply ships to remain off-limits, but a number of jobs that had been open to women under the 180-day rule were suddenly gone.

As Joellen Drag Oslund puts it, "With the stroke of a pen and the change of one word, they limited which ships women could be assigned to. . . . They'd think they had made progress, and then someone reclassified something."

It was carrier qualification all over again. Asked to let women in—in the first case, by Lieutenant (j.g.) Judith A. Neuffer, Ensign Jane M.

Skiles, and Ensign Rosemary B. Conatser, and in the second case, by senators William Cohen and William Proxmire—the navy instead changed the rules and slammed the door shut. As with carrier qualification, the justification was economic: The change would save taxpayer dollars. But Rosemary had a different view: "[It was] a blatant attempt, in my opinion, to keep women off these ships by redefining combat."

It had a damaging effect on careers the navy had promised to women it had actively recruited.

A grand announcement in December 1986 that the navy would add about 1,000 enlisted positions aboard thirty-nine ships hinted at job increases for women. But those were offset by the jobs lost in the former Mobile Logistics Support Force. Then, the new chief of naval operations, Admiral Carlisle A. H. Trost, made known his intention to fulfill his predecessor's goal of cutting the number of women recruited from 51,300 to 46,796. Though Secretary of Defense Caspar Weinberger canceled that reduction, it seemed like the navy was doing everything it could to keep women from getting ahead.

Making matters look even worse, James H. Webb Jr. was soon confirmed as the new secretary of the navy. A marine, Pentagon official, Naval Academy graduate, and decorated Vietnam combat veteran, Webb had published a treatise in the November 1979 issue of *Washingtonian* magazine provocatively titled "Women Can't Fight." In it, he sought to make the case that America's fighting mission was being corrupted and the national defense jeopardized—and that women were largely to blame.

Webb's article attributed an increase in sexual assault and domestic violence in the United States to "the realignment of sexual roles" (with the caveat that "I believe most of what has happened over the past decade in the name of sexual equality has been good") and lamented the loss of the "quintessentially male world" of the military service academies. That included the physical, mental, and emotional abuse of plebes, like the character-building benefits bestowed on him by four upperclassmen who one night beat him with a cricket bat until "they broke the bat on my ass."

The article's framing ran the gamut from sex (admitting women was "poisoning" and "sexually steriliz[ing]" the Academy environment; "the system has been objectified and neutered to the point it can no longer develop or measure leadership") to violence ("Man must be more aggressive in order to perpetuate the human race. Women don't rape men"; "American men are tough and violent"), to sex again (the dorm was "a horny woman's dream," although—in a perhaps unintentional contradiction—"Many women appear to be having problems with their sexuality").

It offered a blanket dismissal of women as a group ("I have never met a woman, including the dozens of female midshipmen I encountered during my recent semester as a professor at the Naval Academy, whom I would trust to provide those men with combat leadership") and of the nation's leaders (the drive for equality is "Civilian arrogance permeat[ing] our government").

As evidence, he quoted an ex-marine who had asked to transfer rather than serve as a woman's subcommander: "I used to look at officers who were Academy graduates and say, 'That man has been through hell. He's earned the right to lead me.' It's not true anymore. The whole place has been pulled down to the level of the women."

Another, who spoke of "women being forced down the brigade's throat . . . it's creating a presumption that women can command troops. . . . There isn't a woman here who could have handled the platoon I was in when I was enlisted."

And a third, for whom the academies and other parts of the military provided "a ritualistic rite of passage into manhood. It was one small area of our society that was totally male. Women now have a full range of choice, from the totally female—motherhood—to what was once the totally male. . . . Males in the society feel stripped, symbolically and actually. . . . The real question isn't the women. The real question is this: Where in this country can someone go to find out if he is a man? And where can someone who knows he is a man go to celebrate his masculinity?"

For all of Zumwalt's efforts, sexism was "still an integral part of the Navy tradition."

"Unless you were at the Academy at the time, it is hard to understand how damaging this article was and how lasting the impact was," retired navy captain Wendy Lawrence, a 1981 Academy graduate, helicopter pilot, and astronaut, told the *Washington Post.* (Lawrence was in the second Academy class that included women; her father, Admiral William P. Lawrence, was the officer about whom Rosemary Mariner made the "radical feminist" remark. He had been Naval Academy superintendent from 1978 to 1981.)

Retired navy captain Barb Geraghty, a member of the first class of female graduates in 1980, said Webb's article "essentially broke the unit cohesion of a brigade of midshipmen at the Naval Academy. I have lost track of how many times men thrust that article in my face and used it as a reason for why I didn't belong."

Decades after its publication, amid protests over an award he was to receive from the Academy, the former Virginia senator and Democratic presidential hopeful apologized—sort of—for his article, which Captain Rosemary Mariner called out for "invidious bigotry."

"Clearly, if I had been a more mature individual, there are things that I would not have said in that magazine article," Webb said. "To the extent that this article subjected women at the Academy or the armed forces to undue hardship, I remain profoundly sorry."

But in 1987, the new navy secretary moved to put those beliefs, which he had repeated in congressional testimony, into practice. He announced that among his first acts would be to give performance in combat assignments—off-limits to women by law—greater weight in the selection and promotion of officers, a process in which men and women were supposed to compete head-to-head.

It was against this backdrop that the DACOWITS fact-finding panel issued its scathing report laying bare a pattern of "morally repugnant behavior" toward navy women. Separately, the Government Accounting Office produced a preliminary report, titled "Combat Exclusion Laws for Women in the Military," that concluded women in all branches were being barred from progress in their chosen careers.

Besides its findings of rampant sexual harassment, discrimination, and refusal by superior officers to address mistreatment of women, DACOWITS uncovered a persistent lack of opportunity and low morale among female navy personnel. The redesignation of the Mobile Logistics Support Force as the Combat Logistics Force was cited specifically.

As DACOWITS vice chairman Judith Gibson testified before Congress:

I found a deep concern among Navy and Marine Corps women, officers in particular, about their prospects for viable careers in their respective services. Directly related to their perceptions of diminishing opportunities and limited promotions is the narrow interpretation by their services of USC Title 10, Section 6015. . . . Navy women consistently referred to their exclusion from the Combat Logistics Force, the CLF ships. With respect to the CLF issue, the DACOWITS recommended at a 1987 spring meeting that the Chief of Naval Operations reevaluate the Navy's assignment policies relating to its interpretation of the Combat Exclusion Law to the extent that it has precluded the assignment of women to the CLF, formerly known as the Mobile Logistic Support Force.

The DACOWITS report and the press coverage it received were so embarrassing that Webb ordered a study of progress of women in the navy. The resulting brief called for reevaluating the meaning of "combat mission," while a follow-up GAO report found that, as the title clearly stated, "More Military Jobs Can Be Opened Under the Current Statutes."

It was a one-two punch. In December 1987, Webb stood up at a Pentagon briefing and announced that any ship or aircraft that does not have "seek out, reconnoiter and engage the enemy" as its primary objective should be open to women. "The difficulty has always been in defining what is combat and what is not," he said. "This represents to me, in naval terms, as far as you can go" without Congress rewriting the law.

It meant, Webb acknowledged, that two-thirds of the Combat Logistics Force—twenty-seven ships—never actually had any sort of combat-related role and therefore should not be off-limits to female personnel in sea and aviation squadrons. In practical terms, this tripled the number of seagoing jobs open to women, from about 5,200 to 15,000. Webb also announced that female pilots would be eligible to fly reconnaissance missions, as long as they were shore-, not carrier-, based. And he ordered that "vigorous corrective and preventative actions" be taken to end the harassment of women uncovered by the DACOWITS panel and his own investigative team of twenty-eight officers and enlisted personnel, who had interviewed 1,400 women in ten sites worldwide and found that half had been sexually harassed and all had witnessed women being victimized.

For many navy women, however, what Webb was touting as opportunities didn't necessarily feel that way.

Although the first navy women were selected for command at sea and the astronaut corps during the 1980s, and six were promoted to admiral, they were the exception. Most women were limited in what they could attain as compared with their male counterparts, and those limits could change practically without warning.

The redesignation of the Mobile Logistics Support Force was a wake-up call. As long as women were legally barred from combat—whatever that meant—the definition could be interpreted, reinterpreted, and twisted at whim. Billets that were available one day could vanish the next. True equality would remain out of reach until the law was changed.

Getting Congress to act meant altering the public perception of what women could and should do. For Zumwalt, that had entailed pushing acceptance of women flying navy aircraft; for Rosemary Mariner, it meant advancing the recognition that women are as capable and qualified as men for the full range of military service, including combat. She would soon attain a position of prominence in which she could not only lead by example, but advocate more forcefully for military women, and, ultimately, engage in a different kind of combat—in speeches, in the press, and in the political realm.

Commander Rosemary Mariner—the college student who had been told women would never fly for the airlines, the trailblazing aviator adamant about not being viewed as exceptional—was about to rack up another of the firsts that defined her remarkable career: the first woman to command an aviation squadron.

VAQ-34 (Tactical Electronic Warfare Squadron) was part of the Fleet Electronic Warfare Support Group at Naval Air Station Point Mugu, California. It was one of two adversary squadrons, with a mission of playing the bad guy: simulating missile attacks on aircraft carriers and airborne forces, jamming radar, and interfering with information-gathering technology in training exercises for ships, air wings, and battle groups. As the United States's great enemy at the time was the Soviet Union, VAQ-34's logo bore a red star, symbol of the USSR. Its aircraft carried equipment very different from that found in most US military jets: jamming devices, missile simulators, transmitters for providing false information to weapons systems, and pods that released chaff to confuse radar.

Rosemary would serve first as executive officer while being groomed to take command, then step up to skipper. She would be in charge of a 300-member squadron, including 50 officers.

It was such a notable achievement that nationally syndicated columnist Paul Harvey gave her a shout-out in an August 1986 column celebrating "under-recognized women in aviation." He listed her in the company of astronaut Sally Ride, the first American woman in space; early aviation pioneer Phoebe Omlie, a barnstormer, Women's Air Derby racer, and the first American woman to serve as a government aviation official and qualify as an airline pilot; and teacher/astronaut Christa McAuliffe, killed in the space shuttle *Challenger* disaster six months before. "Today's superwomen include Lt. Commander Rosemary Mariner. First female to ever fly a front-line tactical A-7E jet. First ever to qualify as officer of the deck on a carrier. An A-7 project pilot, five years in weapons R&D. With 3,000 hours of flight time, don't tell Rosemary Mariner there's an arbitrary ceiling predetermined by sex."

Still, VAQ-34—nicknamed the Flashbacks—was a shore-based squadron; her male peers were going to sea, logging flight hours, and gaining essential experience for the highest reaches of command.

A *Los Angeles Times* story in October 1988 set the scene:

At 35, Cmdr. Rosemary Mariner has spent nearly half her life learning to fly jets, working her way up in the elite society of Navy pilots from whose ranks will emerge future ship captains and admirals.

By all reports, her performance has been stellar, her dedication unquestioned. Self-assured and eloquent, she has been selected by top

*Navy brass to be the commanding officer of a flight squadron, a posi-
tion never before held by a woman.*

*For the female fliers still working their way up in the over-
whelmingly male world of Navy pilots, Mariner's rise is at once
reassuring and unsettling. Mariner has achieved what only a few
years ago seemed impossible, but she is also approaching a limit beyond
which women simply cannot go.*

Having carrier-qualified and earned her credentials as a surface warfare officer, she had been billeted at sea for weeks at a time. But except for
the *Lexington*, female navy pilots still couldn't serve on carriers, the central focus of naval aviation operations. The career path from naval aviator
to carrier command to flag rank was not one that women could follow.

"You cannot get there from here," she told the *Times*. "You cannot,
theoretically, reach the top of this profession because you cannot participate in its fundamental business. In the Navy, the world revolves around
going to sea. That's what we're all about. I have never gone on a cruise. I
don't have any night carrier landings. I've been around fleet pilots enough
to know how much I don't know. I want the opportunity to prove or dis-
prove my ability just like anyone else, but I have not done what men like
my husband do. I haven't paid my dues in carrier aviation like my male
peers, and I understand that."

Another naval aviator quoted in the story, Lieutenant Sali Gear, who
flew T-39s out of NAS North Island in San Diego, said she hoped to
command a carrier but feared she would end up in a desk job in Washington instead. "It's not happening," she said. "You have to punch the
right tickets to do that, and unless things change dramatically in the next
few years, there's no way I can do it. There's no way I could pass through
those gates. . . . Rosemary Mariner was the first female who ever screened
for command of a squadron, and it's wonderful what she's done. But how
many more are going to get to do that? You do everything you can at this
point to plan your career down the road, but you just don't know."

Rosemary, though, was far more hopeful about the future and the
likelihood that women could walk through the doors she had kicked open.

When she joined the navy, she told the *Times*, she'd been told that women

would never go to sea, women would never fly jet airplanes, women would never be able to even carrier-qualify—landing airplanes on board ship. People were emphatic that that would never happen. But two weeks before I entered flight training, people were saying women would never be Navy pilots. . . .

 There's no doubt in my mind that military women, American women, are going to go into combat in the next major war. . . . You're talking about 20 to 30 years of sociological change. You're talking about a time frame now when the American population watched the female astronaut be killed in the Challenger *and nobody sat there and mourned her any more than anyone else. The world has changed.*

 I look at the young women entering the program today who are being told that they can't do many things, as I was told I can't do many things, and there's no doubt in my mind that they may well find themselves leading men and women into combat.

The executive officer of VAQ-34 elaborated on those remarks in a speech at the annual convention of Women Military Aviators, Inc., over Labor Day weekend 1989: "It is my personal conviction that Navy women, especially those in aviation and surface communities, will fight in our next war," Rosemary said. "The combat exclusion law will have to go away. In reality, women have always suffered in war; a dead woman is no more and no less a tragedy than a dead man. That is cold, hard reality. You [women aviators] have to be intellectually honest with yourself and realize that until you share equally in the dangers and the risks, you're not pulling your fair share."

Rosemary's words about war and risk proved prescient. Just three months later, army captain Linda Bray and her company of about thirty military police would end up in a firefight with Panamanian special forces while trying to capture a kennel of army attack dogs during Operation Just Cause. The story made national headlines, and the notion that a woman could not only find herself in a combat situation, but command soldiers in a battle and attain a military objective crashed into the American consciousness. Sociologist Charles Moskos, who would later serve on George H. W. Bush's Presidential Commission on the Assignment of Women in the Armed Forces, called Bray's command of troops in Panama "a shot heard around the world, or at least the Pentagon."

It was becoming clearer that the combat exclusion drew a distinction without a difference. The year before, in response to the DACOWITS report, a Department of Defense task force had attempted to reinterpret the law to make it more consistent across the different branches of the military and address persistent crises in women's morale, careers, and quality of life. The new rule said, "[R]isks of exposure to direct combat, hostile fire or capture are proper criteria for closing noncombat positions or units to women, provided that . . . such risks are equal to or greater than that experienced by associated combat units in the same theater of operations."

But Bray proved that what qualified as combat in theory didn't square with reality. So did the female sailors serving aboard the destroyer tender *Acadia*, when the guided missile frigate *Stark* was hit by Iraqi missiles as it operated alongside in the Persian Gulf. So did the female air force pilots flying tankers to refuel fighters and bombers in dangerous skies.

No matter how carefully the politicians and the brass tried to draw the line, women were in combat, like it or not.

Secretary of the Navy John Warner (right) presented flight training orders to Lieutenant (j.g.) Judith Ann Neuffer in a ceremony at the Pentagon, January 10, 1973.
(GETTY IMAGES)

Joellen Drag poses next to a T-34B Beech Mentor trainer at Naval Air Station Alameda, where she was sworn in by her father, retired Navy Commander Theodore F. Drag. The newspaper caption contained the words "shape of things to come." (UPI)

Lieutenants (j.g.) Judith Neuffer and Barbara Allen, new student naval aviators, pose for publicity photos at Pensacola. (U.S. NAVY/ PHOTOS COURTESY JUDITH NEUFFER BRUNER)

The first three female student naval aviators, from left: Barbara Allen, Jane Skiles, and Judith Neuffer (U.S. NAVY/PHOTO COURTESY JUDITH NEUFFER BRUNER)

Student naval aviators, from left: Rosemary Conatser, Jane Skiles, Barbara Allen, and Judith Neuffer (EMIL BUEHLER LIBRARY PHOTOGRAPH COLLECTIONS, NATIONAL NAVAL AVIATION MUSEUM, PENSACOLA, FLORIDA)

"Janey" O'Dea's flight helmet (EMIL BUEHLER LIBRARY PHOTOGRAPH COLLECTIONS, NATIONAL NAVAL AVIATION MUSEUM, PENSACOLA, FLORIDA)

Lieutenant (j.g.) Barbara Allen holds a snake during survival training at Pensacola while Ensign Jane Skiles looks on. (U.S. NAVY/PHOTO COURTESY JUDITH NEUFFER BRUNER)

Judith Neuffer on *What's My Line?* with host Larry Blyden (PHOTO COURTESY JUDITH NEUFFER BRUNER)

Portion of Lieutenant (j.g) Judith Neuffer's logbook showing first solo by a woman in a Navy aircraft (PHOTO BY AUTHOR/COURTESY JUDITH NEUFFER BRUNER)

Lieutenant (j.g.) Judith Neuffer is congratulated at Saufley Field, Florida, after becoming the first woman to solo a Navy aircraft. (U.S. NAVY/PHOTO COURTESY JUDITH NEUFFER BRUNER)

Certificate commemorating Judith Neuffer's first solo; note the possessive pronoun. (PHOTO BY AUTHOR/COURTESY JUDITH NEUFFER BRUNER)

Certificate marking Barbara Allen's designation as a Naval Aviator (EMIL BUEHLER LIBRARY PHOTOGRAPH COLLECTIONS, NATIONAL NAVAL AVIATION MUSEUM, PENSACOLA, FLORIDA)

Official portrait of Naval Aviator Barbara Allen (EMIL BUEHLER LIBRARY PHOTOGRAPH COLLECTIONS, NATIONAL NAVAL AVIATION MUSEUM, PENSACOLA, FLORIDA)

Lieutenant (j.g.) Judith Neuffer receives her Wings of Gold at Naval Air Station Corpus Christi. (U.S. NAVY/PHOTO COURTESY JUDITH NEUFFER BRUNER)

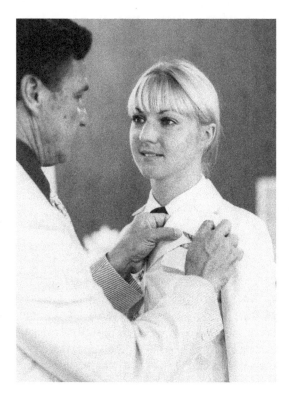

Ensign Joellen Drag, the lone woman in a sea of men, receives her Wings of Gold from her father, retired navy commander Theodore F. Drag.

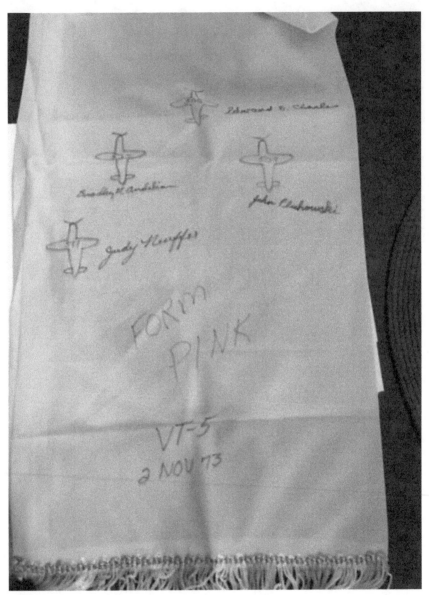

Commemorative scarf signed by members of Judith Neuffer's four-plane formation training team at Saufley Field. Each team was designated with a color; Judy's, of course, was Form Pink. (PHOTO BY AUTHOR/COURTESY JUDITH NEUFFER BRUNER)

Ensign Ana Maria Scott has her flight gear inspected at Helicopter Combat (HC) Support Squadron 6, Naval Air Station Norfolk. (COURTESY TWU LIBRARIES WOMAN'S COLLECTION, TEXAS WOMAN'S UNIVERSITY, DENTON, TEXAS)

Ensign Ana Maria Scott flies the H-3 out of Helicopter Combat (HC) Support Squadron 6, Naval Air Station Norfolk. (COURTESY TWU LIBRARIES WOMAN'S COLLECTION, TEXAS WOMAN'S UNIVERSITY, DENTON, TEXAS)

Ensign Joellen Drag flies the H-46 Sea Knight out of Helicopter Combat (HC) Support Squadron 3, Naval Air Station North Island, San Diego, 1974. (NAVAL HISTORY AND HERITAGE COMMAND)

Lieutenant Joellen Drag Oslund after a flight, Naval Air Station Point Mugu, California, 1978 (NAVAL HISTORY AND HERITAGE COMMAND)

Commander Raymond Lambert, CO of Fleet Composite Squadron
(VC) 2, Naval Air Station Oceana, Virginia Beach, congratulates
Lieutenant (j.g.) Rosemary Conatser upon receiving her commission in June 1975. The first African American CO at Oceana
was a role model for the first woman to command an aviation
squadron. (REPRODUCED BY PERMISSION OF NEW JOURNAL AND GUIDE,
NORFOLK, VIRGINIA)

Ensign Rosemary Conatser
conducts a pre-flight inspection
of the main gear of an S-2
submarine tracker at VC-2.
(NAVAL HISTORY AND HERITAGE
COMMAND)

Jane O'Dea with her father, Paul Skiles, the first naval aviator to pin Wings of Gold on his daughter (PHOTO COURTESY JANE SKILES O'DEA)

Captain Jane O'Dea, commanding officer of the US Navy Recruiting District at Indianapolis, with race car driver Al Unser Jr. at the Indianapolis 500 (PHOTO COURTESY JANE SKILES O'DEA)

Commander Rosemary Mariner is piped aboard as commanding officer of Tactical Electronic Warfare Squadron (VAQ) 34, Naval Air Station Point Mugu, California, 1990. (U.S. NAVY)

Commander Rosemary Mariner, CO of VAQ-34, NAS Point Mugu, California, in her A-7 (NAVAL HISTORY AND HERITAGE COMMAND)

Woman Aviator Pioneer Retires

Capt. Jane Skiles O'Dea, the Navy's senior woman aviator, is "piped over the side" at her 11 April retirement ceremony. One of the initial group of six women to complete Navy flight training, O'Dea received her wings in April 1974. She was the first to achieve command (Navy Recruiting District, Indianapolis) and to be selected for the rank of captain. Assisting as one of the ceremonial sideboys was flight school classmate Capt. Rosemary Conatser Mariner, above right. At right, the two as ensigns 23 years earlier undergoing training at NAS Corpus Christi, Texas. In her career, Capt. O'Dea has logged over 3,000 hours in C-130, C-1A, T-34 and EC-130Q aircraft while assigned to VR-24, VT-2, *Lexington* (AVT-6) and VQ-4.

Captain Jane O'Dea is piped over the side at her retirement. Captain Rosemary Mariner is among those saluting. (NAVAL AVIATION NEWS/NAVY TIMES)

Women In Aviation International Pioneer Hall of Fame induction, 2017. Front row, from left: Rosemary Bryant Merims Conatser Mariner, Ana Maria Scott, Joellen Drag Oslund, Jane Skiles O'Dea, John Rainey (representing Barbara Allen Rainey), Judith Neuffer Bruner, Wes Bruner (Judy's stepson). Back row, from left: Tommy Mariner, Loren Heckelman (Ana Maria's brother-in-law), Dwayne Oslund, Tom O'Dea, Katie Rainey, and Cynthia Rainey Spezia (Barb's daughters) (WOMEN IN AVIATION INTERNATIONAL/JOHN RIEDEL)

Female military aviators gather to remember and honor Captain Rosemary Mariner after her funeral in 2019. Standing, from left: Carey Lohrenz, Peggy Carnahan, Eileen Isola, Marcy Atwood, Lucy Young, Chris Giza, Mary Louise Griffin, Lee Hansen, Judith Bruner, Joellen Oslund. Seated, from left: Barb Garwood, Margie Varuska, Terry Vandendolder, Tricia Wood, Kay Hire (DANIELLE THIRIOT/THE HOOK)

Naval aviators participating in the navy's first all-female Missing Man Formation flyover to honor Rosemary Mariner's life and legacy pose for a photo at Naval Air Station Oceana in Virginia Beach, February 2, 2019. Back row, from left: Lieutenant Commander Jennifer Hesling, Lieutenant Commander Paige Blok, Commander Stacy Uttecht, Commander Leslie Mintz, Lieutenant Commander Danielle Thiriot. Front row, from left: Lieutenants Christy Talisse, Kelly Harris, Emily Rixey, Amanda Lee (U.S. NAVY PHOTO BY MASS COMMUNICATION SPECIALIST 3RD CLASS RAYMOND MADDOCKS/RELEASED)

PART IV

THE 1990S

CHAPTER ELEVEN

Women Take Command

"AN AMES NATIVE WHO GREW UP IN DES MOINES IS ABOUT TO ASSUME command of the US Navy Recruiting District at Indianapolis," reported the *Des Moines Register* in September 1990. "Cmdr. Jane Skiles O'Dea will be in dress blue uniform at the center of a time-honored naval tradition, as her predecessor reads his change of command orders. Then O'Dea will read her orders to assembled subordinates—133 active-duty personnel and six civilians. . . . Although the ceremony has been carried on for years, one thing is different in this case. The command will not pass from a him to a him, but from a him to a her."

It was a milestone for the former "Go-Go Airline Girl" turned aircraft carrier officer of the deck, command and control air warfare officer, carrier-qualified C-1A pilot, communications officer, and Pentagon expert in allied interoperability—coordinating communication with US-allied nations—with more than 3,000 flight hours in her logbook. The career that had taken her around the world was landing her back in the Midwest, where she had grown up.

Jane had hoped for an aviation squadron, but there were advantages to screening for a non-aviation shore command. For one thing, Indianapolis wasn't too far from Des Moines, where her father lived. She was able to visit her dad, who had sparked her passion for aviation when she was just seven years old, often during the last year of his life. For another, it was the home of the Indy 500; a celebrity herself, she loved hanging out with notable personalities, among them championship race-car driver

Al Unser Jr. and famed aviator Chuck Yeager, the first pilot to break the sound barrier.

Attaining command was a turn of events for which she had set the scene the year before, in a Labor Day weekend speech at the 1989 annual convention of Women Military Aviators, Inc. "I've seen changes in the attitudes of men," Jane had said. "They've grown up with us. They know that we've put up with much of what they've put up with. In today's Navy, the junior men are used to having women in leadership roles. It's all just a matter of time."

She had added: "I think that we can all do the same job, but I'll be the first to admit that men and women are different in many ways. With the current laws, women will never be fully integrated into the system. So you have to learn to deal with reality and make a contribution as best you can. Do a good job and establish a degree of credibility first. Then people will listen to what you have to say, and when you have the chance you can bring up issues that are important to you."

That was certainly the case for Commander Rosemary Mariner, about to ascend to a level of national prominence with authority and a bully pulpit to match.

On July 12, 1990, she was installed as commanding officer of VAQ-34—the first woman in US military history to head an operational aviation squadron—with all the pomp and ceremony befitting a career naval officer on the rise. Her promotion had been announced the month before at a conference on the future of women in the navy by Captain Kathleen Bruyere, chief of the navy's women's policies office. Bruyere was the former Kathleen Byerly, one of *Time* magazine's twelve Women of the Year in January 1976 and a plaintiff, with then-lieutenant Joellen Drag, in the lawsuit that had successfully challenged Section 6015.

Rear Admiral Steven Briggs, commander of the Pacific Fleet's Light Attack Wing, presided, calling the occasion a "historic moment in naval aviation." The entire squadron stood at attention as Lieutenant Commander Tommy Mariner, senior missile test officer at Point Mugu's Pacific Missile Test Center, affixed the gold command pin to his wife's uniform. Singing the National Anthem was squadron member Lieutenant Tammie Jo Shults, later to gain international fame as the

Southwest Airlines Flight 1380 captain who landed her crippled jet in Philadelphia in 2018, saving the lives of 143 passengers and crew. In the audience, Shults later wrote in her book, *Nerves of Steel*, were "senators, astronauts, and more admirals than I could count."

In her address, Rosemary harkened back seventeen years, to the day she became one of eight pioneers in integrating women into navy flight training.

"We never accepted that it was okay for 'girls' to accept a lower standard, to expect less of themselves than men," she told the assembled crowd. "Like so many of life's achievements, the key is simple perseverance."

She cited the Ninety-Nines, Inc., International Organization of Women Pilots; her heroines the WASP, at least eight of whom, all in their eighties, came at her invitation; her mother, Constance Merims, the former navy nurse who had launched Rosemary's career with a mailed newspaper clipping; and the 233 women who had earned Navy Wings of Gold in the previous two decades, among them five who had lost their lives. She noted how far female navy pilots had come: "The things that were burning issues of my generation—flying jets, carrier qualifications, and going to sea—are now routine events for women entering naval aviation."

Still, opportunities afforded to her husband remained unavailable. Tommy, she said, "has been my eyes in a world that I am not allowed to see firsthand."

She admitted she had once seriously considered quitting the navy, discouraged by those limitations and tempted by the financial rewards of a career as a civilian commercial pilot. For helping to persuade her to stay the course, she thanked the many navy men who had aided her along the way. "Most of them are combat-experienced aviators who, for various reasons, chose to help female naval aviators by opening policy doors that created new opportunities in the face of stiff and often emotional opposition."

Now, Female Naval Aviator No. 6, the first woman to fly a navy tactical jet, a pilot with more than 3,300 hours logged in fifteen types of aircraft, was taking command of three hundred enlisted and officers, 30 percent of them women, and a fleet of airplanes including her beloved A-7, one of which had her name painted on it.

"Rosemary Mariner is not here because she is a woman," Briggs told the crowd. "She is not here because she is a fine naval aviator. . . . Commander Rosemary Mariner is here simply because her career is marked by distinguished exemplary performance as a superb naval officer, and she is taking merely the rightful place that that performance has earned her."

It was, however, a little more complicated than that, as she had hinted in an interview a few weeks before the change-of-command ceremony. There had been stumbling blocks and pushback—far more than Briggs suggested. And though she had once declined to describe herself as a "women's libber," Rosemary credited the more-militant members of the women's movement of the 1960s and 1970s for inspiring the societal shifts that had enabled Zumwalt's reforms.

"I definitely call myself a feminist—though I don't agree with everything feminists do," she told the *Los Angeles Times*. "It's very important for professional women to acknowledge that a lot of things would not have changed if not for bra-burners."

The paper noted that while the navy overall was 10 percent female, among naval aviators, the proportion was less than 2 percent. A woman couldn't legally lead a squadron in combat. So why put one in charge? Answered Vice Admiral Jeremy Boorda, chief of naval personnel and deputy chief of naval operations, "I am trying to make it as equal as it can be under an unequal situation."

Echoed the spokesman for the Pacific Fleet, Senior Chief Petty Officer Bob Howard, "Mariner has all the attributes and qualities of a good leader and a good fighter pilot. She has punched all the right tickets"—hewing as closely as she could to the career path laid out for her husband and other male naval aviators.

"Rosemary had to overcome a great deal of opposition from male senior officers in her career," her mother told the *Hanford Sentinel*. "She worked very hard to become an effective naval aviation leader. She deserves to command that squadron."

Reflecting back on her career in a 1995 seminar, Rosemary said,

The early experiences in naval aviation ran the gamut of people that did not want us there; many were very adamant. They just threw that in your face. I could tell you stories all day long which resulted from that. When that happened to you, you had no choice but to suck it up. ... What you would hope for is that other people would notice. There were a lot of good people around. There were a lot of fair men and there were, in fact, some very supportive men. Somebody would notice what you were going through and pull off the dogs.

As a consequence, you tend to see women in these early generations having checkered careers. One place they're great, people love them; then they go someplace else where they have a change in reporting senior official. They encounter a bigot, or the terminology I use is the "jerk." When you work for that person, all of a sudden nothing you do is right. If the "jerk" is stupid, he just slam-dunks you and it's obvious. However, a lot of people are much more subtle. They will "damn you with faint praise." They won't give you the jobs that matter. In the aviation world, it was okay for women to be the administrative officer or the safety officer, but don't let them work in maintenance because that's a man's job.

In fact, her road to command did include a stint as a maintenance officer, at Kingsville, as well as surface warfare officer on the *Lex*, safety officer at VX-5, instructor pilot for the A-7E Corsair, and department head with VA-122, a fleet-readiness squadron at Naval Air Station Lemoore in California's San Joaquin Valley, near San Diego.

She had supervised multiple divisions, assumed budgetary responsibility, and modeled military discipline, teamwork, and respect.

She had been a precision pilot, a weapons test specialist, a test pilot, and an accident investigator. As she told the authors of *Ladybirds*: "I have watched my wingman crash and die and known the feeling of total helplessness, for I could do nothing to save him. One can get killed in this business, male or female, without ever being shot at by an enemy. I have also known the total exhilaration that comes from flying an airplane at

500 knots through the weeds and putting one's bombs right on target. I have seen the great beauty of this magnificent country from 30,000 feet and wondered out loud, 'I get paid for this!'"

She had been a mentor and a leader.

Tammie Jo Shults didn't know Rosemary, or know of her, when she joined VAQ-34 in spring 1989, waiting for assignment to train in the A-7 at Lemoore. "When I got there, it was different from any squadron I had ever been in before," she says. "The initial shock was just to see women. I had always been the only woman in the squadron. So I check in, and the executive officer is a woman, there are women pilots, women backseaters, women in every rank. More like normal life. But what struck me was there was not a big deal made about it. It seemed like everyone was busy at the real task at hand and not having fiefdom issues. My initial thought was, okay, fleet squadrons are run differently than training squadrons. It wouldn't be until I got to know more about fleet squadrons and Captain Mariner that [I realized], no, leadership is what sets the tone differently."

By contrast, VA-122, where Shults reported a few weeks later, was "a hostile environment." As she wrote in *Nerves of Steel*: "I immediately felt like I was walking into an enemy camp. . . . Shortly after I arrived, the magazine *Aviation Week* came out with a story about female A-7 pilots. There were only a handful of us at the time, and the cover featured a photo of two of them in front of the aircraft. Before a ready room full of instructors and students, including me—the only woman in the squadron and present in the room—the XO ripped off the cover, crumpled it up, pretended to wipe his rear with it, and threw it on the ground. 'That's what I think of women flying A-7s,' he said."

When an instructor abandoned Shults in a holding pattern in screaming winds and thick clouds after she'd lost her primary flight instruments—leaving her to land partial-panel—and then hanging her "out to dry" after she skidded off a wet runway, Rosemary stepped in. VA-122 wasn't her squadron, but Shults was her pilot, and she took care of her people. Though the brass at VA-122 wanted Shults out and the CO outranked Rosemary, Rosemary called and suggested that the sooner Shults got back in the cockpit, the better. "She watched from afar and didn't meddle with the way they were doing things, but at some point, she interjected," Shults says.

Years later, Rosemary made an off-the-cuff comment. According to Shults, Rosemary said, " 'I called up there just to keep tabs on you because I did that for all my VAQ pilots. [I] wondered if I was going to have to use one of my silver bullets, but it worked out. I was glad to see you got right back into the cockpit. I'm glad to have you here. I'm excited to have you dig in and get busy.' That was it."

Shults, who had been a navy flight instructor herself, in the T-2, adds, "I wasn't a favorite of hers. She hardly knew me. But she kept tabs. She was good about asking questions. She didn't call him up and demand this or that but knew her rights as skipper, shined the light of day by knowing her rights, his rights and my rights. The key to the brilliant thing about Rosemary Mariner's leadership was she never went in guns ablazing, with a pre-made solution. She went in with questions and didn't go in to make any enemies but knew her rights. She knew what the proper way and legal way of doing things were."

After a hearing at which the commanding officer didn't ask Shults a single question to get her side of the story, Rosemary instigated an outside investigation that found no pilot error. Her measured, focused approach to solving problems, in control of her emotions and never letting anyone push her into a reaction, were hallmarks of Rosemary's thoughtful leadership style.

When Shults's new husband, Dean, was scheduled for transfer to the East Coast—even though he was the only Lemoore A-7 pilot who wanted to stay in California—Shults approached Rosemary about a transfer. After asking why, Rosemary called the commanding officer for a quiet chat. Then she let Shults know that she didn't need to put in for a transfer after all; there had been a mistake or misunderstanding. Though the CO had taunted Shults that there was nothing she could do about it, Dean would be staying. The newlyweds would not be split up.

Shults and her husband finished their A-7 training on the same day, but only because, as a female noncombat pilot, Shults learned on an abbreviated syllabus. No weapons training, carrier landings, or aerial combat maneuvers—as she put it, "the fun stuff." So, anticipating the day when female aviators could fly the A-7's entire mission, Rosemary arranged soon after she took command to send Shults back to VA-122 to finish the job.

Shults was one of three VAQ-34 pilots sent to Lemoore for weapons training: another woman and a man. Says Shults, "the guy pressed the target"—released the bomb beyond the normal release point for that particular weapon—"so bad that they said VAQ has to go home." Shults went in and asked whether Lemoore would send all of its own pilots home if just one messed up, and the two women got to stay. But they weren't allowed bombs or bullets.

"I called Captain Mariner and said, 'I don't know what the agreement with 122 is, but I don't see flying a bombing pattern without bombs as advantageous,'" Shults says. " 'How do you know if you're doing it right unless you have bombs to prove you released at the right angle and speed?' [Rosemary] said, 'You don't have bombs?' I said, 'No, they took our bombs and bullets away.'"

Rosemary again stepped in. Shults got in trouble for tattling, but they got their bombs back, although not the bullets. The women loved diving from 10,000 feet, constantly trimming the aircraft as it accelerated to 400 knots to maintain a 45-degree angle at zero G, releasing the bombs on target and then pulling sharply up above the minimum safe altitude. "It takes gender completely out of the equation," Shults says. She didn't get the full syllabus the second time, either, but she at least came home to VAQ-34 weapons-qualified.

Shults's experience echoed an episode from early in Rosemary's own career. As a young lieutenant (j.g.), she was sent with great fanfare to John McCain's squadron in Jacksonville, Florida, for A-7 training. But because of restrictions on women, Rosemary was not allowed to complete the full syllabus. The men finished their qualification and went on to compete to fly in the fleet. But Rosemary was barred.

"That was the most difficult thing—not being allowed to stay with my class," Rosemary told the *Navy Times*. "It was very frustrating not to stay in A-7 training and not have the same shot at a fleet seat as my male colleagues. I was so close—and yet so far." Though she learned to drop bombs from the A-7 at China Lake, Rosemary wasn't permitted to finish the full syllabus for ten years.

This time, history was not going to repeat.

Rosemary Mariner was, Shults says, "an incredible, incredible woman."

Said Lieutenant Sally Fountain, a member of Rosemary's squadron in her fifth year of navy service, "I had not met a leader, a person whose qualities I want[ed] to emulate until I got here. And as a female, when I find another woman, I sit up and take notice because she has done it. And she has done it right. That's how I want to do it."

In fact, Rosemary Mariner's selection as skipper prompted not just robust news coverage, but an *LA Times* editorial calling her out by name and making the case against the combat exclusion:

The newest addition to the local woman-makes-good category is San Diegan Rosemary Mariner, who, at 37, is about to become the first female to command a Navy aviation squadron. Cmdr. Mariner's achievement should be an occasion for unreserved congratulations and acknowledgment of another step in the progress of feminism.

But one cannot take note of Mariner's accomplishment without also recognizing that an anachronistic federal law prevents Mariner from leading that squadron in defense of her country. . . . Women guard bases from Okinawa to West Germany. They were fired upon while flying troops to battle aboard helicopters during the Panamanian invasion. More well-known is Army Capt. Linda Bray's role in an assault on a Panamanian Defense Forces canine barracks unit.

But Congress still has not legitimized women's combat role . . . [A] bill that would have allowed women to participate in all military activities during a trial period is effectively dead for this session of Congress.

Mariner is convinced that manpower shortages forecast for the 1990s mean it is only a matter of time before women are allowed in combat.

"When I hit a wall, I am going to get under it, over it or around it," Mariner said in explaining her climb through the Navy ranks. "Put a wall in front of me and my reaction is to knock it down." We'll cheer loudest when Mariner scales this barrier, or better yet, when it comes tumbling down.

Later, Rosemary would say that wars open a window for change, and the first Persian Gulf War—Operation Desert Storm—soon gave VAQ-34 and its new CO the chance to show what they could do.

When Iraqi dictator Saddam Hussein invaded Kuwait in January 1991, the squadron snapped into action. Simulating attacks by Iraqi forces, VAQ-34 trained seven battle groups at Oceana, San Diego, and Puerto Rico to prepare them for combat. "With the exception of the *Midway*, we worked every Kuwait battle group," Rosemary told the *Hanford Sentinel*.

Shults says this didn't just happen; VAQ-34's new CO "didn't wait for a call for our services. She looked around in the navy to see where we could be used. As a junior officer, I was kind of busy with lower-level management, but I don't remember doing lots of Top Gun work before she became skipper. She would look for places that could use us. For instance, when Desert Storm came about, she offered up our services to test things out at Edwards Air Force Base and China Lake. We hadn't been doing that. . . . Testing jamming equipment and different things out there wasn't part of our normal mission, but we found ourselves doing that."

Rosemary also looked ahead and made sure her squadron's aircraft had all the equipment—moving map displays for navigation in conflict zones, for example—in case they were needed, even if women couldn't fly them.

Before handing the command pin and squadron flag to her successor, Commander Floyd Weaver, the following August and heading for the National War College, Commander Rosemary Mariner received the Meritorious Service Medal. Under her command, mission readiness, number of sorties completed, and consecutive days without damage from FOD (foreign object debris—any loose items left on a runway or taxiway or in a hangar that could harm an aircraft) improved. Marks of good management, all.

The debate over the combat exclusion was heating up again, and Rosemary sensed that change was coming. Shults thinks that's one reason she was sent back to Lemoore to complete her weapons training. "On a personal level, it helped us prepare to transition into a fleet squadron if and when it opened up," Shults wrote. "On a grander scale, she was demonstrating to those who would decide whether to change the policy that it was not only feasible; it had already been done."

CHAPTER TWELVE

The Halls of Congress

"Suppose you had a woman pilot, she's an instructor pilot, superior intelligence, great physical conditioning, and in every way she was superior to a male counterpart vying for a combat position. Would your personal judgment be, because you would not want to see the risk to her life increase by putting her in a combat role, that you would pick the male over the female under those circumstances?"

"That's correct."

"So in other words, you would have a militarily less effective situation because of a personal view."

"I admit it doesn't make much sense, but that's the way I feel about it."

June 18, 1991. Hart Senate Office Building, Capitol Hill. Hearing of the Senate Armed Services Subcommittee on Manpower and Personnel. Subject: Restrictions on women in combat.

For eight months, the American public had watched on TV as soldiers, sailors, airmen, and marines had shipped out for the Middle East during Operation Desert Shield and then Desert Storm, soon to be collectively known as the Persian Gulf War. It wasn't just dads who were deploying in the first major US military engagement since Vietnam; it was moms. The soldier in desert battle gear being interviewed by embedded reporters could well be a woman. The Airborne Warning and Control System (AWACS) planes, tankers, and transports that women flew were tempting, unprotected targets as they provided air traffic control and delivered fuel, troops, equipment, and supplies in the Red Sea,

Persian Gulf, and Indian Ocean. They could be shot at, but they couldn't shoot back. Support squadrons where women were assigned regularly took casualties. So did tactical air bases where women maintained and prepared combat aircraft—the same jobs women were barred from doing on carriers, which were guarded by the fleet.

Female pilots could be put at risk without even a thought. An imaginary line demarcated the combat zone, with Saudi Arabia to the south and Kuwait to the north. Retired captain Dwayne Oslund, Joellen's husband, recalled:

I was assigned to the staff of the Navy's logistics support force in Bahrain where I oversaw the operations of thirty-two shore-based planes and helicopters. One morning the officer-in-charge of one of the helicopter detachments appeared at my office door along with one of the female pilots assigned to the unit. They asked to speak with me, then stepped into my office and closed the door.

"Uh-oh," I thought. "This must not be good."

Turns out the night before, the female pilot was diverted from a routine ship resupply mission and ordered to fly to an oil platform off Kuwait City to pick up Iraqi soldiers who had been captured. Apparently, word got back to the Wing Commander in Virginia that a female crew member had flown into the combat zone, which was not permitted.

I assured the pilot she had done the right thing. As she departed my office, I also reminded the pilot to log combat flight time on her flight reports. My small actions may not have influenced what is the norm today, but it meant a lot to the women pilots for whom I felt a responsibility to treat with fairness and equality. After I passed this situation along to my admiral, I never heard another word. Rules aren't necessarily made to be broken, but this one was out of date.

Oslund later added that after the admiral found out what had happened, he got on the phone to the wing commander with a clear message to leave those pilots alone. The pilots were there, and they were going to be assigned as needed.

It all brought home to America's living rooms the reality that women were fighting, dying, and being taken prisoners of war, combat exclusion or no. As Rosemary Mariner later put it, Americans saw that "The country could not go to war without women."

General Norman Schwarzkopf, commander during Operation Desert Storm, testified before Congress, "I have no doubts that women could perform in Army cockpits—any cockpits." Secretary of Defense Dick Cheney acknowledged that the United States could not have won the war without women.

Members of DACOWITS, after hearing from fifteen female Gulf War vets at its annual April conference, voted to ask Cheney to end the combat exclusion.

So, should the law, on the books since 1948, be rescinded?

Democratic representatives Patricia Schroeder of Colorado and Beverly Byron of Massachusetts thought so. In May 1991, the House of Representatives had approved their legislation to let female aviators in the navy, air force, and marines fly warplanes in combat. It was the first direct challenge to the combat exclusion, and after decades of dithering and debate, false starts and close calls, the Senate began considering whether to follow suit. Or go even further and change the law beyond just female aviators.

Senator William Roth, Republican of Delaware, had introduced a bill, S1076, lifting the ban and authorizing the secretary of defense to prescribe conditions under which women might be assigned to duty in aircraft engaged in combat missions. It was a recognition that, as Roth put it, modern technology had blurred the lines between support and combat functions both inside the battle zone and far beyond the constantly moving front.

Among those in agreement was Republican senator William Cohen of Maine, whose exchange with air force chief of staff General Merrill McPeak about choosing a less-qualified male pilot over a more-qualified woman made national headlines.

Also in the room was Republican senator John McCain of Arizona, ranking member on the subcommittee and Rosemary Mariner's commanding officer at Cecil Field in Jacksonville, where she had first flown the A-7E Corsair in 1976. A few months before the hearing, McCain had said he thought women should be integrated into crews on navy combat ships and fly combat planes and helicopters.

The topic was of such great national interest that Senate offices were flooded with letters representing points of view across the political spectrum. Members of the larger Senate Armed Services Committee sat in on the hearing, including Senator John Warner, Republican of Virginia, who had signed Judith Neuffer's flight training orders at the Pentagon as secretary of the navy in 1973. Warner had written to the secretary of defense that "the face of war has changed significantly while our assignment policies for [military] women has been resistant to change due to what may be antiquated legal restrictions. I believe it is time that Congress again review the combat exclusion laws that limit the assignment of women to many duty positions in our armed forces."

For many military women, including Rosemary—whose entrée into the navy came as the previous war wound down—it was an essential window of opportunity. From 2 percent when the all-volunteer force was implemented in 1973, women now made up 11 percent of active-duty military, meaning some 230,000 female soldiers, sailors, airmen, and marines. There were also some 150,000 in the Reserve—13 percent— including Judy, soon to be promoted to captain, and Commander Joellen Drag Oslund. More than 35,000 women had served in the Persian Gulf, many with distinction.

Much of the public approved of rescinding the law. Subcommittee chairman Senator John Glenn, Democrat of Ohio, a former marine aviator and the first astronaut to orbit the Earth, cited a CBS News survey taken the previous January, just before the outbreak of hostilities. It showed 47 percent of Americans in favor of allowing women to serve in combat; Glenn said he was surprised at how high that number was. McCain described US servicewomen as having demonstrated "outstanding performance" in the Gulf War, and said, "I think it is time we reevaluated the combat exclusion policy for women. Clearly, women have demonstrated they can perform any role they are called upon that any male is called upon to do."

But in testimony, the chiefs of all four branches of the military, with varying degrees of forcefulness, agreed: The combat exclusion was a good thing. General Carl Vuono of the US Army and General Alfred Gray, US Marine Corps chief of staff, were all in. (Said Gray, "We see in the Corps no need to change anything.") McPeak told the senators, "I find great comfort in the law." Chief of naval operations Admiral Frank Kelso, saying he recognized that female naval aviators felt stymied by the restriction, followed a line of reasoning that had guided the navy down through the decades. He did not oppose progress, but one must let those roles evolve. It was a delicate balance. (An editorial in *USA Today*, for one, called out the four chiefs for cowardice, writing, "[T]he leaders of our high-tech military are hiding behind cave-man myths and prejudices.")

As energized as opponents of the combat exclusion were, supporters of restrictions on military women were equally motivated to ensure that the law remained in place. Even after the WASP, the WAVES, and the first female naval aviators proved what women in the armed forces could do; even after McPeak admitted in testimony that female pilots were capable of flying as well as men and could even withstand the same G forces; once the hearing was over, the resistance gained ground. Despite the surprise victory in the House, the same old objections that had kept the combat exclusion in place since 1948—women as a threat to combat readiness, unit cohesion, and morale; traditional gender roles; upper-body strength—seemed to be prevailing. And the war window was closing.

Back in 1983, Rosemary had had the opportunity to meet with Admiral Elmo Zumwalt. She had asked him what it would take to keep the progress he had implemented going. Zumwalt's answer, she said: "The law had to go. Congress passed the law, and Congress could repeal it. But don't expect the navy to take the lead. It was too convenient for military and civilian leaders to justify their policies by blaming Congress and hiding behind the law. It was up to Navy women to make a change."

It was, for her, a time of political awakening. The first strike involved an oiler called the USS *Kalamazoo*, which in 1979 had been promised as a berth for female helicopter pilots. But the navy reneged the following year. The reclassification of the Mobile Logistics Support Force as the Combat Logistics Force in 1986 was strike two. "This wasn't about protecting women or combat readiness," she said. "As I saw it, the people involved said no because they just plain didn't want women at sea and were allowed to get away with it."

Now, with Roth's bill tabled in the Senate, it seemed strike three was imminent. Roth and Democratic senator Edward Kennedy of Massachusetts drew up new legislation to repeal the 1948 ban on female pilots flying combat missions. But the Senate Armed Services Committee leadership was against it.

The best chance for rescinding Section 6015 was in danger of slipping away. It was time to marshal the forces and fight.

The cavalry came in the form of Women Military Aviators, Inc. (WMA), an organization encompassing navy, air force, army, and coast guard pilots and aircrew; officers and enlisted; former WASP; and their families. All told, its hundreds-strong membership covered practically every congressional district in the country.

Commander Rosemary Mariner was WMA's vice president. As she told the Smithsonian audience in 2011:

Women aviators were not going to allow what happened to the WASP in 1944 to happen again. The call went out across the network. Take leave, bring your uniform, come to Washington, DC, and tell your story. Male and female aviators, junior, senior, officer, enlisted, active, reserve, from all the services . . . joined with representatives from numerous organizations including DACOWITS and the National Women's Law Center to set up shop in Senator Roth's office.

The Honorable Carolyn Becraft, with [Women's Research and Education Institute] at the time and a former assistant secretary of the Navy for manpower and reserve affairs, was the head political strategist. . . . WASP in their Santiago blue uniforms turned out in full force to support the younger generation. Retired Air Force Major General Jeanne Holm shared her expertise and encouragement. The president of the Association of Naval Aviation, retired Vice Admiral William P. Lawrence [the "radical feminist" with the daughter at the Naval Academy] was tremendously supportive, writing opinion pieces and writing letters.

So, accompanied by civilians who talked about legislation, military personnel simply told senators and their staffs what they had been doing for twenty years, including their service in the Gulf War.

Then-lieutenant Barbara Bell, first in her class at jet school and the navy's first female test pilot instructor, was one of the legion who turned out. "In 1991, I joined forces with Rosemary and my other women aviator friends on Capitol Hill to repeal the combat exclusions laws," the retired captain wrote in the *Knoxville News* in 2019. "We traversed the halls of Congress educating everyone we came into contact with that women had all the skills needed to fly combat aircraft."

"Educating"—not lobbying, which active-duty military were not allowed to do.

Bell wrote in the funeral home guestbook: "A leader among leaders. Rosemary opened the door for us to follow. Always the consummate professional, she knew that we women must band together to open military aviation to all. The work we performed on Capitol Hill was not for us, but for the many women who now follow."

On the other side was a coalition led by another powerful and accomplished woman: an Illinois housewife, constitutional lawyer, one-time political candidate, syndicated columnist, and brilliantly effective organizer named Phyllis Schlafly. She first rose to prominence in the 1970s, fighting to stop the Equal Rights Amendment—whose expected passage was one driver of Zumwalt's effort to expand opportunity for women in his navy. The chilling specter of females in combat was one of the cudgels she and her grassroots coalition, STOP ERA, had wielded in beating down the amendment (along with claiming, among other things, that it would relieve men of all obligation to support their families). Having succeeded in that campaign, she and her organization, renamed the Eagle Forum, doubled down on their opposition to feminist-supported causes, including women in the military. In her view, the issue wasn't excluding female aviators from flying in combat. It was excluding women from the armed forces entirely. "America is entitled to better protection than women's physical strength can provide," she said.

In 1982, celebrating the defeat of a previous attempt to overturn the combat exclusion, Schlafly wrote, "Except for the tiny fraction of 1 percent of career-age women who volunteer for military service and complete their terms of enlistment, American women still expect their men to protect and defend them. And American men will never stoop so low as to send their wives, sisters, sweethearts and daughters out to fight enemy men. Stereotyped sex roles? Of course. Now and forever."

Eight years later, in her monthly newsletter, she described the quest to overturn the combat exclusion as "the cutting edge of feminist ideology," with the goal of "deny[ing] us our right to make reasonable differences of treatment between women and men." Women, she wrote, were "pushed" into combat-related roles, with the inevitable final result being their mandatory inclusion in a military draft.

"The oft-stated goal of the radical feminists is a totally gender-neutral society," she wrote in 1991, "and the military is the cutting edge."

In a paper written in May 1991, and in a speech before the Heritage Foundation, Schlafly pulled out all the stops in arguing to roll back the clock: Women were inherently unqualified, didn't really want to serve anyway, would behave dishonorably if they did, and were taking away men's rightful role in society.

Letting female pilots fly in combat "would mean affirmative action quotas for women in an occupation in which they cannot compete equally with men" (McPeak's testimony to the contrary).

Military maternity leave discriminated against men because they couldn't get pregnant and use it as an out. ("Pardon me, fellas. I am taking nine months off from flying in order to be pregnant, and then a couple of months more to recuperate. You guys go ahead and kill off the enemy, and I will see you all in about a year.")

There were gender stereotypes: "Men are attracted to serve in the military because of its intensely masculine character. The qualities that make them good soldiers—aggressiveness, risk taking, and enjoyment of body-contact competition—are conspicuously absent in women. Pretending that women can perform equally with men in tasks that require those attributes is not only dishonest; it corrupts the system."

And the claim that there was no real groundswell of support, just unseemly pot-stirring by a small bunch of grasping females who don't know their place: "Only a tiny minority of American women choose a military career at all, and of those only a tiny minority are agitating to get combat jobs. . . . This little group of ambitious women should not be allowed to impose their peculiar views of gender neutrality on our nation. The whole idea of men sending women, including mothers, out to fight the enemy is uncivilized, degrading, barbaric and embarrassing. It is contrary to our culture, to our respect for men and women, and to our belief in the importance of the family and motherhood. And furthermore, no one respects a man who would let a woman do his fighting for him."

Lawrence, for one, disagreed. As he wrote in an op-ed in the *San Diego Union-Tribune* on July 22, 1991:

The true issue is not whether women should be involved in combat. They already have served in combat (with great credit) in Grenada, Panama and the Persian Gulf. Women currently constitute about 11 percent, or 225,000, of the personnel in the armed services. Their roles are so broad and vital to military functions today that they will be extensively involved in any future conflict. The principle [sic] problem which must be solved is that the 1948 law which governs the role of women in the military has become outmoded and inappropriate as the roles and numbers of women have been expanded during the past 40 years.

The law must be modified or abolished if for no other reason than its provisions are being regularly broken. . . . Army women helicopter pilots flew numerous resupply missions into hostile fire zones in Iraq and Kuwait. Women Air Force pilots and aircrews flew in airborne-warning and control aircraft and in-flight refueling tankers within range of enemy aircraft, surface-to-air missiles and anti-aircraft artillery. Women served in Navy logistics ships that were regularly resupplying the aircraft carrier battle groups in the Persian Gulf and Red Sea, constantly [at] risk of being damaged by enemy mines, missiles and bombs.

Were not all of the above cases combat missions? When the Navy opened oil tankers and ammunition ships to women in 1988, a "work around" had to be developed to prevent the appearance of an obvious contravention of the law, because those ships commonly operate in battle zones and high-risk areas. So the problem was solved semantically.

The Department of Defense issued a policy that women would not serve in roles in which they would be involved in "direct combat" with the enemy. It has never been clear to me what "direct combat" means. For example, if a Navy tanker or ammunition ship or an Air Force AWACS aircraft is hit by an enemy missile, is that not "direct combat"? To the persons in those craft who are killed or injured, the distinction between "direct combat" or "indirect combat" is not very meaningful. . . . [T]he laws and policies governing the roles of women in the military are not only irrelevant, they are absurd. It will be difficult to modify them, because wording probably would be developed which is no better than [what] we have now. So the only logical course is to delete sections 6015 and 8549 of Title X. Once this is accomplished, the secretary of defense would be free to employ women as he (or she) feels is most appropriate.

Less than two weeks later, the Senate voted in favor of lifting the combat exclusion—sort of. Women would be allowed to fly combat missions, and the Defense Department could suspend the restrictions to study broader applications of a repeal. The four branches of the military had to reevaluate their individual policies and combat restraints. They didn't have to put women in combat, but if they refused to do so, they wouldn't have the 1948 law to hide behind anymore.

It was, the *Boston Globe* reported, "the first time in seven years that an Armed Services Committee decision was overturned on the Senate floor. . . . Reacting to the Senate's move yesterday, Navy Commander Rosemary Mariner, a pilot who is stationed at a Navy air base in Lemoore, Calif., said in a telephone interview that she would celebrate the victory by going flying. 'We've been waiting almost 20 years for this,' she said. 'I look forward to the fact that all the talented young women and men will have a chance to prove themselves.'"

President George H. W. Bush signed the bill into law in December 1991. But before any changes could be made, a commission would be created to study the effect of servicewomen on combat readiness, unit cohesion, and morale—the same rationales employed forty years before to exclude Blacks from all-white units. The Presidential Commission on the Assignment of Women in the Armed Forces would gauge which other laws or policies needed revision or repeal, consider what modifications would be needed for transitioning women into combat positions, and determine whether there should be different standards for men and women. Forming a study group was a time-honored strategy for avoiding making tough decisions and taking blame for them. ("With the commission, they could stop the train," Becraft noted.) And this one had the backing of both Warner and McCain, in what many viewed as a reversal of their positions of just a few months before.

Several Schlafly allies were appointed to the commission, including a former DACOWITS member named Elaine Donnelly.

Donnelly was executive director of an organization called the Coalition for Military Readiness, which she had founded to counter DACOWITS advocacy in advancing women's roles in the armed forces. According to Linda Bird Francke in *Ground Zero*, Donnelly firmly believed that women weakened the nation's defense and had joined DACOWITS specifically to block that advocacy. As a committee member from 1984–1986, she mounted her own campaign to stoke resistance among men during visits to West Point and military bases—until the Pentagon made her stop.

Having "picked up the Schlafly banner to wage war against women in combat," as Francke put it, Donnelly "had lobbied Capitol Hill by foot and fax and testified against expanded opportunities for women at every congressional hearing since the 1980 hearing on registering women for the draft."

At the April 1991 DACOWITS conference, held just two months before the Senate subcommittee hearing, female pilots from all branches showed up to discuss inequities in the combat law with new members and to advocate for repeal. (Rosemary's pitch: "This is the time to do it because of the tremendous success of Operation Desert Storm. If we hadn't had the Civil War with the resulting legislation and the Fourteenth Amendment to the Constitution, we'd be fighting slavery plantation to plantation. This is what we are doing today in the military.") Donnelly was also there, lobbying those same new members to kill any resolution in favor of overturning the combat exclusion.

Schlafly and Donnelly both submitted written testimony to the Senate Armed Services Subcommittee on Manpower and Personnel ahead of the June 18 hearing, warning of the domino effect that changing the law and letting female pilots fly in combat would set in motion: pregnancy and military motherhood, the risk to "the lives of both men and women, not to mention expensive aircraft," women drafted and forced into foxholes on the front lines, enlisted women sacrificed to the narrow interests of ambitious female officers. It was, in fact, a playbook that some of the senators followed in questioning witnesses at the hearing.

As one air force master sergeant attached to DACOWITS summed it up at the time: "The Schlafly group knows that with the media coverage of women in the Gulf, right now is probably the best time in history to get the law repealed. And they want to counter that. This should not be a political issue, but it absolutely is."

That was crystal clear during a panel discussion on CNN's *Crier & Co.* on July 26, 1991, a week before the Senate voted to lift the ban. And it wasn't just political; it was personal.

In an interview during the show's first segment, Commander Rosemary Mariner staked out her position that it wasn't a matter of gender; the airplane didn't care. Former British prime minister Margaret Thatcher proved how psychologically tough women could be; they were not inherently weaker than men. Senior naval aviators who had flown in Vietnam were among the staunchest supporters of female military pilots. It wasn't a matter of self-interest for Rosemary, as any repeal would come too late for her—the experience needed to fly combat had to be acquired in the first five years of a pilot's career. But it was important for the next generation.

Then, the panel discussion—and the fireworks—began.

Donnelly came out swinging. "I don't think we should allow politics to put women into jobs for which they're really not qualified," she began, running through a series of well-polished talking points—the slippery slope from pilots to ground combat, women in submarines and the draft; pregnancy; harm done to sailors' "quality of life" by accommodating women aboard ship; ambitious female officers seeking "affirmative action."

Rosemary fired back: "I don't know if you can even comment any more than an observer when you make a visit to a ship." And later: "Frankly, I'm quite interested in what your experience is. How much military experience do you have?"—knowing full well the answer was none.

In fact, appearances by Rosemary and other advocates on the talk-show circuit were part of a full-court press against "well-funded conservative opposition." Since the chiefs' testimony in favor of retaining combat limits, resistance to women was building within the military. Schlafly and right-wing commentators were waging a media campaign; Donnelly was roaming the halls of Congress with pamphlets excerpting subcommittee testimony on registering women for the draft, child care, single military moms, and pregnancy—peripheral, emotional family issues that were drowning out the central question of female fliers in military aircraft.

In mounting their counteroffensive, WMA and civilian organizations whose leaders had testified and sent statements to the subcommittee urging repeal decided on personal appeals to senators and congressional staff. But the effort was not as simple and smooth as Rosemary made it seem in her talk at the Smithsonian.

As Francke wrote:

The pilots had one week to mount a counter campaign. . . . Carolyn Becraft faxed the phone numbers and addresses of the members of both houses of Congress to the president and vice president of the WMA. . . . They, in turn, faxed the information to the entire WMA membership of 500, with the most important senators starred. . . . Faxes, letters and phone calls poured into Senate offices from the WASP, the active-duty members of the WMA and their families, friends and supporters. . . . Washington was buried. "I've never seen more faxes and mail over a single issue in my entire career," Tony Cordesman, John McCain's military aide and Gulf war consultant for ABC News, told a friend. . . . Men came to support the women . . . there were F-18 combat pilots on the Hill, enlisted men and retired Navy brass. Retired Admiral Elmo Zumwalt Jr., who had opened Navy aviation to women in 1973, came to continue his stewardship. So did retired Vice Admiral William Lawrence, president of the Association of Naval Aviation and proud father of Lieutenant Commander Wendy Lawrence, who was about to be selected as an astronaut.

The pilots came to support themselves. Navy pilots flew in from Florida, California, Virginia and Missouri. Reservists flew in from their jobs with American Airlines and United Airlines. One Navy pilot flew to Washington for an hour. An Army pilot came for a week.

Under Pentagon rules, service members were not allowed to lobby Congress or to appear on Capitol Hill in uniform unless they were there for a hearing. So WMA president Kelly Hamilton, an air force lieutenant colonel, and vice president Rosemary Mariner, navy commander, drafted some guidelines. Active-duty pilots should get permission from their commanders to come to Washington, take personal leave, and make the trip on their own time. Naval aviators should wear their "leave and liberty" uniforms; army pilots, their Class A uniforms; all participants should make clear they were expressing their own opinions when talking with senators and staff.

As Francke described it:

Forty or so advocates of repeal fanned out from the central command post in Senator Roth's office, armed with fact sheets about the combat exclusion laws and women's historical contributions to the military. Sightings of the uniformed pilots and the civilian lobbyists rippled up and down the Senate corridors. . . . The Senate aides, mostly young, Ivy League graduates with few military contacts, were particularly receptive. "The young staffers, almost to a person, said, 'This is really dumb. What do you mean you can't fly off a ship or fly a bomber? You're pilots,'" says Becraft.

The pilots' corridor campaign met resistance in other Senate offices, especially Senator McCain's, and so infuriated Captain Bud Orr, a former fighter pilot in the Navy's Office of Legislative Affairs, that he called his boss in the Pentagon and persuaded him to punish them. "They weren't supposed to be lobbying in uniform, so I sent a lieutenant to round them up and get their butts over to my office," says Orr. The intimidation campaign was brief. Alerted to the impending reprimand, Senator Roth called the Pentagon. "You got a problem, you call me," a pilot recalls Roth saying to the two-star admiral. But the admiral had already been called off by the secretary of the Navy. "Regrettably, my boss called Larry Garrett and Garrett told him, 'Let them go. It's too hot,'" recalls Orr. . . . And the blitzkrieg continued on the Hill.

On July 25, only six days after the first call went out to the WMA, Senators Kennedy and Roth announced their joint legislation at a press conference. They were flanked by the pilots whose rationale for repeal was just what the senators needed.

With the vote a week later; Bush's signing of the bill in December; and the naming of the commission, the change that Commander Rosemary Mariner, her sisters, and their allies had fought for was tantalizingly close . . . but just out of reach.

As newly elected president of Women Military Aviators, Inc., Rosemary wrote in the organization's December 1991 newsletter:

Hundreds of military women are anxiously awaiting implementation of the FY-92 Defense Authorization Bill that repeals all statutory restrictions on the combat assignment of female military aviators in the armed forces. The House passed their version of the defense bills repealing those laws on May 22, 1991. The Senate, in an overwhelming show of support, voted 69–30 in favor of the Roth-Kennedy amendment (which repealed the statutes) on July 30. While the bill also provides for a Presidential Commission on the Assignment of Women in the Armed Forces, it is clear in both the language, floor votes and extensive press coverage that Congress did not intend to study, or in [any] other manner, delay the combat assignment of female aviators.

Flying military aircraft, just like flying the space shuttle, is strictly a function of individual ability—airplanes don't care about the gender of the pilot. Female military aviators have undergone exactly the same training as their male counterparts to earn their wings for over 16 years. In naval aviation this includes air-to-ground (dropping bombs), air-to-air weapons ("dogfighting") and carrier qualification in tactical jet aircraft.

Army, Air Force and Navy women have been teaching men to fly for over 15 years. Navy female jet instructors teach young Marine Corps student pilots to drop bombs. All military aviators, men and women, have their individual performance "studied," documented on their grade sheets in their training jackets [a folder containing a naval aviator's complete records], throughout their aviation careers. Female aviators in particular have had their individual performance closely scrutinized. Yet after almost 20 years, a woman who finishes at the top of her class in tactical jet training will receive the same orders as a man who finishes at the bottom of the class. The defense bill should put an immediate end to this overt discrimination.

Concerns over "bonding" have no basis in fact. Since aviation opened to women in 1973, men and women have flown together as mature professionals, sharing the dangers, rewards and camaraderie of their service vocation. Women have been flying on men's wings and men on women's wings for years. Male and female aviators have made six-month cruises aboard Navy ships since the early 1980s. They judge one another as individuals. Those people of either sex who can't keep their emotions out of the cockpit shouldn't be flying in the first place.

Concerns over pregnancy have no basis in fact. To entrust a million-dollar aircraft to a woman pilot and then turn around and suggest that she isn't mature enough to control her reproductive choices is not only contradictory but insulting. It is as if the ability to have a child somehow makes one a child. In reality, female aviators plan their families around their flying tours. They invest tremendous time and *effort to fly airplanes, and like all aviators, don't want to do anything that costs them flight time. For those few who have children during flight assignments, no more loss time can be attributed to women as a whole than to men as a whole who suffer long-term, grounding injuries as a result of sporting accidents. . . .*

Concerns that, since women have never flown in combat, we have to "study" them so we know what they will do, is also illogical. First, women have flown in combat. During WWII the Soviets had three squadrons of female combat pilots who flew fighter and night attack aircraft, the famous "Night Witches." Some of these women are still alive today. During Operation Desert Storm numerous women flew in harm's way. Second, all aviators, male and female, have never flown in combat until the first time they fly in combat. Being male is not a predictor of how one will perform under fire. . . . Women aviators, just like male aviators, train as they will fight. But until the individual is exposed to combat, no one knows how he or she will perform. . . . The warrior spirit is [a] function of the heart and mind, not the reproductive organs.

The concept of "we must do a study" is a common political ruse to diffuse accountability and stall action. It is no more valid, especially after 20 years, to claim that we must study women pilots than it is to state we must study female or black astronauts because we don't know what they will do in a space emergency. It ignores the tons of detailed individual records of flight and officer performance. Contrary to those who claimed that there aren't any studies, it ignores the stacks of DOD, DACOWITS, service studies and reports that have been published every year since the inception of the All-Volunteer Force. It assumes that women are some kind of different non-human species, like Martians, instead of individual American citizens. Such commissions and studies are also very expensive and time-consuming. Selective ignorance does not justify wasting the taxpayers' money to study something Congress did not request.

To those who say, what's the rush? What difference is a year delay going to make? I refer them to WMA's young membership for which a one-year delay will prevent them from ever making the transition to a tactical mission. Becoming a combat pilot is like learning a foreign language. If one does not do it early in life they will always speak with an accent. These are demanding skills that must be acquired during the formative stage of an aviator's training and then built upon by ever-demanding tasks and responsibilities. We know from long experience that the failure rate . . . from support mission to dynamic tactical flying is high.

But the biggest problem is the missed leadership experience in the air. We cannot afford senior aviators to make the same mistakes that nuggets make airborne or in execution of their ground responsibilities. In this business, peace or war, people can get killed for such mistakes. To the women who are at this point in their careers now, a one-year delay will mean that their future in military aviation is all but gone. Which also means they have nothing to loose [sic].

The idea of individual rights is a concept that all Americans understand and identify with. It is embodied in the United States Constitution which all service members swear to uphold and defend. It is also one of the principles worth dying for. Women military aviators have been victims of legal discrimination, until this defense bill, for reasons that had nothing to do with ability. This is exactly the same experience millions of black Americans suffered for the same immoral and intellectually bankrupt reasons. All the excuses—like white men wouldn't fight for black men, or blacks were too unreliable to be trusted in combat, or the presence of black men would offend southern gentlemen and therefore adversely affect combat readiness— were used to justify decades of segregation and discrimination. But it all boils down to judging people as individuals and not by gender, race or religion. . . . As Lt. Gen. Charles Horner, USAF, the air commander for CENTCOM during the Gulf War, told the San Diego Kiwanis Club, to deny women the right to fight in combat "perhaps is contrary to what we stand for."

After the contributions of the WASPs and the female military aviators for almost 50 years, there is nothing more to study about men and women flying combat missions. Airplanes have always been gender-neutral. There is no reason to alter military flight training or airplanes—they have been gender-neutral for years. Almost 20 female Army, Air Force and Naval aviators have died in aircraft mishaps since 1980, giving the final proof of their commitment. For years our leaders told us and told the press that the only thing preventing them from putting women in combat cockpits was the law. Following the tremendous contributions of military aviators of both sexes in Operation Desert Storm and strong public acceptance of their sacrifices, the United States Congress did their part and repealed the laws. . . . Hopefully we will soon be told that, just as Congress intended, military aviation is now gender-neutral. Ability, not gender, should decide who fights our next war from the skies.

For eight months, the commission's fifteen members heard testimony from more than three hundred witnesses, among them Phyllis Schlafly and Rosemary Mariner. Schlafly pleaded the case of traditional gender roles and the unsuitability of women to wear the uniform. Rosemary stood up for equality and the ability of women to get the job done, drew parallels between sexism and the military's traditional discrimination against Black service members, and indicted systemic inequality as a root cause of pervasive sexual harassment.

And the first American military woman to fly a tactical jet and to command an aviation squadron—who, as a junior officer under McCain's command, "was not allowed aboard a ship unless on leave, in civilian clothes, accompanied by a male officer, heaven forbid land aboard one"— became a lightning rod.

They called her "combat woman," said Joellen Oslund. It wasn't a compliment.

One *Detroit News* op-ed by a member of Concerned Women for America, an organization allied with Schlafly's Eagle Forum, called Rosemary out by name: "Recent hearings of the Presidential Commission on the Assignment of Women in the Armed Forces featured a number of military women who are dead set on lifting the ban on women in combat. These women claim they only want 'equality,' but the policies they are pushing demand that women and men be treated anything but equally. 'Separate is inherently unequal,' US Navy Commander Rosemary

Mariner stated before the commission. She blamed the ban on women in combat on 'bigotry' within the Armed Forces. If what Commander Mariner said is correct and separate is indeed unequal, then a lot would have to be done to rectify the situation."

In an essay in the October 1992 *National Review* titled "The Feminist Assault on the Military," conservative commentator David Horowitz portrayed Rosemary as a power-hungry proponent of a radical agenda, in league with "gender feminists" who covertly "have little interest in questions of America's national security because they believe America is a patriarchal, sexist, racist oppressor whose institutions must be transformed beyond recognition."

Describing Rosemary as "one of the leading advocates of equal military roles," he dismissed her testimony about institutional bias against women and sexual harassment as emblematic of the "emotional element that is introduced by the moral posturing of the Left." Decrying predatory behavior and demanding justice was really about accumulating power and controlling resources. "Rosemary Mariner is a candidate for admiral," he wrote, though she wasn't even a captain yet.

For her part, Rosemary had some withering words for her critics. In a paper for the National War College, where she earned a master's degree in national security, she singled out Schlafly and placed her in some shameful company.

"The reason why people choose to believe . . . myths of racism and sexism is because they fill a need for recognition without having to earn it," she wrote in the report, which cited, among other sources, the Bible, Machiavelli, Plato, Ralph Ellison, Shelby Steele, and W. E. B. Du Bois. "The Ku Klux Klansman who burns crosses to intimidate black families or misogynist who physically assaults a female soldier are extreme examples. The pettiness of a male officer who must constantly badmouth females or the vocal 'combat lawyer' are more common examples. A strong personality, such as David Duke or Phyllis Schlafly, can successfully employ these themes by playing to the abject, fearful side of human nature. The degree of hostility displayed towards blacks or women is directly proportional to the depth of insecurity in the bigot."

She added this during a seminar in 1995:

What you have with a lot of women [is that] the idea of equality is very frightening. What you are hiding behind is the myth of what we call the true woman . . . the whole idea that women have a higher, different moral reasoning than men. It goes back to this myth that women are somehow inherently different than men when it comes to issues of character or spirit.

In order to maintain the pretense that it's okay to want to be a coward and to hide behind your sex, you have to make all women like this, not just yourself. To me, that in a nutshell is the whole driving philosophy behind Phyllis Schlafly. The genesis of the anti–Equal Rights Movement and the backlash to the equity feminism, as it's called now, goes back to the idea that, "I would be judged by the same standards, potentially as harshly as men, if I enter this world." So, for example, in Phyllis Schlafly's day, the epitome of being a woman was to marry well, be attractive, be smart and all these other things, and have a family. She had achieved that. Now, in order to gain the same recognition, she would have to go spend eight years in medical school and be a brain surgeon. Maybe she wouldn't see her family every night. Maybe she would have to make some of those difficult choices that men have always had to make, the sacrifices in their personal lives and all the hard work that's involved to get the same recognition.

But it wasn't just outspoken conservatives who opposed rolling back the combat exclusion.

In an op-ed responding to an appearance by servicewomen, including Rosemary, on the *Today* show, a self-described feminist wrote:

There aren't many advantages to being the weaker sex, but being denied equal access to napalm and shrapnel has to be one of them. Demanding the right to get blown to smithereens or shot out of the sky has to be one of the stupidest things feminists have done this century. If it were up to me, I'd be real quiet about this combat deal and hope that no one notices that women don't get drafted.

My apologies to the female pilots who distinguished themselves during Desert Storm and the women reservists who were called up and went and sometimes left little children behind. What these women did for their country is more than heroic. I can understand why they want to be able to rise through the ranks and exercise their talents as fully as any man. It's fine to say that if a woman can fly a plane as well as a man, drive a tank, shoot an M-16 rifle, her gender shouldn't prevent her from doing all that she is able. But if there were ever a time that women should be careful what they ask for lest they should get it, this is it. . . .

Even Cmdr. Rosemary Mariner, a Navy flier and proponent of women in combat . . . acknowledged that only 12 percent of the military women surveyed said they would volunteer for combat. Mariner's argument was classic feminist theology: "Those who are qualified should be allowed to compete." . . . That sounds good in theory and works in civilian life. But war isn't theory. And it isn't civil. When it comes to equal opportunity to die in combat, this is one feminist who'll pass.

Chapter Thirteen

Tailhook

On the day Captain Kathleen Bruyere announced Commander Rosemary Mariner's selection as skipper of VAQ-34 before an audience of two hundred navy women, she had come to their conference directly from an investigation into sexual harassment at the Naval Academy. Among the incidents was an attack six months before, in December 1989, on a midshipman named Gwen Dreyer. Male classmates had handcuffed her to a urinal and taken pictures; one of the guys had pantomimed urinating on her as others applauded.

Academy officials took two months before deciding to hold a hearing. Some of the accused warned Dreyer, the third generation in her family to attend the Academy, not to testify. Her father was told by the brass that they had the pictures in their possession, and they proved she was complicit, since they didn't show her crying or screaming.

After an internal investigation, Academy officials ruled the attack was not premeditated, and so didn't rise to the level of hazing, which would have been grounds for expulsion. When it was all over, two of the male midshipmen got demerits and a loss of leave time. Six got written warnings. The punishment for an assault brushed off as an "isolated incident," "good-natured hijinks," and "a good-natured exchange" that got out of hand was roughly equivalent to the penalty for being drunk in uniform.

"After the whole thing was over, one of the guys told my roommate that this kind of thing was going to keep happening until we, the female midshipmen, got a sense of humor," Dreyer told the *Los Angeles Times*.

Frustrated with the Academy's response, she resigned after final exams at the end of the semester.

Commander Mary Purdy, adviser to the Academy's superintendent on women's issues, told the *San Diego Union-Tribune* that women had trouble being accepted "not because of our minority status; it's the fact we don't go into combat roles." Agreed one male graduating senior, "The big problem you run into here is that once they (women) graduate, they cannot serve in a combat assignment. That . . . generates some bad feelings."

An aggravating factor, said retired vice admiral William Lawrence, was James H. Webb's 1979 magazine article, "Women Can't Fight." It was, Lawrence said, "one of the most difficult problems I had to deal with" as the Academy's superintendent from 1978 to 1981, when the first female midshipmen graduated—among them, his daughter, Wendy. The article "dropped on us like a bombshell," he said. "It had a great impact on morale" among the women, and it took "a great effort to deal with the young macho male types" who saw the article as permission to victimize their female classmates. Its influence was insidious. When Lawrence returned to teach at the Academy after retiring in the mid-1980s, the paper reported, he "discovered that some male midshipmen had formed a 'cult' around Webb's article, distributing copies to new male midshipmen and plastering excerpts on walls where the women would see them."

It all set the tone for a culture that budding officers absorbed early, said one female midshipman: "When a kid comes here from high school, he doesn't come with those ideas that women are inferior, that women don't belong in the Navy. A lot of it is learned here." Upperclassmen set the example for the young midshipmen. "It's very hard to change attitudes," she said.

The type of harassment Dreyer experienced, the everyday hostility, and the casual attitude from up the chain were exactly what members of a DACOWITS fact-finding panel had encountered in their investigation of treatment of women at military bases around the world.

At the 1987 hearing where DACOWITS vice chairman Judith Gibson testified about rampant sexual harassment and stonewalling by superior officers, Carolyn Becraft told the House Armed Services Committee Subcommittee on Military Personnel and Compensation:

What is the biggest obstacle . . . that military women face in their profession today? It has to be sexual harassment. Nowhere has it been more graphically detailed than in the 1986 and 1987 DACOWITS reports. Secretary Weinberger and the military service secretaries have issued policy statements that sexual harassment will not be tolerated in the armed forces. Yet it is tolerated. Women do not trust the military system to deal with this critical issue.

Sadly, their fears seem to be justified. Attempts to address discrimination and sexual harassment in the military environment are oftentimes met with derision. Actions of the perpetrators of this harassment and discrimination are dismissed with phrases such as, "Boys will be boys," "It was just a crude and tasteless joke," or "That's life." Most often the harasser of military women is a member of the chain of command. . . . Although DOD and the services have issued direct policy statements prohibiting such conduct, which is clearly illegal, rarely have courts-martial been used to punish incidents of sexual harassment. Enforcement has obviously not been rigorously pursued. . . .

Is there anyone in this room who would choose to work and live in the conditions experienced by women in the military as described in the DACOWITS reports or in other press accounts? . . . Would any of us like to live in a community where women cannot walk down the street without being verbally abused or being grabbed by US military men?

Officially, the answer was no, and it seemed the situation had improved, to some degree.

"People are less afraid to report instances of harassment," Bruyere told the two hundred assembled navy women at the conference. "When they are reported, they are dealt with very swiftly."

In March 1990, the navy instituted a formal policy against sexual harassment to codify stricter enforcement and penalties that had been implemented the year before, when new navy secretary Lawrence Garrett declared there would be "zero tolerance." While the Naval Investigative Service (NIS) found a 55 percent increase in reported rapes and sexual assaults at installations worldwide from 1987 to 1990—up to 240 from

155—there was a sense that it was the number of reports, not necessarily the number of assaults, that was on the rise.

A fact-finding panel formed partly in response to the Dreyer attack issued 150 recommendations intended to improve the treatment of women. The panel's chair, Rear Admiral Roberta Hazard, called those recommendations "a recognition that progress has been made," though work still needed to be done. Said Bruyere, "Things are not perfect, but they're getting better. We took a temperature check and the patient is certainly improving."

At the June 1991 Senate subcommittee hearing on women in combat, where air force general Merrill McPeak and Senator William Cohen got into their well-publicized scrap over female aviators, subcommittee chair Senator John Glenn noted: "The integration of women into our all-volunteer force has not been without problems. There were some tough institutional biases at the outset, which were quite daunting. Some of these biases have been overcome but others still remain. For example, even though substantial progress has been made with regard to the problem of sexual harassment in the workplace, the problem still exists and has not been completely corrected."

It was, perhaps, a bit of an understatement. Rosemary Mariner used to say that 10 percent of the people navy women dealt with were very supportive, while 10 percent were jerks who blamed others for their own failings—and women were a particularly easy target. The other 80 percent didn't care about gender as long as everyone did his or her job. But that second 10 percent could do a world of harm, and just three months after Glenn made his assessment, a scandal hit the headlines that focused the worst kind of attention on naval aviation.

The first indication came in response to a question posed at the thirty-fifth annual convention of the Tailhook Association—an independent, navy-sanctioned organization of 18,000 active-duty and retired naval and marine aviators. Some 1,500 officers had been flown to Las Vegas to take part in the September 1991 confab, at a cost to the navy of more than $190,000.

Naval aviator Lieutenant Monica Rivadeneira stood up and asked nine admirals on a symposium panel when women would be allowed to fly tactical combat missions off aircraft carriers. It was the same question Tailhook member Rosemary Mariner, at the time known as Lieutenant Rosemary Conatser, had asked at the 1979 Tailhook convention.

The response to Rivadeneira from the floor was hisses, jeers, and catcalls. The admirals on the dais remained silent. It was a betrayal from within, from comrades and colleagues. But it was nothing compared to what was to come.

Tailhook conventions had always been known for rowdiness and drunken debauchery, and 1991's was no exception. On the third floor of the Las Vegas Hilton, twenty suites catered to tailhookers with booze, porn, strippers, and scantily clad bartenders serving up drinks in penis-shaped vessels, to the tune of about $140,000. For three nights, the hallway outside was a "hot drunken mess," packed with inebriated officers in civilian clothes ambushing women and shoving them through a gantlet of grasping hands, pinching fingers, and biting teeth. Female officers, enlisted women, even hotel guests who just happened to step off the elevator were groped, slapped, and stripped. Anyone trying to get through would spend twenty minutes stumbling down the 140-foot corridor.

As Lieutenant Paula Coughlin, the navy helo pilot who was the first victim to come forward, described it: "The man . . . put both his hands down the front of my tank top and inside my bra where he grabbed my breast . . . I dropped to a forward crouch position and placed my hands on the wrists of my attacker in an attempt to remove his hands. . . . I sank my teeth into the fleshy part of the man's left forearm, biting hard. I thought I drew blood," she said. "I then turned and bit the man on the right hand," she continued. "The man removed his hands and another individual reached up under my skirt and grabbed the crotch of my panties. I kicked one of my attackers . . . I felt as though the group was trying to rape me. I was terrified and had no idea what was going to happen next." Colleagues whom she begged for help did nothing.

"I was attacked by naval officers and marine officers that knew who I was, and it was a sport to them. It was a good time," Coughlin told ABC News. "And it's not a good time. It's against the law. It's criminal. And it's wrong. They wouldn't have done it to their sister. They wouldn't have done it to their wife. They'd be mortified if someone did it to anyone they love. But for them, it was a sport."

Coughlin later told an interviewer: "I've worked my ass off to be one of the guys, to be the best naval officer I can, and prove that women can do whatever the job calls for. And what I got: I was treated like trash. I wasn't one of them."

An admiral's aide, Coughlin sent complaints up the chain of command. They went nowhere. And she got blamed.

"That's what you have to expect when you go up to the third deck with a bunch of drunk aviators," she was told. When a probe was finally launched, one of the investigators propositioned her. Some 1,500 interviews conducted by the Naval Investigative Service turned up not one aviator or senior official initially willing to admit any knowledge of the attacks. A Pentagon report found that "Navy officials deliberately undermined their own investigation to protect their colleagues."

Frustrated with the lack of results, Coughlin went public in July 1992.

"I had an obligation as an officer to stop what was going on in that hallway," she told the *Navy Times*. "I have an obligation as a human being to let everyone know you have to come forward when something bad like that happens. People I don't even know have called and said, 'You did the right thing. . . .' But there are a lot of guys out there who still don't get it."

Ultimately, the probe found that at least twenty-six women, half of them officers, had been assaulted. More victims had simply fled, unidentified. Others stayed quiet or declined to press charges because they somehow felt they were responsible for what happened. Several ultimately filed multimillion-dollar lawsuits against the Tailhook Association and the navy. The navy itself cut ties with the group; after thirty-five years, there would be no more free office space at Naval Air Station Miramar, no more free transportation to the conference, no more time off to attend. (The association formally apologized in August of 1992, promising to ban alcohol and hospitality suites and to establish a free sexual harassment reporting hotline.)

Some 140 navy and marine corps officers were referred for possible disciplinary action, but none went to trial. For half, the charges were dropped. The other half went "to the mast," an administrative proceeding addressing unseemly behavior rather than sexual assault. Participation at the convention was noted as a black mark on any aviator's service record, and thousands of attendees' promotions were delayed.

A separate inspector general's investigation found "a marked absence of moral courage and personal integrity" in the naval aviator community and blamed a failure of leadership.

Garrett, who had attended Tailhook, was removed. So was NIS commander Rear Admiral Duvall Williams, who had likened female naval aviators to "go-go dancers, topless dancers or hookers." So was the navy's judge advocate general, and its inspector general.

For Coughlin, there was punishment as well. She got support from navy women but a chill from navy men. She was grounded, in what she feared was the beginning of a campaign to drive her from the service. Ultimately, she transferred to another unit and got back in the air, flying the CH-53 Sea Stallion with a helicopter combat support squadron out of Norfolk. "You say to yourself, 'I did the right thing, I'm a good person.' But I've run into attitudes, people who don't acknowledge me in a room. After a while you think, what's my job here? To endure, or to come to work and do my job?"

She added: "If it happened all over again, I would do the same thing, probably sooner. I look at many of these guys (who still don't get it) and I think to myself, 'It was their Navy. It's soon going to be my generation's Navy.'"

To Commander Rosemary Mariner, "a minority of jerks" was giving naval aviators a bad name, and she spoke out on Coughlin's behalf in a 1993 interview: "Paula did what any self-respecting naval aviator would have done if they felt they'd been attacked or abused. She stood up for herself and kept with it."

Rosemary, seeing parallels between women's struggle for equality and the civil rights movement, compared Coughlin to Rosa Parks. "The fact that she had the courage to take a stand—that always makes a difference. When one individual has the courage not to accept something that's wrong, it inspires other people to have the courage to stand up."

Had just one admiral at the symposium voiced support for female aviators when the catcalls started, she told the *Los Angeles Times*, "Do you think the group of junior officers on the third floor would have thought of that when they decided to have a little fun? . . . Sexual harassment will continue to be a problem in the military services as long as women are barred from combat duty—as long as we are considered institutionally inferior. Just as in matters of race, separate is inherently unequal."

The day after the investigation ended, with no assault charges or courts-martial, Coughlin resigned, writing, "The physical attack on me . . . at the 1991 Tailhook convention, and the covert and overt attacks on me that followed, have stripped me of my ability to serve."

A 1992 analysis of the scandal's roots blamed what new navy secretary Sean O'Keefe called "a cultural problem which has allowed demeaning behavior and attitudes towards women in uniform," caused in large measure by restrictions on career assignments that perpetuated a view of women as unequal and inferior. It cited an updated report on the progress of female navy personnel that described a "warrior mentality," implying that "women don't belong."

None of this was a surprise to Commander Joellen Drag Oslund. The attacks, attitudes, and outcomes were all sickeningly familiar.

During her first two-week deployment with Commander Fleet Air Mediterranean Reserve Unit 1082 in Naples in February 1989, four officers, including the CO, came to her hotel room. She was the unit's administrative officer, one of perhaps five women among twenty-two or so men. It was a "red light" visit—unannounced—late at night. Drunk, the four barged in. Two unzipped their pants and lounged around, having a conversation, with their genitals hanging out. When she told them they needed to leave, she was thrown onto the bed, pinned down, and groped under her sweater. Finally, they left. She filed charges the next day.

"You don't think those kinds of things are going to happen to you as a senior officer," she says. "It did, and it was horrible." She was lucky; things could have gotten much worse.

There had always been pushback against women doing "men's" jobs, she says, but in the late 1980s and early 1990s there was a groundswell of antagonism. "Women were becoming senior officers," she says. "That's when things get bad. Junior officers are no threat. Six pilots are no threat." But with their numbers growing, women were increasingly moving into areas that men felt were their domain, and they didn't want to share. "They were extremely resentful of the fact that women were flying jets," says Joellen. "It just escalated. The Good Old Boys' Club was not in the least interested in giving that up."

Her commanding officer was relieved of duty at their Louisiana-based unit and court-martialed in Pensacola on charges of sexual harassment, assault, and indecent exposure. Joellen testified; three enlisted women, she said, had told her of a pattern of harassment in the unit, a "steady stream of harassing remarks." The skipper admitted exposing himself in the Naples hotel room but tried to laugh it off as a joke. Joellen, the defense claimed, had enjoyed the party.

In October 1989, he pleaded guilty to conduct unbecoming an officer and was dropped to the bottom of the seniority list for captains in the Reserve. Two of the other officers received admiral's mast administrative hearings. The fourth was disciplined within the unit.

After returning to her unit for monthly drills, Joellen encountered a hostile environment. Like Coughlin, she transferred out.

"Knowing what I knew at the time, Tailhook came as no surprise," Joellen says. What had happened to her in Naples was different only by a matter of degree.

Had her attackers been disciplined more severely, she believes, Tailhook might not have happened. The navy, she said in a 1992 interview, "passed up a good opportunity to do something about sexual harassment three years ago."

Embarrassed on an international scale by Tailhook, the navy decided to "do something about" it. In spring 1992, Admiral Frank Kelso, chief of naval operations, announced a regimen of instruction and discipline for all navy personnel, starting with trainees at Pensacola, to combat sexual harassment in the ranks. He said navy men would have to "make fundamental changes in some of our behavior and our way of dealing with women, and even in some of our long-held traditions." By the following September, everyone in the navy would have to undergo a daylong sexual harassment seminar. Offenders found guilty of harassment would be discharged.

Still, on June 18, during something called the "Tomcat Follies," sexual slurs were lobbed at Representative Patricia Schroeder in a lewd skit at the Miramar Officers' Club. Schroeder had introduced the House bill two years before to remove the restriction on female aviators flying in combat, and she had sharply criticized the navy's handling of the Tailhook scandal.

Nationally syndicated columnist Ellen Goodman connected the dots in a scathing July 1992 article headlined "Navy Must Learn Harassment Won't Be Tolerated." She began by describing the endurance and bravery of a female Gulf War POW who had been brutalized and sodomized by Iraqi troops and then asked, "But what of the military women who suffered from what can only be called 'the friendly fire' of sexual assault? The women who were attacked by the men on their side, our side. The women brutalized by their officers, or their peers. American men who treated American women as if they were the enemy?"

She continued: "Rosemary Mariner, the president of Women Military Aviators and a member of Tailhook herself, compares these assaults to what happened to blacks in the old South. She calls them a 'tar and feathering.' She believes the atmosphere was poisoned not just by booze and strippers and porno flicks. Psychological permission for the disparagement of women was also granted at the Tailhook symposium, says Mariner, when a chant went up against women pilots on aircraft carriers—'No Women in TAC Air!' No senior aviator stopped it. Such hostility was seen two years ago when a female Naval Academy student was chained to a urinal by male midshipmen. It was seen three weeks ago, when an obscene banner directed at Rep. Pat Schroeder, member of the Armed Services Committee, was unfurled at Miramar Naval Air Station in California. The backlash, the gantlet, is not just on the third floor of the Hilton Hotel in Las Vegas."

For his part, conservative columnist David Horowitz, in the same essay that disparaged Rosemary as a power-hungry proponent of a radical feminist agenda, dismissed the entire chain of events: "A series of relatively trivial incidents (a joke about women's sexual excuses, a skit mocking a female member of Congress) and a drunken party at which crotches were grabbed in a gauntlet ritual have fueled a national hysteria about 'sexual harassment' and a political witch hunt that is threatening to deconstruct the military in the way other institutions have been deconstructed before."

By Rosemary's reckoning, some deconstructing was definitely in order.

"Despite the fact that many officers, including senior officers, refused to cooperate with the official [Tailhook] investigation, the Navy's only formal action was to send 'training packages' to fleet units in 'an attempt to help Navy people shape important "core values" that would keep them from wanting to commit harassment,'" she wrote in a report at the National War College. "The reason why a minority of men harass women is because they can get away with it. They get away with it because, no matter how many messages or training packages are sent proclaiming 'zero tolerance of sexual harassment,' the fact is that civilian and military leadership still holds, by word and deed, that women aren't good enough to fight. From the constant verbal abuse so many military women put up with to the criminal acts of a Tailhook debacle, sexual harassment will continue because the combat exclusion laws and policies make women institutionally inferior."

And not long before she took up her post with the Joint Chiefs of Staff, she said on *The MacNeil/Lehrer NewsHour*: "All of my twenty years . . . in this business tells me that if you cannot share the equal risks and hazards in arduous duty, then you are not equal. And if the institution can discriminate against you, then it's not a big leap for . . . bigots to decide that, 'Well, I can harass you and I can get away with it.'"

The *New York Times* highlighted that quote in an editorial: "The best guidelines . . . may have been proffered already—by Cmdr. Rosemary Mariner, a former naval aviator and commander of a jet squadron, during a recent interview. . . . In short, what has been proven true for minorities is just as true for women. Unless people get the chance to prove they can do as good a job as the next guy, whether on an assembly line or in aerial combat, the next guy's going to push them around."

Pointing out that she was speaking for herself, not the navy, Rosemary provided some valuable context to interviewer Judy Woodruff: "I was of a generation in the early '70s . . . in which this kind of thing was more common. And one of the things that has happened over the last twenty years is that it is not as common as it used to be, that women are not in a position where they are defenseless. But it is up to them and up to the commanding officers that are responsible for them to make sure these incidents come forward."

In Tailhook, she saw a silver lining of sorts to a very dark cloud.

The scandal kept navy women's second-class status "in the public eye, and that helped," she told the *Los Angeles Times.* "The Navy leadership has always wanted to do the right thing. And Tailhook maybe helped them focus on what the right thing is."

Several senior officers saw their names pulled from nomination for promotion in the aftermath of the scandal, one because of his handling of the Dreyer case at the Naval Academy. And Kelso, who called Tailhook a "watershed event"—though other officers termed it a witch hunt—would retire early, in April 1994, to "close this difficult chapter."

CHAPTER FOURTEEN

The Exclusion Finally Falls

THE HEADLINE IN THE *BOSTON GLOBE* SAID IT ALL: "NAVY LEADS IN Opening Combat Roles to Women."

For eight months, the Presidential Commission on the Assignment of Women in the Armed Forces had taken testimony from more than three hundred witnesses at thirty public hearings and visited thirty-one military installations, at a cost of $4 million in taxpayer dollars.

Finally, on November 3, 1992—Election Day—the commission's nine men and six women voted 8–7 to recommend that women be allowed to serve on navy combat ships, except submarines and amphibious vessels. But they should not participate in ground combat and needed to be shielded from any hypothetical draft, and Congress should reinstate the combat ban on female pilots, of whom, throughout the military, there were nearly nine hundred.

Former navy secretary Sean O'Keefe called the commission's recommendations "a fish and rabbit stew" that, in putting women on combat ships but not in combat cockpits, was thoroughly lacking in logic.

The formal report issued a week later "had a little bit to make everybody mad," commission member Charles Moskos, a sociology professor at Northwestern University, told the *Tampa Tribune*. "We gave a mixed message. But that reflects Department of Defense thinking and public opinion. I hope it was all worth it."

He noted that rather than focusing on the capabilities of women or military readiness, much of the commission's debate centered on the political and social. Shirley Sagawa of the National Women's Law Center, one of the organizations involved in lobbying the Senate to repeal the combat exclusion, told the paper, "A lot of the testimony was along the lines that a woman's place is in the home. Some expressed concern that if more women are placed in harm's way, there would be less [public] support for military intervention."

Several weeks before the report's formal release, Sagawa had written this evaluation of the commission's efforts in a "Women in the Military Issue Paper": "Although members of the Commission have made efforts to ensure that relevant issues are fully and fairly aired, draft findings have been strongly biased against increasing assignment of women."

She noted that while the panel included no active proponents of increasing women's military roles, it did have several long-standing opponents, and they had used the commission to promote their views. Among these was Elaine Donnelly, who had gone head-to-head with Commander Rosemary Mariner on national television. She and four other commission members had walked out of the voting—"The Fade-out Five," the *Navy Times* called them—and had demanded, and gotten, their own section in the final report, titled "Alternative Views: The Case Against Women in Combat."

Sagawa echoed Moskos's observation that cultural issues ate up time that should have gone to discussion of military effectiveness—and generally took the perspective of right-wing organizations. The conversation focused on problems, not solutions, and the final report, she wrote, omitted expert witness testimony about ways to make changes work. There was also no inquiry into problems posed by restrictions already in place, and the panel chose not to conduct any research or gather any empirical evidence beyond an opinion poll, relying instead on witnesses' experiential, anecdotal, or opinion testimony.

Among those opinion witnesses was Phyllis Schlafly, who testified that "mothering is more important than flying a plane or driving a tank," and told the *Tampa Tribune*, "It's contrary to our culture to send our women to kill our enemies, and it would make our country the laughing-stock of the world." Then, invoking the Tailhook scandal, Schlafly added: "If these women can't protect themselves in a Las Vegas hotel, how can they protect themselves in combat?"

In the same article, Rosemary countered that—speaking from personal experience—male pilots accept female pilots who can do the job: "When the shooting starts, it's the size of the fight in the dog—not the size of the dog."

But in the end, the commission's vote didn't really matter. Neither did its report, which had been submitted to President George W. Bush but whose recommendations would have to be implemented—or not—by his successor, Bill Clinton.

Opportunities for military women, particularly in the navy, were already expanding. Female sailors had been serving aboard a "combat-equipped ship," the frigate USS *Bowen*, since February 1992. Its designation as a training ship for reservists opened a loophole that made the assignment of eleven enlisted women and one female officer legal. Even before the presidential commission issued its findings, the navy named its own advisory group that recommended accelerating equal opportunities for female naval aviators and, until Section 6015 was rescinded, reclassifying combat ships as support vessels to open those billets to women. The navy also looked to draw up legislation ending the ban. Maritime surveillance aircraft that flew with all-male crews would be opened to female pilots.

In the wake of Tailhook, the navy was working to integrate women as never before. There was mixed-gender boot camp, where men and women slept in separate quarters but otherwise trained together from wake-up at 0330—3:30 a.m.—until lights out. (Some men "just got mad because I could always do the push-ups," a female recruit told the *St. Louis Post-Dispatch*; a female chief petty officer said the women wanted to keep up with the men, while for out-of-shape men, being beaten by women was a huge incentive to raise their game.) There were also tough rules against sexual harassment, formal anti-harassment training, clearer definitions of off-limits behaviors, and a complaint resolution system spelling out everyone's responsibility, "from the victim and the perpetrator to the commander and the co-worker."

But with the post–Cold War drawdown, the military needed to shrink, and the navy risked losing billets for women it was trying so hard to attract and retain. For example, the training carrier *Forrestal*, whose crew included six hundred female sailors, was scheduled for retirement.

Submarine and destroyer tenders, support ships where many women served, were to be taken out of service. The air force, Rosemary told her Smithsonian audience in 2011, "announced that it was eliminating some eight hundred Training Command instructor pilot billets, jobs like flying T-38s, T-37s that women had held for years. Navy women jet pilots were being told by their detailers that if combat aviation didn't open up soon, they might as well get out of the navy. Female military aviators were being driven out of tactical aviation."

Finding more slots for women was essential.

Moskos drew a direct line between the navy's push to open more jobs to women and its need to counter the fallout from Tailhook, especially as release of the official report on the scandal loomed in the months following Clinton's January 1993 inauguration.

Sean O'Keefe, who had been brought in to clean up the mess, called it "institutional shock therapy."

Or, as the *Boston Globe* put it: "The Navy, embarrassed by its aviators' demeaning treatment of women in the Tailhook scandal, has suddenly become the driving force behind the Clinton administration's determination to let women fight for their country alongside men" (though combat wouldn't fully open to women until 2015).

The *New York Times* summed it up nicely in an editorial on April 12, 1993:

Last year, a commission on expanding women's roles in the military delivered a remarkably unhelpful report to President Bush. Some members focused on what really matters: performance. But others bent their minds to irrelevancies like male gallantry and "commonly shared cultural assumptions defining how men should treat women."

Adm. Frank B. Kelso 2d, the Chief of Naval Operations, has already taken a more straightforward view, in effect junking the commission's work. He wants to expand the role of women, first by opening up the number of shipboard jobs and eventually by allowing women to serve in combat.

There may be a public relations motive here; the admiral's initiative could sweeten the aroma that's sure to rise from the Navy's final report on the 1991 Tailhook convention—a reunion of aviators featuring blue movies, male streakers and a gantlet of drunken gropers through which female guests, among them 15 officers, were forced to run.

No matter. The admiral's concern with giving women a fair chance speaks directly to the point raised by a former naval aviator, Cmdr. Rosemary Mariner: "If the institution can discriminate against you, then it's not a big leap for . . . bigots to decide that, 'Well, I can harass you and I can get away with it.'"

While Admiral Kelso is trying to widen women's roles in the Navy, the Air Force seems bent on shrinking them. It plans to stop training female students on high-performance training aircraft; such training is an essential step toward flying combat aircraft. Meanwhile the Army, as one general put it, is keeping "its head down."

Defense Secretary Les Aspin can't afford to keep his head down. Last week he spoke of the need for "consistency" among the services' deployment of women, and the need "to do something on it." Admiral Kelso's bold proposal, and gender-neutral testing for specific jobs, makes a fine starting point.

Just a few days later, the issue came up, as these things seemed to, at the DACOWITS spring meeting.

Rosemary described the scene during her Smithsonian speech:

On April 18, 1993, DACOWITS held their spring conference in Washington, DC, hosted by the Air Force. The opening session was chaired by Chief of Staff General Merrill McPeak, who gave the standard remarks and then opened the floor to questions. Immediately, hands went up from a row of good-looking women pilots in their uniforms.

Knowing that General McPeak would lock on the best-looking one, navy lieutenant Kara Hultgreen stood up, and he took her question. She asked why he needed to wait for the secretary of defense to act when the law had been repealed two years ago. General McPeak answered by saying he thought it was a mistake to put women in bombers and fighters. And then he talked about unit cohesion. Kara came right back at him—my husband had to hold her down. At first, it looked like the general was going to dress the lieutenant down. But then he reversed and became philosophical, mentioning that his feelings didn't fit Aristotelian logic.

A few questions later, General McPeak called on another good-looking navy pilot, F-18 test pilot Lieutenant Commander Lori Melling Gattuso. In a precise way, Lori began, "You say that it is unit cohesion that makes you oppose women in tactical aviation squadrons. Correct?" He affirmed the premise. She then continued: "And you had men and women flying together in tanker and transport squadrons, including AWACS, during Desert Storm. Did you have a problem with unit cohesion in those squadrons?" He hesitated and said, "Not that I'm aware of." "So," she finished, "why do you think that your fighter pilots are any less professional than the rest of your male pilots?"

General McPeak started to ramble. Something about not having to experience a thing to know that it is evil. Going into a burning building. And there, in front of DACOWITS and the press, General McPeak spun out of control. However, General McPeak, God bless his honesty, is a good fighter pilot, and he lived to fight another day.

Several weeks later, when combat aviation was opened to women, he beat out the navy by staging the first press conference, making it look like the air force was going to have fighter pilots before the navy.

So finally, on April 28, 1993, now-Secretary of Defense Les Aspin held a major press conference with the service chiefs standing behind him, announcing that he was now directing the services to open combat aviation to women, and ordering the Navy to draft legislation to repeal the remaining law dealing with ships. The fight to fly at sea had finally been won.

Now that women could fly combat, where was the military going to find them?

An Associated Press headline on April 28, 1993, had something of an answer: "At Long Last, Rosie the Riveter Can Be a Top Gun." The story introduced Air Force 2nd Lieutenant Jeannie Flynn, who had graduated first in her flight school class but hadn't been allowed to fly jet fighters. Now—despite what McPeak described at the DACOWITS conference as a "culturally based hang-up; I can't get over this image of old men ordering young women into combat"—she was about to begin training in the world's most advanced fighter, the F-15E Strike Eagle. The navy identified about one hundred of its top-rated female aviators as potential candidates for transition to such combat aircraft as the carrier-based A-6 Intruder bomber. The army tapped about a half-dozen of its female combat support and observation helo pilots to begin flying Apache and Cobra attack helicopters. The Marine Corps, which had no female aviators, would start remedying that "by the day after tomorrow," said Commandant Carl Mundy.

"The essence of the new policy is that the military services are to open up more specialties and assignments to women," Aspin said at the press conference announcing the changes. "The services will be able to call on a much larger pool of talent to perform the vital tasks that our military forces must perform in the post–Cold War world." Kelso, whose branch was far out ahead of the others, told the assembled reporters that the navy was "good to go." But he was upstaged by McPeak, who—apparently having gotten over his "hang-up"—staged a press conference immediately after Aspin's to introduce to the media three future female air force combat pilots.

In a *USA Today* story headlined "Search On for Female Pilots // Candidates for Combat Role Sought," Kate Walsh O'Beirne—one of the presidential commission's "Fadeout Five"—predicted that women aviators would be "leap-frogged" over men for combat slots. "We're going to have an affirmative action Air Force," O'Beirne said.

Responded US Navy Admiral R. J. Zlatoper: Women "will displace no one," as assignment to aircraft would be gender-neutral. "The bottle-neck is the training squadron. Obviously, there's a one-to-one swap-out. If a woman goes into a combat squadron, then someone else has to go to a support squadron."

The story continued: "Cmdr. Rosemary Mariner, the first woman to command a Navy aviation squadron and now working for the Joint Chiefs of Staff, said 'some small number' of men will conclude 'that "someone is getting my F-18."' But I don't think that's going to be a major issue. I am absolutely personally opposed to any kind of quota or ceiling."

"The more people you have competing for the jobs, the higher the quality you'll get," Rosemary told the Associated Press in the "Rosie the Riveter" story.

"If only one female Naval Aviator qualifies for a combat slot," she added in *USA Today*, "it doesn't matter."

In fact, many more than one qualified. Though female naval aviators had to catch up on some specialized training in warfare tactics that men routinely received, they were already working as test pilots, landing on carriers, simulating aerial attacks in aggressor squadrons, and teaching male pilots to fly some of the nation's most advanced fighters. Within just a few months, women were training in combat billets and completing night carrier qualifications, and by April 1994, more than sixty female pilots and flight crew members had received orders to combat squadrons. Hundreds of navy women, including helo, EA-6B Prowler, and F/A-18 jet pilots, were being assigned to the aircraft carriers *Eisenhower* in the Atlantic and *Abraham Lincoln* in the Pacific, bound for duty in the Mediterranean and Persian Gulf.

It was too late for the original female naval aviators; now, it was up to the next generation to make history of its own.

Commander Rosemary Mariner offered some perspective in a February 1994 CNN discussion of women in the military post-Tailhook, after Kelso announced his early retirement in hopes of closing the book on the scandal once and for all (questions below are paraphrased, but Rosemary's responses are direct quotes):

Q: *How have things changed in the three years since Tailhook?*

A: I remember how things were when I first entered the navy and when "politically correct" meant no women. Things have changed in the last several years because there is an awareness that when you mistreat any sailor or soldier, that that is improper and unprofessional behavior. And that lesson was driven home very much that—all the circumstances surrounding Tailhook—that we have that obligation as members of the service.

Q: *Was your career hampered by your own lack of combat experience?*

A: I was able to succeed because I had the support of many good senior men and women and also the support of my juniors. So people like me succeed because we had that, and in an environment that made it otherwise difficult. It's not an issue for me because of my relative seniority. I'm too old to play in this now. . . . I would love to have the opportunity to be twenty-two and start over again. And yes, I very much wanted to [fly combat], particularly when I first entered the navy. The perspective I think we need to retain on this is that many of these changes were already going on prior to Tailhook. The combat exclusion law concerning aviation was repealed before Tailhook occurred, and it was a result of Desert Storm. So what Desert Storm showed is that women had already been in combat—you were good enough to die for your country—so the issue became, were you good enough to fight. . . .

If my daughter wants to aspire to some of these positions, I certainly don't want her to be artificially restrained from doing so, based on some factor other than her competence to do so. [Her daughter, Emmalee, was born later that year.]

Q: *What are your thoughts on strength / endurance / unit cohesion arguments against servicewomen in combat?*

A: When women first entered naval aviation, the same things were said about women flying military aircraft and our ability to bond with our male counterparts. These things are evolutionary. It took twenty years to reach this point in military aviation. It took ten years with women aboard ships, and I think that eventually you will see that happening in other areas, such as ground combat.

Q: *What are your thoughts on persistent sexism?*

A: The only way that you convince people . . . who doubt is for them to see with their own eyes. They have to work with these people, and the women that pioneer these fields have got to be tough. There is no easy way. You just go do it.

If there was any doubt about their continuing place in history, the headline in the April 5, 1993, issue of *Navy Times* spelled it out: "New Captains Have Flown Against Tradition." It was an announcement of four new captains-select: Jane O'Dea, Rosemary Mariner, Joellen Oslund, and Commander Lin Hutton, a member of the second class of female naval aviators and the first woman to command a fleet support squadron.

Trailblazers, pioneers, the vanguard—whatever the word, these four women have lived a life of firsts. . . .

Now, Cmdrs. Jane O'Dea, Rosemary Mariner, Linda Hutton, and reservist Joellen Oslund have all added to their list—first female aviators to make captain, and all on the first try.

Their lives have not been easy, and they are not thin-skinned.

They have at times faced the open hostility of some men, constant presumption in the early years that they could not do the job, battles for equal flight training with men and the court fight that opened the way for women to at least be temporarily detached to ships.

In fact, Judith Neuffer Bruner had made captain two years before, in November 1991, in the Reserve. No longer serving in flying assignments, Judy had had three command tours, all in Washington: She had served as skipper of a computer processing unit at the Navy Yard; as director of the Science and Technology Reserve Program; and as skipper of the head-quarters unit at the Office of Naval Research and of the reserve logistics unit at OP 04 at the Pentagon. At the time the others were selected, Judy was a branch head at NASA's Goddard Space Flight Center.

Jane was skipper of the Navy Recruitment Command in Indianap-olis; Rosemary was with the Joint Staff at the Pentagon; and Joellen was stationed in Florida with her Reserve unit while her husband was serving with the US Central Command.

For Joellen, the promotion came as a surprise, because she was already retired from the navy. Or so she thought.

It was an echo of what had happened twenty-one years before, when Lieutenant (j.g.) Joellen Drag wrote to the secretary of the navy seeking permission to land on ships with the rest of her squadron. She sent her letter of resignation up the chain of command—and it vanished.

"I don't know what happens with my letters," Joellen says, "but they seem to get lost. I waited for a reply and heard nothing. Then I got a call at home. My husband picked up the phone, and it was an administrative person from the Reserve unit in Tampa. He says, 'Can I speak to Captain Oslund?' My husband says, 'Speaking.' The caller says, 'No, the other Captain Oslund.'

"I got promoted after I resigned."

Being one of the "women that pioneer these fields," as Rosemary Mariner put it, was a double-edged sword.

An F-18 lieutenant commander quoted in the Associated Press "Rosie the Riveter" story inadvertently foreshadowed what was to come. Male or female, he said, pilots who didn't meet the same strict standards of performance would be weeded out. But: "The first time we kick a gal out, I'm sure there's going to be all kinds of flak."

What happened turned out to be far worse.

The "gal" was Lieutenant Kara Hultgreen, the same naval aviator who had confronted McPeak at the DACOWITS conference. And she wasn't kicked out—she was killed.

Hultgreen was the navy's first fully qualified female fleet fighter pilot, assigned to the *Abraham Lincoln*. It was a billet she'd wanted, badly. She'd repeatedly put in for transfers and roamed the corridor at DACOWITS conferences in her flight suit, advocating for her chance. But just months after she qualified for combat, Hultgreen lost her left engine while lining up to land on the carrier as it prepared for deployment off Naval Air Station Miramar. Coming in at an approach angle too steep to recover as the carrier pitched and rolled at sea, the F-14A Tomcat crashed in the Pacific Ocean. Her navigator ejected; she didn't get out in time.

In the previous two years, nine male naval aviators had died in training accidents in that same hard-to-handle aircraft. But none had received the attention that was focused on Hultgreen. Faxes and anonymous phone calls to local media in San Diego blamed political correctness that had supposedly lowered standards for women to hurry them into combat carrier billets. They claimed her flight skills were inadequate, though navy records showed that Hultgreen was an average to above-average aviator, third of seven in her class. The official accident report and video blamed

engine failure far more than pilot error. Eight of nine attempts to repli-
cate the incident in a flight simulator ended with a crash.

"All too often we forget how narrow the margin of safety is in naval
carrier aviation," said Vice Admiral Robert J. Spane, Commander, Naval
Air Force Pacific. "This pilot did her best to keep this aircraft flying under
conditions that were all but impossible."

While male pilots' crashed F-14s were left on the ocean floor, the
navy spent more than $100,000 locating and raising Hultgreen's Tom-
cat and recovering her body, still strapped into the pilot's seat. She was
buried with full military honors at Arlington National Cemetery in a
ceremony attended by top navy brass. The men were not. Their obituaries
appeared in their hometown papers; hers made national headlines.

The whisper campaign, couched as promoting the interests of safety
and combat readiness, seeped into the national consciousness. "It was an
unheard-of breach of naval aviation etiquette to question the flight record
of a pilot who had gone down," Jean Zimmerman wrote in *Tailspin*. "It
was just not done. Except with Kara Hultgreen."

Even worse, portions of her confidential training records, and those of
another female combat pilot, were stolen by a crew member and illegally
given to Elaine Donnelly. (The carrier by now had been nicknamed "the
Babe-raham Lincoln." Its counterpart in the Atlantic, the *Eisenhower*—
the Ike—was similarly dubbed "the Dyke." There had been predictions
that because of the five hundred women in the crew, the *Eisenhower*
would be unable to leave Norfolk for the Mediterranean on time. It did.)
Donnelly, Rosemary Mariner's longtime opponent on matters of women
in the military, published excerpts from the training records in a report
that billed them as proof of a double standard.

A second navy investigation into Hultgreen's accident refuted those
allegations but emphasized pilot error more prominently than the first
report did; investigators, including members of her squadron on the carrier, noted that all of the *Lincoln*'s pilots had met the same standards, but
the women had received more help.

Rosemary was having none of it. It was, she said, "the sliming of
Kara."

She was the keynote speaker at the dedication, in Hultgreen's memory, of an F-14 displayed outside the Arnold Engineering Development Center aerospace test facility in Tennessee. That particular jet had been flown in Hultgreen's unit, the Black Lions of Fighter Squadron 213. Rosemary told the story of Hultgreen's encounter with McPeak; comparing flying an F-14 to dancing with an elephant, she said Hultgreen had grown to love it and gotten good at it.

The plaque on the display read: "Lt. Kara Hultgreen, USN, naval aviation pioneer."

Donnelly's report spurred new efforts to have Congress reinstate the ban on women in combat aviation. She claimed in the *Chicago Tribune* that there was a navy cover-up of supposed pilot error by Hultgreen and that women were being pushed into fighter jets in an attempt to burnish the navy's tarnished image after Tailhook.

But her allegations were belied by the service of America's female combat pilots. Hultgreen was one of 54 in the navy; the air force had 316, 8 of them flying bombers; the army, 367 flying combat helos, including 8 in attack helicopters. The 14 women aviators and aircrew members on the *Lincoln* and the 12 on the *Ike* completed their first cruises admirably and without incident. They flew patrols off Haiti and Bosnia, and over Iraq and Kuwait, just like their male counterparts. And in accomplishing their mission, they made history of their own.

Still, in light of Donnelly's report, seven female naval aviators, including three of the six on the *Lincoln*, were reevaluated for flight duty, with the risk of losing their wings. From the navy to the National Guard, there was forceful pushback against female fighter pilots in particular. Posting their pictures in bathrooms was a favorite tactic for making aggrieved men's feelings known. One female veteran test pilot, whose otherwise all-male squadron decided she simply "would not fit in," was made to repeat qualifications already successfully completed. Denied training, support, encouragement, and mentorship that kept novice male fighter pilots from washing out, female aviators were ostracized and disparaged, then faulted for receiving extra training, which was then cited as evidence of favoritism. One navy helicopter commander refused to fly with women during a mission in Haiti, over what he said were religious objections.

The women pushed back, saying that yes, a double standard was at play, but cutting the other way: Errors overlooked in male pilots drew laser-focused attention when committed by a woman.

Some of the worst offenders in fostering a climate of hostility and discrimination saw their careers stalled. But skilled female pilots, trained at great expense and entrusted with multimillion-dollar aircraft, were driven out.

There was, as predicted, "all kinds of flak."

Again, Rosemary Mariner was called upon to offer context. Noting that reevaluation was fairly common in carrier aviation, which required high skill levels and allowed virtually no margin for error, she told the *Chicago Tribune*: "In the overall picture, I am very satisfied. There is room for improvement, but I have to make the analogy to racial integration. There's a world of difference between 1955 and 1995 in the status of relations in racial integration. We are just now beginning that process regarding women in combat aviation, and I am optimistic we will do that successfully."

It was just one of a string of continuing appearances in the media. As a member of the Joint Staff at the Pentagon, commander of Naval Air Station Meridian, Mississippi, professor of military strategy and holder of the Joint Chiefs Chair at the National War College, and a member of the Naval Institute *Proceedings'* Editorial Board, Rosemary was a go-to for comment in opinion columns, news stories, and TV talk shows about anything military when women were involved.

A sample:

Autumn/Winter 1994–1995—*Joint Force Quarterly*, "Lessons Learned" column, contributed by Captain Rosemary B. Mariner, USN Exercise and Analysis Division (J-7) Joint Staff, "based on the winning entry in the 1992 Lt. Col. Richard Higgins, USMC, memorial essay contest sponsored by the National War College class of 1985": "The same principles that military leaders have used for centuries to forge effective fighting forces, namely, discipline and accountability, underpin gender integration. Successful integration is dependent on a common identity and purpose: a soldier is a soldier. The initial step, both for those doing the integration and those undergoing integration, is to regard themselves and each other first and foremost as officers or as soldiers, sailors, marines and airmen."

June 2, 1996—*Orlando Sentinel / Baltimore Sun* op-ed column, "Women Enhance Military's Power": "Women have always 'been in combat.' The consternation over women warriors is a peacetime one, because in war necessity is the overriding concern. Anyone selling the notion that women and children are somehow protected from war's horrors need only read the newspaper accounts of Bosnia or Rwanda, let alone the Bible. While women are invariably among war's many innocent victims, they have also taken up arms and fought back. . . . The combat laws were repealed by Congress, in accordance with our system of government, following a two-decade debate that culminated with the Gulf War. Those who think this happened overnight were simply not paying attention. Nor is the participation of women incompatible with national security. Rather, it ensures the strongest possible defense by increasing the pool from which to draw the best qualified individuals."

November 19, 1996—CNN, *Talkback Live*, on a sexual assault scandal at the army's Aberdeen Proving Ground in Maryland: Q: *Should military men and women be separated?* A: "Frankly, I think the idea, after all these years, of going back to early 1970s, 1960s-style segregation is absurd. We work together, we train together, and we fought the Gulf War together. And the idea that we would go back in time makes as much sense as going back to racial segregation because we still have racial tensions or bigots in our ranks."

November 20, 1996—NPR, *All Things Considered*, on fraternization and accountability in the Aberdeen scandal: "Having spent my entire adult life in uniform, I also have perspective. And like most first females who pioneered nontraditional fields, I have my own share of horror stories. However, the pervasive natures of these charges surprised even me. . . . It is . . . important to emphasize that the vast

majority of uniformed men and women are honorable professionals who do their jobs as true teammates. . . . What is the command
climate, and who is in charge? The problem of seniors abusing their
authority over juniors is not new and not limited to women. The
profession of arms has dealt with this issue for centuries, establishing
strict taboos against fraternization. . . . Accountability resides at the
highest levels of leadership. . . . Yet another sexual harassment study
is not the solution. Going back to 1960s-style gender segregation in
the military is just plain silly and violates the principle of train-as-
you-fight. Top uniformed and civilian leadership must accept their
responsibility and return to the tradition of vertical accountability.
For the real issue here is not women in the military, but the integrity
and readiness of the armed forces."

May 11, 1997—*Washington Post*, op-ed column, "The Military
Needs Women":

*In 1973, when I joined the Navy, going into the military was one
of the most politically incorrect things a young person could do. At the
end of the Vietnam War, my decision to become a Navy pilot made
me a "baby killer" in the eyes of many college classmates. Twenty-four
years later, in the wake of the Army's sexual misconduct scandals, I
am again pilloried for wearing the uniform of my country—this time
because I am a woman.*

*In the twisted commentary surrounding the Aberdeen miscon-
duct cases, one might get the impression that female soldiers are just
problems, forced into uniform by radical feminists who strike terror in
the heart of combat-hardened generals. . . . Anyone who doesn't agree
with this view is "politically correct." . . . Contrary to culture war
propaganda, women serve in the armed forces because they directly
contribute to our central mission, national defense. Integrating large
numbers of high-quality female recruits into nontraditional fields
made the All-Volunteer Force possible. As a result of the Gulf War,
women serve in all combat positions except those classified as "direct
ground combat" and aboard submarines. Desert Storm demonstrated
that combat exclusion policies do not protect women from coming*

home in body bags or becoming POWs. Rather, such arbitrary restrictions hurt combat readiness by limiting the flexibility of commanders to use all their soldiers, however needed, especially under fire. In terms of plain fairness, if American women are good enough to die for their country, they are good enough to fight. . . .

The vast majority of American men do not want to be in the military, let alone in combat positions. Next year, the armed forces must enlist more bright young people than ever to replace those leaving active duty. If women were forced into an ancillary role, the Defense Department would have to significantly increase the number of lower mental category men and high school dropouts. Even if force structure is dramatically cut, the declining pool of eligible youth does not alter the demographic imperative. In the age of "dominant battle space maneuver" where brains are more important than brawn, the nation would be faced with the absurd prospect of conscripting unmotivated men to replace quality female volunteers.

Today, with almost 15 percent of the total force female, including women warriors, ours is the most combat-ready peacetime force in history. Military women are not a social experiment but an integral part of the armed forces. . . . [W]e dare not squander our success by pandering to a few vocal critics pushing an anti-woman social agenda at the expense of national security. No amount of nostalgia over manly warriors protecting fair maidens erases the fact that this country cannot go to war without women on the front lines. . . . Either women serve honorably and equally, or we draft men. Turning back the clock on gender integration means a return to the broken force of the early 1970s. Those of us who served then, know there is no going back.

August 22, 1997—*USA Today*, "Muscular 'G.I. Jane' Pumps up Navy Dramatics": Was Demi Moore's portrayal of a Navy SEAL in the film, with its rain-soaked troops eating out of trash cans, sleeping in bare-bones, open barracks, and sporting buzz cuts, accurate? "Who cares?" Rosemary asked. "The big thing is you have to make up your mind you're not going to quit. You've got to dish it back. [Moore] stood up to them."

PART V

THE 2000S

CHAPTER FIFTEEN

Piping Over the Side

"THEY SOARED HIGHER THAN MOST WOMEN AND MANY MEN," THE *NAVY Times* reported on May 19, 1997.

They pushed to the far horizons the boundaries for all military women. In the end, however, stars eluded them, and now the Navy is bidding good-bye to its two most senior female warriors and aviators.

Capt. Jane Skiles O'Dea, informally the Navy's female "gray eagle," was piped ashore for the last time on April 11 in a retirement ceremony at Washington's Navy Memorial. She plans to go work for a defense contractor in the area.

This summer, Capt. Rosemary Mariner, after a few months herself as senior female aviator, will retire to her husband's cattle farm in Tennessee and write a book on gender integration.

It was a fitting and well-deserved tribute that recognized the end of a history-making era, a milestone also noted on NPR and in *Naval Aviation News.* "Pausing to reflect, Naval Aviation . . . acknowledged the legacy of opportunity left by retiring Captains Jane Skiles O'Dea and Rosemary B. Mariner," read *NAN Year in Review.*

According to the *Navy Times* story:

Both women acknowledge some disappointment that they did not have more opportunities, or the chance to make admiral. It would have been difficult for them to make admiral because they were not allowed to punch the same career tickets as the men who entered at the same time, they note. When combat aviation was finally opened to women, in 1993, they were too senior to get the jobs that could have brought them into the ranks of the stars.

"I'm maybe a little disappointed but not bitter. There comes a time in your life when you have to move on," O'Dea says.

"I have no regrets. I enjoyed the Navy," says Mariner, who decided to retire before she went up for flag rank. "I had a wonderful, adventurous, interesting experience in the Navy. But there comes a point where you have to move on. I made that choice."

At her Piping over the Side ceremony—a formal navy farewell symbolically marking the departure of a distinguished personage from a ship—Jane thanked all those who had helped her succeed in her storied career.

"We've flown airplanes together, we've gone to sea, we've traveled the world, we've stood watch in the dark of night, we've toiled in the Pentagon," she said. "You're my senior officer mentors, who advised me during my career. You're my cousin, who was a role model for me as a seventeen-year-old girl. You're my steadfast carpool mate who drove my girls to swim practice when I was doing navy business. You were all truly the wind beneath my wings. Thank you all."

Jane also had this advice for the next generation: "Dig in and scrap for every opportunity they'll give you and be prepared to work hard to prove yourself. Women still have to work harder. And do what your male counterparts are doing. Don't do the traditional shore types of jobs. Go to sea, fly airplanes, do everything you can to get those warfare qualifications. That's what counts when you get to the top."

Which she did.

Her résumé includes a stint as skipper of the Navy Recruiting Command in Indianapolis, where she won the award for top navy enlisted recruiting district in 1992.

"Command was wonderful. I loved to command," Jane said. "I thought everyone would do what I said." When they didn't, "It was a surprise. My husband gave me a plaque, which I had on my desk. It said: 'When all else fails, do what the captain suggests.'"

There were posts in the Space and Electronic Warfare Directorate in the office of the Chief of Naval Operations and with the Naval Computer and Telecommunications Command in DC, NATO-related flights to Brussels with the Joint Staff, and a round-the-world trip inspecting communications stations in London; Sicily; Diego Garcia; Christchurch, New Zealand; and Sydney—"Aussies really know how to party!"

"I've had a great career," Jane said. "I've done things that some people only dream about."

Post-retirement, she earned a master's degree in computer systems management, worked in information services for Boeing, took a civil service post for the Space and Naval Warfare Systems Command, and became a professor at Defense Acquisition University in San Diego, teaching program management and systems engineering.

"I will always miss the smell of jet fuel and salt air," Jane said. Among her personal memorabilia is a plaque made of wood planking from the deck of the Lady Lex.

For Rosemary Mariner, life as a retired navy captain solidified her status as one of the nation's foremost experts on women in the military. She was a frequent TV commentator and opinion columnist, a consultant for ABC News, a lecturer in the history department at the University of Tennessee, and a scholar-in-residence at the university's Center for the Study of War and Society.

In news stories, she weighed in on such topics as a possibly reckless military training flight in Italy (NPR); whether continued animosity toward women is keeping female aviators from choosing the jet pipeline (*San Antonio Express-News*); whether men and women should be separated for part of basic training (CNN); women's "warrior mentality" (*Florida Times Union*); character training in the navy (*Chicago Tribune*); the status of the war in Iraq (NPR); Iraq War POW Jessica Lynch (*San Antonio Express-News*); the death of a female army helicopter pilot in Iraq (*Los Angeles Times*); honor and the Swift Boat controversy involving

Vietnam War hero and presidential candidate John Kerry (*Washington Post*); and a captain relieved of command over a series of racy shipboard videos (NPR).

She was one of eight essayists writing for NPR about the investigation, impeachment, and trial of President Bill Clinton.

She penned an op-ed about her appreciation for Admiral Elmo Zumwalt in a *Washington Post* piece headlined "Adm. Zumwalt Changed My Life."

As a panelist/interviewee on television and radio, she discussed fighter pilot culture (NPR); co-ed military training and the history of legislation regulating women in combat (NPR); a bill prohibiting women from serving in infantry, armor, or artillery units (ABC); pregnancy in the army (NPR); women serving on board submarines ("We will have made progress when this is not a newsworthy event. . . . Is this news anymore, really? Not like it would have been in 1975") (*Washington Post*); and cultural/technological changes in the military (NPR).

And she co-edited a book of essays about American culture and the atomic bomb.

Rosemary Mariner was, wrote Deborah G. Douglas in *American Women and Flight since 1940*, "one of the nation's leading advocates for equal opportunity for women in the military."

US Naval Reserve captain Joellen Drag Oslund retired in January 1998—for real this time.

After she stopped flying in 1984, she had a billet at the Navy Command Center at the Pentagon, standing watches, handling crises, war-gaming, briefing the chief of naval operations. Then, on to Corpus Christi; Hawaii, where she was commanding officer of a small maintenance unit for P-3s; a volunteer training unit in Florida; and, last, a post as navy liaison officer to the Federal Emergency Management Agency (FEMA), in the San Francisco Bay Area.

Having sort of run out of billets and completed her twenty-five years, she once again sent a letter informing the navy of her intention to retire. "That one," she says, "apparently found its way to the proper people."

She became a stay-at-home mom, raising her two children, Kenny and Cassie, while her husband traveled for work. She got involved in community affairs, running an equestrian program for the local 4-H club and teaching dozens of boys and girls how to ride and compete. She participated in public speaking programs, giving presentations to community and military groups, and recorded an oral history for the Smithsonian Institution. At one event for elementary and middle schoolers about famous women in history, with participants dressed in period costume, she portrayed a groundbreaking female aviator, wearing a survival vest and helmet. At the end of the program came the big reveal—she was portraying herself! The kids loved it and mobbed her, wanting to try on her gear.

She and her husband are both dedicated advocates for military women.

Judy Bruner had performed the same calculations as Jane and Rosemary and arrived at the same conclusion.

She'd had three tours as CO, but they were surface commands, and for an aviator to make flag, he or she needed to command an aviation squadron. There was a rule in the Reserve that an officer could be skipper for only two commands at a given rank, and Judy had already had two as a captain: back-to-back tours at headquarters of the Office of Naval Research, overseeing sixteen units nationwide, and at OP 04. She kept getting good billets—her next post, after her third CO tour ended in 1996, was at Readiness Command 6, as mobilization officer for the Washington, DC, region. But there was no opportunity for another command, and she realized she had gone as far as she could. "So I figured it was time to get out of the way so some guys behind me could get those good billets and make flag," she says.

After twenty-eight years in the navy—ten years on active duty and eighteen in the Reserve—Captain Judith Neuffer Bruner retired in October 1998.

The first one in was the last one out.

She spent New Year's Eve 1999 in the SOHO (Solar and Heliospheric Observatory) control center at NASA's Goddard Space Flight

Center in Greenbelt, Maryland, making sure the Y2K bug didn't cause any problems. She led the team that returned SOHO to routine operations after losing contact with it in summer 1998, and implemented a new vision for the Wallops Flight Facility, NASA's launch range in Virginia. And she was director of safety and mission assurance for six years at Goddard, responsible for the physical safety of the center, its ten thousand employees, and five other sites, as well as for making sure any spacecraft would do what it was supposed to when it arrived at its destination—for example, Jupiter.

On November 5, 2014, she received the Katharine Wright Memorial Trophy, presented by the National Aeronautic Association. Named for Wilbur and Orville's sister, the award, according to an NAA press release, is "awarded annually to a woman who '. . . has contributed to the success of others, or made a personal contribution to the advancement of the art, sport and science of aviation and space flight over an extended period of time.' Ms. Bruner is being recognized 'for over 40 years of distinguished and historic contributions as one of the first female Naval Aviators, a pioneering research pilot and a senior NASA Technical Leader.'"

Ana Maria Scott had been out of the military at this point for nearly two decades. She flew domestic routes for FedEx, then started flying in Europe, staying in Madrid or Paris for weeks at a time. She had always wanted to live abroad, so after she retired in 2011, she stayed. She'd had no contact with the others for years; even while in the navy, their paths rarely, if ever, crossed. Though the first six female naval aviators were often referred to as being in the same class, this was somewhat of a misnomer, as they trained, and served, in different squadrons and at different bases at different times. A few had been temporarily stationed near each other—Jane and Rosemary on the *Lex*, Ana Maria and Joellen at North Island—and some saw each other at conferences and meetings of professional organizations. But the original female naval aviators were never in the same place at the same time.

Then, in 2017, Ana Maria received word that the six had been chosen for induction into the Women in Aviation International (WAI) Pioneer Hall of Fame.

The gala celebration, at the twenty-eighth annual WAI Conference in Lake Buena Vista, Florida, brought Rosemary Bryant Mariner, Ana Maria Scott, Joellen Drag Oslund, Jane Skiles O'Dea, and Judith Neuffer Bruner together in the same room for the first time. John Rainey was there representing his wife Barbara Allen Rainey, Female Naval Aviator No. 1, who died in a flight training accident in 1982. Escorted by family and feted by friends, including more than fifty women wearing Wings of Gold, the six were honored for their groundbreaking bravery, commitment, and service.

The WAI tribute video, *First Class of Women Naval Aviators*, included this citation:

In January 1973, eight female trainees were selected to train as United States Naval Aviators. Four months later, the women reported to Pensacola, Florida, for flight training. Six of the original eight women went on to earn their Wings of Gold and became the first women to be designated full-fledged military pilots.

The first class of women Naval Aviators includes Judith Neuffer, Barbara Allen, Jane Skiles, Ana Marie [sic] Scott, Joellen Drag and Rosemary Merims. These dedicated women became fully integrated into their squadrons, eventually commanding some of these units. While there were difficult circumstances along the way, these six women persevered, and made lasting contributions. Their success made it possible for subsequent female Naval Aviators.

These six pioneers clearly demonstrated that women had the physical and mental capacity to fly not just naval aircraft, but perform all military missions. Their success set an example for the US Army, US Air Force and US Coast Guard to emulate. These services subsequently opened pilot training to women, forever changing the face of military aviation. Their courage and determination in the air, at sea, and on the ground paved the way for all future female military aviators by constantly being [the] first women in opening new aircraft types and missions.

Some nineteen years later, the opportunity for women to fly all types of aircraft in the military inventory became a reality. Standing on the shoulders of the WASP, their successes proved the ability of women to fly, and serve their country, anytime, anywhere.

When the video concluded, some 1,500 conference attendees leapt to their feet in applause.

As the most senior of the six, Judy was asked to make an acceptance speech.

On behalf of the first group of women who went through Navy flight training, I would like to say how honored and humbled we are to be recognized here today.

I am sure I speak for all of the women who went through flight training early on when I say we didn't do it to be the first, and while luck played no part in our selection or success, certainly we were fortunate to be there at a point in our country's history when we were given the amazing opportunity to become a Navy pilot.

While we are humbled by the title of "pioneer," we know that we were not the first female aviators to fly military aircraft. That honor went to the WASP, who played a vital role in piloting military aircraft in World War II. They were the true pioneers, but they did not receive the formal recognition for the fact that they were, indeed, the first. Hopefully, we built on their legacy and made them proud.

Initially, there were many restrictions to the aircraft we could fly and the missions we could support. Today, those restrictions are gone. There are female Naval Aviators in every aircraft on every platform, both as crew members and as the leaders of these organizations at all levels. We are very proud and humbled by the role we played in helping to make that happen.

Again, we thank you for this wonderful honor.

Epilogue: The Flyover

On February 2, 2019, the skies over Maynardville, Tennessee, were filled with the roar of four F/A-18F Super Hornets streaking overhead in close formation. In each aircraft were two young female fliers, executing the first all-woman missing man formation flyover in navy history. As the four jet strike fighters reached New Loyston Cemetery from the northeast, the second pilot from the right pulled up, climbing toward the heavens in an aerial salute to a fallen comrade. The other three flew on, the gap in the formation symbolizing the emptiness of a wingman lost.

From the combat pilots in the air to the sailors in the ground crew, every participant in the "Sabre 9" mission was a woman based at Naval Air Station Oceana. There, four decades before, Rosemary Mariner had made history as the first female naval aviator to enter the jet pipeline.

It was a sad but fitting honor on a day of mourning and celebration. "One of those young women [flying in the tribute] was born the year Rosemary took command of her squadron," retired navy captain Mary Louise Griffin told the *Washington Post* on her way to the funeral. "She would have liked that. We spent almost twenty years getting doors open, and we just keep rocking on."

Griffin, who helped coordinate the flyover, was one of four naval aviators who spoke in the packed church that day. Retired captain Joellen Drag Oslund, retired commander Tommy Mariner, and former lieutenant Tammie Jo Shults also addressed the mourners, many prominent pilots among them. These included retired captain Judith Neuffer Bruner and dozens of members of Women Military Aviators, the professional organization Rosemary once led.

Rosemary's death on January 24, 2019, from ovarian cancer at the age of sixty-five drew expressions of sympathy and accolades from across the country. A tribute was entered into the *Congressional Record* by Tennessee senator Marsha Blackburn on behalf of herself and fellow Tennessee senator Lamar Alexander.

As with many of the milestones in Rosemary's storied career, the flyover made national headlines.

On Twitter, in videos produced by the navy, and in comments to the press, the flyover pilots—who hadn't even been born when the original female naval aviators started forging the path they would follow—reflected on the past and looked ahead to the future.

Said Commander Stacy Uttecht, "Sabre 9" mission commander, who was a teenager when the ban on female combat pilots was repealed: "Captain Mariner truly was a trailblazer. She basically made it possible for us to do our jobs that we're doing today. I've never had anyone tell me no in the Navy. No one's ever told me I couldn't go on deployment or fly in a jet aircraft, and those are the types of things that women like Captain Mariner were up against . . . To be able to pay a tribute to someone who truly made it possible for me to follow my dream from when I was a little girl is something that I'll never forget. . . . Without her, I would not be able to stand here and be the commanding officer of an F-18 squadron. . . . We have a lot more females that are flying in the Navy, especially in tactical aircraft, than there were even fifteen years ago, and that all started because of women like Captain Mariner."

She added: "If Captain Mariner and her colleagues had not been such advocates for equality, we might not have had female combat veterans to conduct the flyover. She lived her life to ensure a better tomorrow."

Said Lieutenant Christy Talisse: "Seeing strong female mentors throughout my career, as well as men, has inspired me and pushed me to be better, and to hear Captain Mariner's story and realize the legacy she left behind is really empowering. . . . Between the female maintainers and technicians that maintain our jets and do a great job and work hard day in and day out, and women that don't see themselves as any different and just want to fly and pursue their dreams, I think it's sort of becoming the new normal. And I love that."

"Because of Captain Mariner, all of us are fortunate enough to stand here in these uniforms," Lieutenant Kelly Harris told the *Virginian-Pilot*. "She was able to blaze the trail for us, and so today, and for years to come, decades to come, her history and her legacy will live on in us and for future naval aviators."

Rosemary had already been diagnosed with the cancer that would take her life when Lieutenant Commander Danielle Thiriot met her at the Women in Aviation International Pioneer Hall of Fame induction. "She showed up and had her full dress uniform on," Thiriot told the *Courier News*. "She was always so humble."

The flyover, Thiriot said, was "sort of her last flight."

"We're all combat veterans, and we were honoring Captain Mariner and what she did for us," Thiriot told the paper. "We stand on the shoulders of giants, and hers were the tallest." She added: "It was really emotional, being a part of this. Our hearts were pounding a little bit too, just understanding that gravity."

After the funeral and flyover, everyone gathered back at Rosemary's home. Recalled Lieutenant Amanda Lee: "As we walked up to the late Captain Mariner's farmhouse for the reception, the mood was surprisingly joyous, and we were met with smiling faces and an overwhelming round of applause from some of the most influential women in Naval Aviation that I have ever had the honor to meet. For them, I think, it was the culmination of all they had to endure, all they fought for, and their dreams [had] come true. They did it. That realization was the most rewarding part of this unforgettable experience."

Joellen Oslund, Rosemary's friend for forty-six years, returned the compliment. Of the flyover pilots, she said, "I was so impressed by their professionalism, dedication to our country, and sense of history."

Lieutenant Commander Paige Blok, who had also had the opportunity to meet Rosemary in person, perhaps put it best: "As we gracefully crossed over the cemetery and Lieutenant Commander Thiriot began her pull to the heavens, the symbolism of the tribute became pointedly clear to me. Captain Mariner's life's work was on display, exemplified by eight women in four fighter aircraft. We are her legacy. We are thankful, and it was a great honor to fly her home."

GLOSSARY OF NAVY/AVIATION TERMINOLOGY

aircraft commander   pilot in command of aircraft and crew

angle of attack   angle at which an aircraft's wing meets the relative wind, generating lift

backseater   navigator or weapons specialist who flies with the pilot

billet   job assignment or post

BOQ   bachelor officer quarters

BuPERS   Bureau of Navy Personnel, now called Navy Personnel Command

CENTCOM   Central Command

checkride   flight serving as a final exam that determines whether a pilot is qualified to fly a particular aircraft

CINCLANTFLT   Commander-in-Chief, Atlantic Fleet

CINCPACFLT   Commander-in-Chief, Pacific Fleet

CNATRA   Chief of Naval Air Training

CNO   Chief of Naval Operations

COMNAVAIRPAC	Commander, Naval Air Forces, US Pacific Fleet
DACOWITS	Defense Advisory Committee on Women in the Services
detailer	official who assigns navy personnel to their next billet
fixed-wing aircraft	airplane
flag rank	in the navy, admiral or higher
flag secretary	aide who manages an admiral's calendar
FLETRAGRUPAC	Fleet Training Group Pacific
FNA	female naval aviator
FSNA	female student naval aviator
get behind the airplane	stop "thinking ahead of the airplane" and anticipating what will happen next during the flight
hit the boat	land on an aircraft carrier
jacket	folder containing complete records of a naval aviator's training and service
MAAG	Military Assistance Advisory Groups
nugget	a novice naval aviator
OPNAVINST	Office of Chief of Naval Operations Instruction
PEP	Personnel Exchange Program

piping over the side   ceremony symbolically marking the departure of a distinguished personage; holdover from a time when visitors had to be hoisted up and over the side of a sailing ship

rates   designations of enlisted navy personnel according to pay grades and ratings

ratings   occupational specialties for enlisted navy personnel

restricted line   specialized training for officer candidates

rotary aircraft   helicopter

Sacred Twenty   original members of the Navy Nurse Corps, established in 1908; the first women to officially serve in the navy

SNA   student naval aviator

surface warfare officer (SWO)   navy officer whose training and duties focus on ships at sea; SWO qualification is required for future surface command

TACAMO   Take Charge and Move Out: command system that includes airborne communications links with the nation's strategic nuclear weapons arsenal

traps   aircraft carrier landings

unrestricted line   unspecialized training for officer candidates

VFR   visual flight rules

WASP   Women Airforce Service Pilots; female aviators recruited to fly for the army during World War II

WAVES

Women Accepted for Volunteer Emergency Service; a women's Reserve created in 1942; disbanded in 1948 under the Women's Armed Services Integration Act

Wings of Gold

official winged-anchor insignia denoting a naval aviator

WOS

Women's Officer School, Newport, Rhode Island; disbanded in 1976 and integrated into Officer Candidate School

Sources

Prologue: The Flyover

"She Made History as a Navy Pilot. An All-Female Squadron Just Flew Over Her Funeral," *Washington Post*, February 2, 2019.

"Rosemary Mariner, Pathbreaking Navy Pilot and Commander, Is Dead at 65," *New York Times*, February 1, 2019.

"Captain Rosemary Mariner, USN (2 April 1953–24 January 2019)," Naval History and Heritage Command, February 4, 2019.

" 'A Badass Pilot': Capt. Rosemary Mariner, First Woman to Fly a Tactical Fighter Jet, Dies," NBCNews.com, February 4, 2019.

"Rosemary Mariner, Spurned by Airline Executive, Led Way for Female Pilots in US Navy," *Wall Street Journal*, February 15, 2019.

"Remembering Barrier-Breaking Naval Aviator Rosemary Mariner," NPR.org, January 28, 2019.

"Navy's First Female Jet Pilot Dies at 65 After Losing Battle with Ovarian Cancer," ConnectingVetsRadio.com, January 28, 2019.

" 'Mission Success': Navy's First Woman Fighter Pilot Honored in Tennessee with Historic All-Female Flyover," knoxnews.com, February 2, 2019.

"Rosemary Mariner Honored with Flyover," University of Tennessee, YouTube, February 4, 2019.

"Navy Selects First Women Flight Candidates," *Pittsburgh Post-Gazette*, January 11, 1973, 3.

"The Careers of the First Four Female Naval Aviators in Celebration of the 40th Anniversary of Women in Naval Aviation," MadisonNavyLeague.org.

"Barrier-Breaking Naval Aviator Encourages Students to Persevere, Network," University of Tennessee News, November 16, 2017.

"For Women in the Navy, Rough Waters Run Deep," *Los Angeles Times*, June 28, 1992.

"NAS Oceana Pilot Interviews," Defense Visual Information Distribution Service, January 30, 2019.

Deborah G. Douglas, *American Women and Flight since 1940* (Lexington: University Press of Kentucky, 2004).

"Success and the '80s Working Woman," *Glamour*, March 1982, 222.

"Women with Navy Wings," *All Hands*, April 1975.

"Women in the Training Command," Naval Aviation Training, 1987, 16.
Navy Women in Ships: A Deployment to Equality, 1942–1982, https://issuu.com/navalhis
toricalfoundation/docs/women_in_ships_1978_20160207.
"The Military Needs Women," *Washington Post,* May 11, 1997.

Chapter 1: Essential but Expendable

"100 Years of Naval Aviation," *Air & Space,* March 2011.
"From Typewriters to Strike Fighters: Women in Naval Aviation," exhibit, National
Naval Aviation Museum, Pensacola, Florida.
"A Naval Aviator in the Making," *Proceedings,* June 1928, USNI.org.
"The History and Development of Fighter Plane Weapons," War History Online,
November 8, 2017.
"WWII Aircraft," Smithsonian Air & Space Museum.
Douglas, *American Women and Flight since 1940.*
Wright-Brothers.org.
"Naval Aviation's First Year," *Proceedings,* May 1961, USNI.org.
"Naval Aviation: The Beginning," *Proceedings,* January 1971, USNI.org.
"The Work Ahead of Naval Aviation," *Proceedings,* March 1915, USNI.org.
"The History of the US Air Service in World War I," Centenaire.org.
"Organisation of Military Aeronautics, 1907–1935," *AAF Historical Studies,* No. 25, 26.
"Materiel Research in the Army Air Arm," *AAF Historical Studies,* No. 50, 17.
"The Ten Most Pivotal Events in US Naval Aviation," *Proceedings,* May 2011, USNI
.org.
"Sixty and Counting, 60th Anniversary Commemorative Collection, 1929–1989," *99s
News.*
"Media Life: Pioneer World War II Pilot Betty Wood Forgotten in Auburn," Gold-
CountryMedia.com, February 3, 2011.
"Curtiss Flies to Cruiser," *Washington Post,* February 18, 1911.
"Our History," The Ninety-Nines, International Organization of Women Pilots.
"Girl Pilots," *Life,* July 19, 1943, 73–81.
"The Greatest Magazine Ever Published," *Slate,* December 27, 2013.
"General Arnold's Final Speech to the WASP," WingsAcrossAmerica.org.
"US Navy Aeronautic Detachment No. 1," Naval History and Heritage Command.
"Origins of Navy Patrol Aviation, 1911 to 1920s," *Dictionary of American Naval
Aviation Squadrons,* Vol. 2, Naval Historical Center, Department of the Navy,
Washington, DC, 2000.
"WASPs Pioneered Military Flying," *San Antonio Express News,* March 10, 1991.

Chapter 2: Equal Means Equal

Elmo R. Zumwalt Jr., *On Watch* (New York: Quadrangle/*New York Times* Book Co.,
1976), 167–265.

"Navy Reformer Elmo Zumwalt Dies," *Washington Post*, January 3, 2000.
"Elmo R. Zumwalt Jr., Admiral Who Modernized the Navy, Is Dead at 79," *New York Times*, January 3, 2000.
"List of Z-grams," Naval History and Heritage Command.
"The WAVES' 75th Birthday," Naval History and Heritage Command.
"Wave Navigators on Duty in Navy Planes," *New York Herald Tribune*, July 22, 1945, A10.
"Waves Air Navigators Charting a New Course," *Aviation History*, January 1999, 34–40.
"L.A. Then and Now—Elite Female Navigators Quietly Made WAVES," *Los Angeles Times*, April 14, 2002, B4.
Jean Ebbert and Marie-Beth Hall, *Crossed Currents: Navy Women from WWI to Tailhook*, 3rd ed. (Washington, DC: Brassey's (US), 1999), 61–115, 123–25.
Linda Bird Francke, *Ground Zero: The Gender Wars in the Military* (New York: Simon & Schuster, 1997), 25.
Chester G. Hearn, *Carriers in Combat: The Air War at Sea* (Mechanicsburg, PA: Stackpole Military History Series, 2005).
"The African American Experience in the US Navy," Naval History and Heritage Command.
"Women's Armed Services Integration Act of 1948," Public Laws, Chs. 447–449, June 10, 11, 12, 1948.
Navy Women in Ships: A Deployment to Equality, 1942–1982.
"Inside the Historic Decision to Deep-Select the Navy's Top Officer," *Navy Times*, August 6, 2019.
"Navy Pilot Blazes Trail for Other Women Fliers to Follow," *Los Angeles Times*, June 25, 1990.

Chapter 3: The Word Goes Out

Ebbert and Hall, *Crossed Currents*, 182, 266–69.
"Navy Pilot Blazes Trail for Other Women Fliers to Follow."
Transcript, *Face the Nation*, John Warner interview, November 1972.
"She's Got Grit: From Small Town Iowa to Naval Aviation History," Medium.com, September 14, 2017.
"Women with Navy Wings," 32–37.
"Launch," *The Hook* (Winter 2010), 29–33.
"Rosemary Mariner Obituary," *The Times* of London, March 21, 2019.
"Women Start Training to Become Navy Pilots," *Courier-News*, March 2, 1973.
"Girl Flier Gets Kiss, Wants Combat, Too," *Courier-Post* (UPI), January 11, 1973.
"Rosemary Merims Begins US Navy Flight Training," *Daily Herald* (Jasper, Indiana) (UPI), January 17, 1973.
"Navy Miss Wants to Fly," *South Bend Herald* (AP), January 17, 1973.
Zumwalt Jr., *On Watch*, 245–60.
Douglas, *American Women and Flight*, 214.

Linda Maloney, *Military Fly Moms: Sharing Memories, Building Legacies* (New York: Tanenbaum, 2011).
"Navy's 1st Woman Flight Cadet Says She'd Like Astronaut Duty," *Burlington Free Press* (Associated Press), January 11, 1973.
"Navy Puts 1st Woman in Pilot Training," *New York Times*, January 11, 1973.
"Navy Flight Cadet Is a She (the First)," *Philadelphia Inquirer*, January 11, 1973.
"Gal Seeks Those Navy Wings," *The Home News* (New Brunswick, New Jersey), January 11, 1973.
"The Expanding Role of Navy Women," *All Hands*, April 1973, 20–27.
"The Blue Yonder's Wild About Her," *Stars and Stripes*, March 31, 1975, 1.
"100 Years of Naval Aviation 1911–2011," advertising supplement to the *Washington Post*, February 9, 2011, H11.
Guestbook, *East Montgomery County Observer*, legacy.com.
News release #097-73, Navy News Bureau, February 27, 1973.
"Public Affairs Guidance Pertaining to Flight Training for Women," unclassified US Navy document, September 9, 1972.
Basegram 1520, unclassified, "Eligibility for Flight Training for Navy Women," official announcement from chief of naval operations, November 2, 1972.
"Navy Plane Is Flown by Woman," *Austin American Statesman*, August 7, 1974, 6.
Henry W. Holden and Captain Lori Griffith, *Ladybirds: The Untold Story of Women Pilots in America* (Randolph, NJ: Black Hawk Publishing, 1991).
"Fighter Pilot Flies in Face of Sexism," *Los Angeles Times*, Ventura County Edition, June 25, 1990, B1.
"Gender, Stress and Coping in the US Military," Vol. II, *Historical Perspectives on Acculturation, Performance, Deployment, and Contingency Stress*, seminars held as part of research sponsored by the Surgeon General, US Air Force, as part of the Defense Women's Health Research Program, FY 94, Department of Psychiatry, F. Edward Hebert School of Medicine, Uniformed Services University of the Health Sciences, Bethesda, Maryland, October 1995, 27–55.

Chapter 4: Women's *Officer Training*

Directions (DM), Navy Internal Relations publication, March–April 1973, 48.
"Answering the Call: 'For a Woman of My Generation, Serving in the Military Was a Godsend,'" *Proceedings*, August 2011, USNI.org.
Ebbert and Hall, *Crossed Currents*, 134.
"The Fight to Fly at Sea," retired captain Rosemary Bryant Mariner, speech, National Air and Space Museum, GE Aviation Lecture Series, October 27, 2011.
"New Group of Women Is Ready to Try Their Wings," *Pensacola Journal*, June 8, 1973, C1.
"2 Women Quit Navy Program," *Burlington Free Press* (Associated Press), June 11, 1973, 7.
"Navy Pilot Blazes Trail for Other Women Fliers to Follow."

"Ladies Wear the Blue," video, US Navy Reserve (excerpt of Neuffer solo on Face-book)—"Reel America," C-SPAN3, American History TV—credit US Navy. C-SPAN broadcast, "Women in Combat, Past Integration Efforts," panel discussion, February 1, 2013.

"One of Navy's First Women Pilots Has Her Head in Air," *Los Angeles Times*, August 15, 1974.

"Women with Navy Wings," 32–37.

"'Nobody Asked Me, But . . .': The Female Naval Aviator: A Free Ride?" *Proceedings*, September 1975, USNI.org.

"Wings No Pushover for Women—or Pushup," *Los Angeles Times*, February 24, 1974.

"Military Service No Longer a Man's World," *Christian Science Monitor*, August 13, 1973, 9.

"Female Drives 'Charlie,'" *Pensacola Journal*, June 22, 1978, 1.

"Public Affairs Guidance Pertaining to Flight Training for Women."

Memo, unclassified, NO1542, "Women Naval Aviators Trial Program," January 16, 1973.

"Evaluation of Undergraduate Pilot Trainees," April 2, 1973, US Navy document

Chapter 5: No Place to Land

"Women with Navy Wings," 32–37.

"The Expanding Role of Navy Women," *All Hands*, April 1973, 20–27.

"In Arms the 'MS' Gains Equality," *Legion*, March 1977.

"They're Delighted with Long-Haired Navy Pilot," *Staunton* (Virginia) *Leader* (Associated Press), July 23, 1974, 7.

"Pieces of History: First Female Pilot Arrives at Oceana," retrospective, MilitaryNews .com, March 21, 2013, militarynews.com.

"First Female C-130 Pilot Completes Course at LRAFB," *The Drop Zone*, Little Rock AFB publication, July 22, 2005.

"Navy Plane Is Flown by Woman."

"Navy Pilots," *Burlington Free Press* (Associated Press), September 19, 1974.

"No Place to Land," *Atlanta Constitution*, May 24, 1974.

"She Made History as a Navy Pilot."

Holden and Griffith, *Ladybirds*.

"Female Navy Pilots Taking Off in Derby," *Arizona Republic*, July 4, 1975, B4.

"Flight Log," *The Times* (San Mateo, California), July 12, 1975, 4A.

"People" column, *St. Louis Post Dispatch*, February 1, 1976, 7A.

"Plane Lady," *The Record* (Hackensack, New Jersey), February 1, 1976, 2.

"She Passes with Flying Colors," *St. Petersburg Times*, December 14, 1976, 12B.

Capt. Rosemary Bryant Mariner Guest Book, Legacy.com.

Judith Stiehm, *Arms and the Enlisted Woman* (Philadelphia: Temple University Press, 1989), 39.

"Command History of Attack Squadron ONE SEVEN FOUR for Calendar Year 1976."

"'Nobody Asked Me, But . . .'"
Memo, unclassified, NO1542.
"The Fight to Fly at Sea."
Maloney, *Military Fly Moms.*

Chapter 6: Lessons from Integration

"Like a Date with a Pretty Girl," *Norfolk Journal & Guide,* June 21, 1975, 1.
"Lambert Squadron Tops," *Daily Express* (Newport News) (Associated Press), July 25, 1975, B4.
"The Fight to Fly at Sea."
"Barrier-Breaking Naval Aviator Encourages Students to Persevere, Network," *University of Tennessee at Knoxville News,* November 16, 2017.
"High-Flying Ladies," *Naval Aviation News,* February 1981, 6–15.
"100 Years of Naval Aviation 1911–2011."
"Women Military Aviators 1989 Convention," *Naval Aviation News,* November–December 1989, 10–12.
Holden and Griffith, *Ladybirds.*
"Legal Impediments to Service: Women in the Military and the Rule of Law," *Duke Journal of Gender Law & Policy,* Vol. 14:1061 (2017).
"Female Pilot Resigned Over Navy Limitations," *New York Times,* November 27, 1977, 20, New York Times.
"The Blue Yonder's Wild About Her."
Maloney, *Military Fly Moms.*
"Pregnant, Iowan Gets Navy Flak," *Des Moines Tribune,* July 15, 1976, 1.
"The Fight to Fly at Sea."
"D.M. Woman Makes Navy History," *Des Moines Register Sun,* December 19, 1976, 7C.
"Navy's 1st Woman Pilot Raps Career Limitations," *Pensacola News,* November 25, 1977, 1A.
"Woman Pilot: There's No Such Thing as Equality in Navy," *Courier-News* (Bridgewater, New Jersey) (Gannett News Service), November 26, 1977, A-10.
"The US Navy in Review," *Proceedings,* May 1998, USNI.org.

Chapter 7: Owens v. Brown

Ebbert and Hall, *Crossed Currents,* 182, 242–50.
Navy Women in Ships: A Deployment to Equality, 1942–1982.
Francke, *Ground Zero,* 32.
Owens v. Brown, 455 F. Supp. 291 (D.D.C. 1978), Justicia.com.
Stiehm, *Arms and the Enlisted Woman,* 47–49.
Holden and Griffith, *Ladybirds.*
Bernard D. Rostker, *I Want You! The Evolution of the All-Volunteer Force* (Monograph, RAND Corp., 2006), 564.

Jeanne Holm, *Women in the Military: An Unfinished Revolution* (New York: Presidio Press, 1992), 382.
"For a Trail-Blazing Navy Flier, Happy Landings on an Aircraft Carrier," *New York Times*, December 1, 1979, 48.
"People, Planes, Places," *Naval Aviation News*, December 1980, 32.
"The Fight to Fly at Sea."

Chapter 8: "The Honeymoon Is Over"

Video: "Women in Combat, Past Integration Efforts," C-SPAN, February 1, 2013.
Rostker, *I Want You!*, 564.
Stiehm, *Arms and the Enlisted Woman*, 49–50, 53.
"Naval Pilot Decries Limitations," *Florida Today* (Cocoa, Florida), August 22, 1984, 6B.
"Women Move Up in the Military, But Many Jobs Remain Off Limits," *Wall Street Journal*, March 14, 1985.
"Norton Sound: A Troubled Ship," *Boston Globe*, August 20, 1980, 3.
"Highlights in the History of Military Women," The Women's Memorial.org.
"Becoming a Female Naval Aviator," *Proceedings*, October 1986, 105–06, USNI.org.
"Increasingly, Naval Aviation Is Women's Work, Too," advertising supplement to the *Washington Post*, February 9, 2011, H11.
"Women Fliers in Race with Changing Times," *Washington Post*, July 29, 1991
"Naval Pilot Decries Limitations," 6B.
"Up Front with Judy," *Naval Aviation News*, July 1977.
"High-Flying Ladies."
Holm, *Women in the Military*, 276–77, 343–44.
"Sexual Harassment Cited in Navy and Marine Corps," *The Morning Call* (*New York Times* News Service), September 17, 1987, A9.
Women in the Military: Hearings Before the Military Personnel and Compensation Subcommittee of the Committee on Armed Services, House of Representatives, One Hundredth Congress, First and Second Sessions, Hearings Held October 1, November 19, 1987, and February 4, 1988.
"Women Will Get Bigger Navy Role," *Orlando Sentinel* (Reuters), December 19, 1987, A1.
"Sexual Harassment of Women in the Military," Women in the Military Issue Paper, Shirley Sagawa and Nancy Duff Campbell, National Women's Law Center, October 30, 1992.
"Equal Opportunity: DOD Studies in Discrimination in the Military," US General Accounting Office Report to the Ranking Minority Member, Committee on National Security, House of Representatives, April 1995, 17.
"Judith N. Bruner—Serving Our Country in the Navy and at NASA," Goddard Space Flight Center, August 26, 2014.
"Navy's First Female Pilot Killed," *Burlington Free Press* (Associated Press), July 15, 1982.

Chapter 9: Down to the Sea in Ships

"High-Flying Ladies."
"Female Drives 'Charlie.'"
"Moms at Sea," *Wifeline*, Department of the Navy, 1984, 8.
Maloney, *Military Fly Moms*.
"Naval Pilot Decries Limitations," 6B.
"Navy to Honor First Woman Fighter Pilot, UT Lecturer with All-Female Flyover at Tennessee Funeral," KnoxNews.com, February 1, 2019.
"'We Have the Watch'—All-Female Naval Aviators Fly High for the Late Capt. Rosemary Mariner," TheCourierNews.com, February 6, 2019.
"'She Knew Women Could Fly—Rosemary Mariner's Inspiring Legacy," TheDaily Independent.com, February 7, 2019.
Douglas, *American Women and Flight*, 204.
WASP Newsletter, second quarter, 1985.
"Meet the First Woman OOD on a Carrier," *Campus*, Vol. 10, Issue 2, February 1981, 25.
Francke, *Ground Zero*, 142.
"Woman Pilot Aims for Combat Status," *Cedar Rapids Gazette* (United Press International), March 14, 1982, 3B.
"Women in Naval Aviation: From Plane Captains to Pilots," *Naval Aviation News*, July 1977.
"Success and the '80s Working Woman."
Holden and Griffith, *Ladybirds*.
Holley-Gamble Funeral Home, Capt. Rosemary Bryant Mariner Guest Book.
Capt. Rosemary Bryant Mariner Guest Book, Legacy.com.
"Command Change at First Female-Led Squadron," *Hanford* (California) *Sentinel*, August 8, 1991, 3.
"Women Move Up in the Military, But Many Jobs Remain Off Limits."
"Careers Are Adrift; Female Pilots in Navy Can Only Fly So High," *Los Angeles Times*, October 10, 1988.
"100 Years of Naval Aviation 1911–2011."
Navy Women in Ships: A Deployment to Equality, 1942–1982.
"Flyover to Honor 1st Female Fighter Pilot," *The Tennessean*, February 2, 2019, 1.

Chapter 10: What's in a Name?

Sylvia Marie Rafels, "Women and Combat: Impediments to the Total Integration of Women in the Military," dissertation, Western Michigan University, ScholarWorks at WMU, 38–44.
Michael J. Crawford, ed., *Needs and Opportunities in the Modern History of the US Navy* (Washington, DC: Naval History and Heritage Command, Department of the Navy, 2019), 245–46.

Emerald M. Archer, *Women, Warfare and Representation: American Servicewomen in the Twentieth Century* (London: Bloomsbury Publishing, 2017), 52–53.
"Department of Defense Authorization for Appropriations for Fiscal Year 1982: Hearings Before the Committee on Armed Services," US Senate, Ninety-Seventh Congress, First Session, US Government Printing Office, 1981.
"Women Can't Fight," *Washingtonian*, November 1, 1979.
"The Fight to Fly at Sea."
"Under Pressure, Jim Webb Declines to Be Recognized as a Distinguished Naval Academy Graduate," *Washington Post*, March 28, 2017.
"Careers Are Adrift; Female Pilots in Navy Can Only Fly So High."
"Ceiling Limited for Navy's Women Fliers," *Los Angeles Times*, October 12, 1988, 3.
"Webb's Views Opposing Women in Combat Called 'Propaganda,'" *Baltimore Sun*, April 6, 1997, 3A.
Women in the Military: Hearings Before the Military Personnel and Compensation Subcommittee of the Committee on Armed Services, House of Representatives.
Francke, *Ground Zero*, 22.
"Wanted: More Women for Sea Duty; Navy Secretary Also Orders Crackdown on Sexual Harassment," *Washington Post*, December 22, 1987, A23.
"Webb Adds Jobs for Navy Women, Will Fight Sexual Harassment," *Orlando Sentinel* (Associated Press), December 22, 1987, A4.
"Navy Expands the Roles of Women," *New York Times*, December 22, 1987, D23.
"Women on the Way Up," *Johnson City* (Tennessee) *Press*, Paul Harvey, syndicated column, August 27, 1986, 4.
"Unique LNAS Squadron Packs It In," *Hanford Sentinel*, September 28, 1993, 3.
The Naval Officer's Career Planning Guidebook, Naval Military Personnel Command, 1990, 15.
"First Woman to Lead GIs in Combat—and Look at the Thanks She Got," *Seattle Times* (Associated Press), January 25, 2013.
Holm, *Women in the Military*, 408–14, 424–36.

Chapter 11: Women Take Command

"Former Iowan to Take Command of Naval Unit," *Des Moines Register*, September 21, 1990, T3.
"Naval Pilot Decries Limitations," 6B.
"Her Most Impossible Mission Yet," *Los Angeles Times*, June 26, 1990, B6.
"Ex-LNAS Pilot to be Navy's First Female Squadron Leader," *Hanford Sentinel* (Associated Press), June 5, 1990, 1.
"S.D. Native Becomes First Woman to Lead Jet Squadron," *Los Angeles Times*, July 13, 1990, B2.
"Command Change at First Female-Led Squadron," *Hanford Sentinel*, August 8, 1991, 3.
"Woman Will Command Jet Squadron," *Newark* (Ohio) *Advocate* (Copley News Service), June 6, 1990, 6.
"Squadron Gets a Change," *Hanford Sentinel*, August 11, 1991, 4.

"Navy Fighter Pilot Flies in Face of Sexism," *Los Angeles Times*, June 25, 1990, VCB1.

Tammie Jo Shults, *Nerves of Steel* (Nashville, TN: W Publishing Group, an imprint of Thomas Nelson, 2019).

"New Captains Have Flown Against Tradition," *Navy Times*, April 5, 1993, 4.

Holden and Griffith, *Ladybirds*.

Chapter 12: The Halls of Congress

Senate Armed Services Subcommittee on Manpower and Personnel, hearing, restrictions on women in combat, C-SPAN, June 18, 1991.

"Ban on Women in Combat Divides Service Chief," *New York Times*, June 19, 1991, A16.

"Drop the Ban on Women in Combat," *USA Today*, June 20, 1991, A10.

"Military Cool to Women in Combat," *Chicago Tribune*, June 19, 1991.

"Feb. 9 Deadline for Draft Info," *Philadelphia Daily News*, January 25, 1980, 5.

"Joint Chiefs Testify Against Allowing Women in Combat," *Pittsburgh Post-Gazette*, June 19, 1991, 2.

Ebbert and Hall, *Crossed Currents*, 291.

"Women in Military Combat? What It Means for American Culture and Defense," Phyllis Schlafly, Heritage Foundation, May 28, 1991.

"Eternal Differences," Phyllis Schlafly, letter to *The Wilson Quarterly*, Summer 1982.

"Schwarzkopf: Expand Combat Role for Women," *Chicago Tribune*, June 13, 1991.

Rafels, "Women and Combat," dissertation.

"Senate Votes to Lift Ban on Women War Pilots / Repeal Passes by 69–30; A Key Panel Is Ignored," *Boston Globe*, August 1, 1991.

Commander Rosemary Bryant Mariner, "A Soldier is a Soldier: Successful Gender Integration in the Armed Forces," report, National War College, 1992.

David Horowitz, "The Feminist Assault on the Military," Center for the Study of Popular Culture, October 5, 1992.

"Women in Combat: The High Price of Equality," *Detroit News*, July 23, 1992, 14A.

"Capt. Rosemary Mariner Was a Leader among Leaders," KnoxNews.com, March 4, 2019.

Francke, *Ground Zero*, 33–40, 189, 230–40.

Holm, *Women in the Military*, 435, 470–509.

"Combat Flights by Women Backed," *Washington Post*, May 9, 1991, A1.

"The Fight to Fly at Sea."

"The President's Corner," Newsletter, Women Military Aviators, Inc., December 1991.

"Lift Barriers for Women in Military," *San Diego Union-Tribune*, July 22, 1991, B-7.

"Military Fights Gender Battle," *Tampa Tribune*, November 7, 1991, 1.

Dwayne Oslund, USN (Ret.), "Excluding Women from Combat Is Just Plain Wrong: A Navy Captain's Story," ACLU blog, May 31, 2013.

Crier & Co., transcript, CNN, July 26, 1991.

"Equal Right to Die in War? No Thanks," *Press Democrat*, November 18, 1992, B5.

"Women in the Military, Part I," *Morning Edition*, NPR, May 12, 1997.

Holley-Gamble Funeral Home, Capt. Rosemary Bryant Mariner Guest Book.

Chapter 13: Tailhook

"Ex-LNAS Pilot to be Navy's First Female Squadron Leader," *Hanford Sentinel* (Associated Press), June 5, 1990, 3.

"Top Brass Oppose Women in Combat," *Chicago Tribune* (Scripps Howard News Service) July 31, 1992.

"Women and Stone Age Warriors," *New York Times*, July 8, 1992, A18.

"Gender, Stress and Coping in the US Military," Vol. II.

"The Social History of the US Navy, 1945–Present, A Historiographical Essay," Navy History and Heritage Command.

"Midshipman Recalls Her Rough Seas at Annapolis: Harassment: Resignation from the US Naval Academy after Male Colleagues Handcuffed Her to a Urinal Has Brought Unwanted Attention to the 19-Year-Old Encinitas Woman," *Los Angeles Times*, May 23, 1990, Los Angeles Times.

"15 Years Later, Annapolis Women Battle for Acceptance," *San Diego Union-Tribune*, May 31, 1990, A-1.

"Sordid Doings at Annapolis: How the Navy Reacted," *Chicago Tribune*, May 25, 1990.

Gregory L. Vistica, *Fall from Glory: The Men Who Sank the US Navy* (New York: Simon & Schuster, 1997), 294.

Women in the Military: Hearings Before the Military Personnel and Compensation Subcommittee of the Committee on Armed Services, House of Representatives.

Horowitz, "The Feminist Assault on the Military."

"The Sex Life of the Navy," *Washington Post*, May 24, 1992.

Ebbert and Hall, *Crossed Currents*, 300–10.

"Navy Will Hold Sexual Harassment Trial," *Times-Picayune*, June 13, 1989, B-6.

"Reserve Officer Admits Bad Conduct," *Times-Picayune*, August 10, 1989, B-6.

"Concern Lacking in '89, Navy Assault Victim Says," *Times-Picayune*, July 20, 1992, A-1.

"Sex Harassment at Party Reveals Problem's Depth with US Navy Aviators," *Democrat and Chronicle* (Rochester, New York) (*New York Times* News Service), June 14, 1992, 8A.

"Sexual Harassment of Women in the Military."

"Navy Hit Over Harassment Case," *San Antonio Light*, July 21, 1992, A6.

"Sex Harassment Called Pervasive in Navy; Internal Study Recommends Changes in Policies Affecting Women," *Washington Post*, April 4 1991, 4.

"A Scandal Too Big to Live Down," *San Francisco Chronicle* (Reuters), April 24, 1993, A2.

"Navy Must Learn Harassment Won't Be Tolerated," Ellen Goodman, syndicated column, *State Journal-Register* (Springfield, Illinois), July 8, 1992, 5.

"Officer Who Went Public Toughs It Out," *San Francisco Chronicle*, April 24, 1993, A2.

"Key Tailhook Accuser Has No Regrets," *Los Angeles Times*, April 23, 1993, p. 1.

MacNeil-Lehrer NewsHour, transcript, July 1, 1992.

"Navy Admiral Issues a Profuse Apology for Miramar Incident," *Los Angeles Times*, July 3, 1992.

"Navy Plans Training to Fight Sexual Harassment," *New York Times*, June 6, 1992.

"For Women in the Navy, Rough Waters Run Deep."
"Navy Taking on Tough Mission of Torpedoing Sex Harassment," *Las Vegas Journal-Review,* June 29, 1992, 1A.
"Navy Women Hope Tailhook Brings Reforms," *The Advocate* (*Los Angeles Times*), April 25, 1993, B1.
"An Injustice Faced by Our Military Women," Captain Joellen Drag Oslund (USNR Ret.), ACLU blog, November 29, 2012.
Video: "Stand with Service Women," Captain Dwayne Oslund, USN (Ret.) and Captain Joellen Drag Oslund, USNR (Ret.), ACLU blog.

Chapter 14: The Exclusion Finally Falls

"Report to the President," Presidential Commission on the Assignment of Women in the Armed Forces, November 15, 1992.
Francke, *Ground Zero,* 246–60.
"Navy Assigns Women to a Combat-Equipped Ship," *New York Times,* March 1, 1992, 24.
"Women Fliers in Race with Changing Times."
"Women Pilots Face Military Resistance," *Chicago Tribune,* November 14, 1995, D-1
"Women and War," *New York Times,* April 12 1993, A-16
" 'Tailhook' Disclosures Called Catalyst for Change: Navy Has Come a Long Way, Observers Say," *St. Louis Post-Dispatch,* April 22, 1993, 1-C.
"Women Ready to Fly for Navy, or Flee It," *New York Times,* April 23, 1993, A14.
"Senate Votes to Lift Ban on Women War Pilots."
Shirley Sagawa and Nancy Duff Campbell, "Women in Combat," Women in the Military Issue Paper, National Women's Law Center, October 30, 1992.
Rafels, "Women and Combat," dissertation.
"Gender, Stress and Coping in the US Military," Vol. II.
"Military Fights Gender Battle," *Tampa Tribune,* November 7, 1992, 1.
"For Women in the Navy, Rough Waters Run Deep."
"The Sky No Longer Has Limits: Female Fighter Pilots and the Combat Exclusion Policy," *The Unwritten Record,* National Archives, October 3, 2019.
"New Captains Have Flown Against Tradition."
Ebbert and Hall, *Crossed Currents,* 313–32.
"Navy Leads in Opening Combat Roles to Women," *Boston Globe,* April 29, 1993, 1.
"At Long Last, Rosie the Riveter Can be a Top Gun," Associated Press, April 28, 1993.
"Search on for Female Pilots: Candidates for Combat Role Sought," *USA Today,* April 29, 1993.
"Women in Combat," press conference, C-SPAN, April 28, 1993.
"Navy Chief Kelso to Retire Early," *Christian Science Monitor* (Associated Press), February 17, 1994.
Newsmaker Saturday, transcript, CNN, February 19, 1994.
"Flying into the History Books: The Navy's First Female Combat Pilot," *Baltimore Sun,* October 2, 1994.

Francke, *Ground Zero*, 256–60.
Susan H. Godson, *Serving Proudly: A History of Women in the US Navy* (Annapolis, MD: Naval Institute Press, 1991), 283.
"Women in the Military, Part I."
"Women in Combat: Issues for Congress," Congressional Research Service report, December 13, 2016.
Jean Zimmerman, *Tailspin: Women at War in the Wake of Tailhook* (New York: Doubleday, 1995), 219, 292–95.
"Woman Combat Pilot Killed on Training Mission; Lt. Kara Hultgreen Flew Navy F-14s," *Baltimore Sun* (Los Angeles Times), October 27, 1994.
"Flight Rating of Navy Pilot Who Crashed Is Made Public," *New York Times* (Associated Press), November 21, 1994, A16.
"Double Standards in Naval Aviation," Center for Military Readiness, June 1995.
"A Pilot and a Fighter," *San Antonio Express-News*, November 15, 1998.
"AEDC Honors Pioneer Female Flyer," *Times-Gazette* (Shelbyville, Tennessee), March 31, 2007.
Kara Spears Hultgreen, Lieutenant, United States Navy, ArlingtonCemetery.net.
"Aircraft Dedicated to Fallen Navy Aviator," news article, Arnold Air Force Base, March 30, 2007.
Rosemary Bryant Mariner, "A Soldier is a Soldier," *Joint Force Quarterly* (Winter 1993–94).
Rosemary B. Mariner, "Women Enhance Military Power," opinion column, *Orlando Sentinel*, June 2, 1996.
"Army Sex Scandal," transcript, *Talkback Live*, CNN, November 19, 1996.
"Military Women," transcript, *All Things Considered*, NPR, November 20, 1996.
Rosemary B. Mariner, "The Military Needs Women," opinion column, *Washington Post*, May 11, 1997.
"Muscular 'G.I. Jane' Pumps up Navy Dramatics," *USA Today*, August 22, 1997.

Chapter 15: Piping Over the Side

"Closing Out First-Filled Careers: Navy's Female 'Gray Eagles' Are Calling it a Day," *Navy Times*, May 19, 1997, 16.
"People, Planes, Places: Woman Aviator Pioneer Retires," *Naval Aviation News*, June 1997, 43.
"Women in the Military, Part I."
"Year in Review 1997," *Naval Aviation News*, July–August 1998, 11–12.
"Co-ed Training in the Military," transcript, *Crossfire*, CNN, December 16, 1997.
"Not a Good Idea," *All Things Considered*, NPR, December 16, 1997.
"Possible Segregated Training in the Military," *CNN Worldview*, January 2, 1998.
"Training Flights," All Things Considered, NPR, February 4, 1998.
"Few Women Choose Jets; Navy Denies Limited Options," *San Antonio Express-News*, November 15, 1998.
"These Women Don't Mind Being Ignored," *Florida Times Union*, December 19, 1998.

"Eight Essayists Explain What They Have Learned during the Investigation, Impeachment and Trial of the President," *All Things Considered*, NPR, February 12, 1999.

Rosemary B. Mariner, "Adm. Zumwalt Changed My Life," opinion column, *Washington Post*, January 9, 2000.

"Interview: Captain Rosemary Mariner Discusses Fighter Pilot Culture," *All Things Considered*, NPR, April 13, 2001.

"Character Counts in Navy Basic Training," *Chicago Tribune*, May 5, 2002.

"Analysis: Military Analysts Give Assessment of War So Far," special report, NPR, March 20 2003.

"Analysis: Iraqi Air Defense Threats to US Pilots Gauged," NPR, March 22, 2003.

"Female Warriors Advancing; Reaction to Lynch Ordeal May Mean More Acceptance," *San Antonio Express-News*, April 13, 2003.

"War Comes Home in a Coffin; Kimberly Hampton, Like Most of the Soldiers Killed in Iraq, Was from a Small Town. And for Everyone There, Her Death Was a Big Deal," *Los Angeles Times*, February 2, 2004.

"Disband of Brothers; A Split in Ranks of Veterans over Kerry Has Its Roots in the Concept of Honor," *Washington Post*, August 26, 2004.

"Women in Combat: Rules and Reality" *Talk of the Nation*, NPR, May 19, 2005.

"US House Debates Role of Women in Combat," US Federal News Service, Washington, DC, May 22, 2005.

"Women in Combat," *Burlington Free Press*, May 25, 2005.

Rosemary B. Mariner and G. Kurt Piehler, eds., *The Atomic Bomb and American Society: New Perspectives* (Knoxville: University of Tennessee Press, 2009).

"What Private Life Is When You're in Uniform," *Talk of the Nation*, NPR, December 23, 2009.

"Increasingly, Naval Aviation is Women's Work, Too."

"Captain Honors Relieved of Command in Video Flap," *Talk of the Nation*, NPR, January 4, 2011.

"What's Changed in the Military, and What's Next," *Talk of the Nation*, NPR, June 24, 2013.

Douglas, *American Women and Flight.*

"Judith Bruner to Receive Katharine Wright Trophy," press release, National Aeronautic Association, September 29, 2014.

"Forming a More Perfect Union: Honoring Women in Naval Aviation," *Naval Aviation News* (Spring 2016).

Video: "The First Class of Women Naval Aviators—WAI 2017 Pioneer Hall of Fame," Women in Aviation International.

Epilogue: The Flyover

"Meet the Aviators Who Will Honor Female Naval Aviation Pioneer," US Navy Album, Facebook, January 31, 2019.

Video: "All-Female 'Missing Woman' Flyover Honors First Female Navy Jet Pilot," USNI News, February 3 2019.

"The Navy Is Flying Its First Ever All-Female Missing Man Formation to Honor a Trailblazing Aviator," *Virginian-Pilot*, February 2, 2019.
"We Have the Watch," *Courier News*, February 6, 2019.
"She Made History as a Navy Pilot."
Senate Resolution 61: Honoring the Life of Rosemary Mariner, Congressional Record, Vol. 165, No. 24, US Senate, February 7, 2019.
Videos: NAS Oceana pilot interviews, first all-female flyover formation in tribute to Rosemary Mariner, Defense Visual Information Distribution Service.
" 'Trailblazer in the Sky' Capt. Rosemary Mariner," *All Hands*, March 2019.
"Historic Tribute to Capt. Rosemary Mariner," *The Hook*, magazine of the Association of Naval Aviation (Spring 2019).

Index

Carnahan, Peggy, *168*
carrier onboard delivery (COD), 135, 136
carrier qualifications, 79–81, 99, 112, 120, 130, 135, 138, 149
Carter, Jimmy, 111, 113, 121
Cecil Field, 77
Celestial Link flight simulator, 24
Center for the Study of War and Society, 90, 239
Central Command (CENTCOM), 249
Challenger disaster, 148, 150
Chambers, Washington Irving, 6
"Change in Flight Training Syllabus; request for" (Neuffer, Skiles, J., and Conatser, R. B.), 79–80
checkride, 249
Cheney, Dick, 186
Chief of Naval Air Training (CNATRA), 79–81, 249
Chief of Naval Operations (CNO), 249; combat exclusion laws and, 146; Hayward as, 113, 120; Holloway as, 111; Kelso as, 188, 214, 221; McCain report to, 78; physical fitness standards and, 55; Space and Electronic Warfare Directorate under, 239; Trost as, 143; Watkins as, 142; women flight training and,

41, 55, 79–80; Zumwalt, E., Jr., as, xiv, 15–16, 22, 45
children, 92–94
China Lake, 182
CINCLANTFLT. *See* Commander-in-Chief, Atlantic Fleet
CINCPACFLT. *See* Commander-in-Chief, Pacific Fleet
CINCPACFLT 5720.2H, 105
Claytor, W. Graham, 100, 111
CLF. *See* Combat Logistics Force
Clinton, Bill, 220, 240
CNATRA. *See* Chief of Naval Air Training
CNN, 38, 195, 225; *Talkback Live*, 232
CNN discussion, 225–26
CNO. *See* Chief of Naval Operations
Coalition for Military Readiness, 194
Coast Guard, 105
Cochran, Jacqueline, 3
Cochran, John, 42
COD. *See* carrier onboard delivery
Cohen, William, 143, 186, 209
combat exclusion laws, 83–84, 138, 145, 146, 150, 218
"Combat Exclusion Laws for Women in the Military" (GAO), 145
Combat Logistics Force (CLF), 142, 145, 146, 188
combat support units, 142